Bounded Ratic
Economics and

edited by

Christian Richter

LIT

Bibliographic information published by the Deutsche Nationalbibliothek
The Deutsche Nationalbibliothek lists this publication in the Deutsche
Nationalbibliografie; detailed bibliographic data are available in the Internet at
http://dnb.d-nb.de.

ISBN 978-3-8258-1614-8

A catalogue record for this book is available from the British Library

© LIT VERLAG Dr. W. Hopf Berlin 2008
Verlagskontakt:
Fresnostr. 2   D-48159 Münster
Tel. +49 (0) 2 51/620 32 - 22   Fax +49 (0) 2 51/922 60 99
e-Mail: lit@lit-verlag.de   http://www.lit-verlag.de

Auslieferung:
Deutschland/Schweiz: LIT Verlag Fresnostr. 2, D-48159 Münster
Tel. +49 (0) 2 51/620 32 - 22, Fax +49 (0) 2 51/922 60 99, e-Mail: vertrieb@lit-verlag.de
Österreich: Medienlogistik Pichler-ÖBZ GmbH & Co KG
IZ-NÖ, Süd, Straße 1, Objekt 34, A-2355 Wiener Neudorf
Tel. +43 (0) 2236/63 535-290, +43 (0) 2236/63 535 - 243, mlo@medien-logistik.at

Distributed in the UK by: Global Book Marketing, 99B Wallis Rd, London, E9 5LN
Phone: +44 (0) 20 8533 5800 – Fax: +44 (0) 1600 775 663
http://www.centralbooks.co.uk/html

Distributed in North America by:

Transaction Publishers
New Brunswick (U.S.A.) and London (U.K.)

Transaction Publishers
Rutgers University
35 Berrue Circle
Piscataway, NJ 08854

Phone: +1 (732) 445 - 2280
Fax: + 1 (732) 445 - 3138
for orders (U. S. only):
toll free (888) 999 - 6778
e-mail:
orders@transactionspub.com

Acknowledgements

This volume of Bounded Rationality in Economics and Finance is the outcome of a workshop on the same topic at Loughborough University in December 2006. This workshop was organised by the *INFER* working group on Bounded Rationality in Economics and Finance. This was the first workshop on this topic. As the topic suggests, half of the papers were from the Finance area and the other half came from Economics.

We hope that the collection of papers in this volume are a good starting point for further workshops and research in this topic. Readers interested in joining this working group and *INFER* may have a look at *INFER's* webpage at www.infer-research.net.

We would like to thank all participants, who came from different countries for their participation in discussions and presenting their research. We are also grateful to the *INFER* board for generous support.

Last but not least, we would like to thank the Department of Economics at Loughborough University for financial support.

Christian Richter
Loughborough, December 2007

List of Contributors

Simone Alfarano
Institute of Economics, Business and Social Sciences
Olshausenstraße 40
24118 Kiel
Germany
Email: alfarano@bwl.uni-kiel.de

Iván Barreda-Tarrazona
Departamento de Economía
University Jaume I
Avda. Sos Baynat s/n
12071 Castellón
Spain
E-mail: ivan.barreda@eco.uji.es

Eva Camacho-Cuena
Dept of Economics
Departamento de Análisis Económico: Teoría Económica e Historia Económica
University Autónoma of Madrid
Carretera de Colmenar Viejo Km 15
2049 Madrid
Spain
Email: eva.camacho@uam.es

Andrew Hughes Hallett
School of Public Policy
MS 3C6
George Mason University
Fairfax, VA 22030
USA
Email: ahughesh@gmu.edu

Frederic B. JENNINGS, Jr.
Center for Ecological Economic and Ethical Education
Ipswich
Massachusetts
U.S.A.
Email: ecologicaleconomics@yahoo.com

Ioannis Krassas
Dept. of Business
City College - Affiliated Institution University of Sheffield
546 24 Thessaloniki
Greece
Email: ikrassas@city.academic.gr

Laurent Percebois
Centre d'Economie de la Sorbonne
Université Paris I Panthéon-Sorbonne-Matisse
106-112 Boulevard de l'Hôpital
75647 Paris Cedex 13
France
Email: laurent.percebois@malix.univ-paris1.fr

Christian Richter
Dept. of Economics
Loughborough University
Loughborough, LE 11 3TU
UK
Email: c.r.richer@lboro.ac.uk

Federico Sallusti
Dipartamento di Economia
Facoltà di Economia "F. Caffè"
Università degli Studi Roma Tre
Via Ostiense 139
00154 Roma
Email: sallusti@uniroma3.it

Tom De Schryver
Faculty of Economics
Universiteit Antwerpen
Groenenborgerlaan 171
2020 Antwerpen
Belgium
Email: tom.deschryver@ua.ac.be

Contents

Introduction

So far, the dominant hypothesis in (neoclassical) economics has been the assumption of prefect rationality. Rationality means here that individuals use *all* relevant information in their decision making process. Indeed, this assumptions (almost) guarantees market efficiency, so that there no market inefficiencies such as price stickiness or inflexible labour markets.

However, there are two dilemmas for this assumption: Whenever it was used the empirical evidence turned out to be against it. Secondly, this assumption is far from reality. Individuals usually do not possess all relevant information, which – as Simon argued - may actually be rational (for some circumstances).

On the other hand, once one deviates from perfect rationality, it is often claimed that these approaches are "ad hoc", in terms of a missing microfoundation. The question arises though, why perfect rationality should be less "ad hoc" than its counterpart bounded rationality? As a result, bounded rationality in economics (not so much in finance) is still somewhat like an outsider, despite the fact that this direction of economics has won the Noble price (e.g. Kahnemann).

Hence, there is a need for more research in this direction. This volume therefore presents some more recent results of research in this area.

This volume contains three parts. The first part investigates bounded rationality in financial markets. *Andrew Hughes Hallett* and *Christian Richter* use an empirical approach to find out whether capital market participants are really rational. They investigate the German and UK capital. The result is that both markets are not fully efficient. They find that although not efficient, those market relationships are very stable and that the risk premium carries most of the adjustment. Moreover, market adjustments to shocks can take considerable time, which also indicates market imperfections. So that capital markets do not appear to be efficient. The second paper in this part is by *Simone Alfarano, Iván Barreda-Tarrazona*, and *Eva Camacho-Cuena*. They analyse heterogeneous and imperfect information in an experimental asset market and find asset markets are not efficient in transmitting information. Moreover, observed transaction prices always deviate from those implied by the fundamentals. Besides, those traders who buy and use information about the dividends obtain higher payoffs at the end of the experiment than the other traders, thus indicating that they are able to exploit their private information.

However, the presence of more information in the market has some effects: a lower variance of the trading prices around those implied by the fundamental value could be observed.

The last paper in this part is by *Ioannis Krassas*. His paper examines how investors react to profit warning announcements under the scope of trading volume. The main finding shows that investors do trade excessively despite having common prior and posterior beliefs which implies differential beliefs revisions. Furthermore the level of trading activity is positively related to the magnitude of the surprise induced by the profit warning announcements, a result which complements previous studies related to EPS announcements.

The second part of this volume investigates the effects of bounded rationality on industrial organisations. *Tom De Schryver* investigates the impact of strategic changes of small firms. His starting point is that the lessons from large-scale change are not sufficient to study small strategic changes. A shift from research on large-scale change to research on a variety of small, specific strategic responses brings along specific and more complex research questions. He highlights theoretical and methodological tools from organizational learning theory to answer which parts of the strategic content are changed, how, when and why. He also shows that organizational learning theory is good soil for studying small strategic changes.

The second paper in this part is by *Frederico Sallusti*. He investigates the organisational structure of companies. The starting point is that the definition of the nature of a firm as a structure is not entirely ruled by the mechanisms of the market, but rather as a replica, on a different scale, of the transactions of the market. The principal aim of this work is the proposition of a scheme consistent with instability, assuming that agents are characterised by bounded rationality and that the variations of the decisional context are not entirely derivable. The abandonment of the logic of a-temporality are reflected in the analysis of two different moments: one defined as static – with an unvaried environment – and one dynamic – with a varying environment, which shows how process phenomena may be developed in response to variations that have taken place.

The simultaneous presence of learning and adaptation processes allows, on one hand, a definition of the sterilization of bounded rationality and management of complexity of interaction processes that determine the internal structure, and, on the other, a tool for describing and analysing the evolutionary path of firms, that is, their innovation capabilities and growth trends.

Furthermore, though this theoretical approach is evidently general in scope, it will be particularly suitable for analysing some categories of problems associated with peculiar forms of entrepreneurial organization. The strong link between knowledge and information in fact allows a better interpretation of the dynamics of the firm, which are strongly characterised by more flexible, rather than particularly mechanised, structures of interaction. From this perspective, there is an evident difference between firms in the industrial and service sectors. On the other hand, such a model would also allow an interpretation of the capability of innovation of enterprises of different sizes, even in the same sector. This means we can analyse the structure in terms of flexibility/rigidity, both as independent and dependent variables, and in other terms both as a structural feature that differentiates firms, and as strategic variables that influence its path of development, in both innovation and growth.

The third part of this volume deals with bounded rationality in price theory, environmental economics and public management. *Frederic Jennings* introduces a horizonal theory. The starting point of the argument is that information economies suffer problems of interdependence similar to ecological living systems and transportation networks: all encounter a nondecomposable mix of sub-stitution and complementarity at every turn. Networks have no exclusively par-allel links – like firms in an industry – and no rising cost to keep power in check. Increasing returns and concerts of value raise issues standard theory avoids with its suppositions of substitution and decreasing returns. Scarcity in the presence of complementarity yields no value: ubiquity augments worth in networks! Sub-stitution no longer applies; complementarity rules.

Here the notion of planning horizons is used to unbind the imbroglio: first, a horizonal theory of pricing by single agents is introduced, and then ex-tended through an inclusion of external profit effects to yield a static measure of interdependence within any grouping of firms (so replacing our 'industry' con-cept). Then the interrelation of planning horizons is shown to alter the balance of substitution and complementarity in an orderly way, due to contagious 'horizon effects.'

With interhorizonal complementarity, longer horizons shift our relations of interdependence away from substitution in favor of complementarity, yielding a case for complementarity as "far more important" than substitution, confirm-ing Kaldor's contention. The new information economy has a lot to teach the economist: substitution (negative feedbacks and tradeoffs) cedes to complemen-tarity (positive feedbacks and network connections) in a horizonal economics, suggesting cooperation is more efficient than a competitive frame (which short-ens planning horizons).

The second paper in this part is from *Frederic Jennings* as well. In this paper he applies the horizonal theory to environmental economics. The core of ecological economics is interdependence: substitution and complementarity. Yet orthodox economics stands on substitution assumptions as the universal human relation. A theory so founded does not apply to a complementary realm. The optimal organizational form in a world of substitution is competition among our resources. Where complementarity rules, however, this is precisely wrong: cooperation is sought instead.

Interdependence is also the basis for bounded rationality theories. If consequences sweep outward forever, our prior anticipation of those outcomes shall be contained. The range of our understanding – called the planning horizon in choice – sets the boundedness of our rationality into an ordinal frame. Especially in the presence of complementarity, impacts grow as they spread, displacing competition for cooperation as our welfare ideal.

Examples are found in ecology, education and ethical culture: none are well served by competition. The health of ecology lies in complementarities sundered by competition. The educational system in its intangible information may be our clearest case of complementarity: it is a good illustration of failure. The ethical manifestation of this problem is short horizons, a culture ruled by myopic concerns. Such conclusions are framed within a horizonal theory of foresight, to be explained below.

Prices, economic growth and most of our ecological losses are tied to planning horizons, which extend through learning and trust. Longer planning horizons transform substitutes into complements, a shift of interdependence calling for institutional change. Without adapting incentives to cooperation, progress is slowed: horizon effects show why. A horizonal economics of complementarity is introduced and discussed.

The last paper in this section is by *Laurent Percebois*. He investigates public administrations; in particular, public administration reform. Public administration reform constitutes a lively field of interest for academics and practitioners, and there is now a strong impetus for efficiency-prone reforms. Moreover, since Herbert Simon's groundbreaking works, several decades ago, the central issue of rationality in administration has been regarded as a crucial topic. Since decision-makers cannot exhibit perfect rationality, due to problems in information diffusion and hierarchical dysfunctions, improving performance could be a difficult matter, even if it is nowadays privileged by reformers. The New Public Management (NPM) stands for the heterogeneous current set of reforms whose goal is to increase efficiency and accountability in public administration, often by means of devices taken from private management traditional routines. However, this managerial, legal and economic approach to public administration reforms generally pays little attention to the economic issue of rationality, despite Simon's results.

The objective of this paper is to try to combine and to reconcile Simon's traditional views of bounded rationality, as well as subsequent developments by his academic followers, and modern theories and practices of reforms, which deeply emphasize efficiency but rarely explicitly refer to bounded rationality.

The methodology employed here makes reference to the economics of public administration and bureaucracy. The paper compares the consequences of bounded rationality on public bureaucracy and the NPM's logical approach. It advocates the inclusion of the bounded rationality issue in the study of public management reforms. A simple model displays the trade-off between management delegation in public bureaucracies and centralization, taking into account possible flaws arising from bounded rationality. Eventually, bounded rationality should be given greater importance in theoretical public management, which hopefully should result in better performance.

Part I: Bounded Rationality in Financial Markets

On the Dynamics of Capital Markets – An Analysis of the Short End of the Term Structure of Interest Rates in Britain

Andrew Hughes Hallett and Christian R Richter

1 Introduction

This paper builds on the discussion in behavioural finance (*Barberis et al*, 1998, 1999; *Daniel et al*, 1998; *Shefrin*, 1999, *Shleifer*, 2000, and *Thaler*, 1994, for example), which we try to transfer to economics. A standard paradigm in economics, and in financial markets in particular, is that markets are efficient. And conventional wisdom is that efficient markets are more stable (less volatile) because the adjustment to equilibrium is faster, and destabilising speculation would prove unprofitable in the longer term[1]. Especially if agents would be perfectly rational, there would be no reason why markets should inhibit large volatilities: adjustment to a new equilibrium would be instantaneous, since all agents possess the same information and all agents would process this information identically. Therefore, if markets were inefficient, we would expect to see a large influence of very short cycles, of less than one or two months say, increasing the volatility of the observed time series.

But to examine efficiency in that sense, that is in the speed with which they incorporate all the available information in their price signals as well as the fact that they incorporate all that information, will take a detailed dynamic and spectral analysis of the data. The analysis of the lag structure allows us to investigate how much time it will take to incorporate (all) information, i.e. when the equilibrium is reached again (if the model is stable in that sense). The (cross) spectral analysis tell us whether the interest rate relationship causes longer cycles rather than shorter cycles. If long cycles dominate, the observed time series is less volatile. Moreover, if agents are learning then there is no reason that the lag structure and therefore the cross spectra are constant over time. Indeed the more agents learn the shorter should be the adjustment time to a new equilibrium. That is to say that at the beginning of a sample the adjustment time should be relatively long and as time passes by, the adjustment period should become shorter. In that sense, we have to put the dynamic analysis into a time-varying framework itself: the lag structure cannot be assumed to be constant (*Sheffrin*, 1996)[2]. The dynamics of any financial market can therefore be expected to reflect both within and between period adjustments to an equilibrium path which is itself adjusting to learning, the resolution of uncertainty and the costs of in-

---

[1] Indeed the discussion whether speculation is stabilising or destabilising is still not solved and goes back at least to *Kaldor* (1939) and *Baumol* (1957).

[2] That does not exclude that the lag structure is constant. What we are saying, is that, it is very restrictive to assume from the beginning that the lag structure is constant.

formation gathering. As we will show below, if the lag structure is not constant anymore so is the cross spectrum not constant anymore.

In terms of econometrics that causes severe estimation problems. Using a normal OLS and searching for structural breaks could result in the problem that the subsamples are too small so that no estimation can be done. More severely: a direct estimation of the spectrum of an observed time series may be impossible since a large sample is usually required to estimate the spectrum of a time series directly. One way to overcome the last problem is to use wavelet analysis. Wavelet analysis has become increasingly popular in recent years (e.g. *Percival/Walden*, 2000; and *Gençay et al.*, 2002). Wavelet analysis basically investigates the change of the importance of certain frequencies over time. The disadvantage is that firstly only a few frequencies can be analysed, since the number of frequencies investigated is depending on the sample size (which is usually small in macroeconomics). Secondly, we cannot test economic hypotheses, i.e. whether underlying relationships changed. So, what we need is a way to overcome the "small sample" problem, to analyse all frequencies at all times, and to test economic hypotheses, in order to allow for bounded rationality.

We model bounded rationality in terms of time-varying coefficients, in particular using the Kalman filter[3]. That results in within and between period adjustments (i.e. "deterministic" and "stochastic" adjustment (*Sheffrin*, 1996)). This in turn enables us to perform a time-varying spectral analysis.

Our approach is to exploit a technique for calculating the necessary spectra indirectly; that is from the kind of dynamic regression or VAR models that have proved so popular in the literature in recent years. This can be done in the case where the parameters of the underlying market structure may be time varying for the reasons we have mentioned. *Laven/Shi* (1993), *Nerlove et al.* (1995), and *Wolters* (1980) have each shown that a dynamic regression equation can be used to derive the *autoregressive distributed lag model*. Here we show how to extend such a model to yield the spectra and cross-spectra needed for a proper frequency domain analysis of the data. We use these tools here to analyse the relationships of the British and German capital markets, before and after the collapse of the ERM system in 1992-3.

At that time the UK was participating in the "hard ERM", and that therefore effectively fixed their exchange rates in a world that guarantees free mobility of capital. If the markets were efficient, then the UIP condition would hold and the pricing mechanisms would show a stable relationship at all but the very shortest cycle lengths as the markets adjust.

We in fact find the opposite. The UIP relationship does not hold. Hence these financial markets were not efficient in our sense. However, and contrary to much conventional wisdom, they have not been more unstable as a result of be-

---

[3] See also *Garratt/Hall*, 1997a, b.

ing inefficient[4]. On this "behavioural finance" view, systematic and significant deviations from efficiency can be expected and may well persist for long periods of time (*Shleifer*, 2000; *Shefrin*, 1999; *Thaler*, 1994)[5].

This paper is structured as follows: in the first section we show the link between the time domain and the frequency domain. For the ease of exposition we repeat the results in a non-time-varying framework. In the second section we put the results from the first section into a time-varying framework. In the third section, we derive our uncovered interest rate parity (UIP) approach. We then present our results for the British economy in the time domain. In particular we analyse the lag structure and the adjustment towards the equilibrium after a shock occurred. The fourth section shows the results in the frequency domain. Here we analyse the volatility implied by relationships of the interest rates.

2 The Relationship between the Time Domain and the Frequency Domain

2.1 Introduction

Frequency analysis in general and cross-spectral analysis in particular, has gained popularity again with the introduction of wavelets into economic analysis (e.g. *Percival/Walden*, 2000; and *Gençay et al.*, 2002). Wavelets show how pre-assigned frequencies vary over time. In this paper, we present an alternative approach to generating a time-varying frequency analysis without having to pre-specify which frequencies should be examined. That will be determined by the data. However, for the ease of exposition we first discuss our techniques for the case of time-invariant spectral analyses. Once we have investigated this case, we show how to introduce time variation.

The spectrum shows the decomposition of the variance of a sample of data across different frequencies. Hence, the power spectrum describes the cyclical properties of a particular time series. It is assumed that the fluctuations of the underlying process are produced by a large number of elementary cycles of different frequencies, and that the contribution of each cycle is constant throughout the sample. The power spectrum then gives the relative contribution made by these elementary cycles to the variance of the process overall. Our job in this paper is to show how to do that when the contribution of each cycle may

---

[4] This may simply be a consequence of the cost of gathering information, or the cost of adjusting to a new equilibrium, the process of learning, or the asymmetries of information (*Black*, 1989; *Easley/O'Hara*, 1992).

[5] In this case, movements to equilibrium will arise only when the profit opportunities are large enough to compensate investors (agents) for the costs of information gathering and then trading to adjust their stocks of assets (skills, goods). But, as they do so, they are likely to affect what other agents then perceive (but not necessarily know) to be their equilibrium state. Indeed, if information deficiencies underlie these disequilibrium movements or changes in the perceived equilibrium path, it would hardly be sensible to model these markets as if they had strictly rational expectations and efficiency (*Frydman*, 1983), and that prices reflect all the available information.

vary over time. To do so we use an approach introduced by *Hughes Hallett/Richter* (2002, 2004), which we briefly summarise here.

Suppose, we are interested in the relationship between the variables, $\{Y_t\}$ and $\{X_t\}$ say, which are assumed to be related in the following way[6]:

(2.1) $Y_t = A(L)X_t + u_t$,

where A(L) is a filter, and L is the lag operator such that $LY_t = Y_{t-1}$. We want to derive an approach for calculating the gain in Y_t at different frequencies, given X_t, from an estimated model like (2.1). We can define the *cross-covariance generating* function as (Wolters, 1980)

(2.2) $g_{YX}(z) = \sum_{\tau=-\infty}^{\infty} \gamma_{YX}(\tau)z^\tau$

where $\gamma_{YX}(\tau)$ is the covariance between Y and X, and γ_{XX} is the variance of X:

(2.3) $\gamma_{YX}(\tau) = E(Y_t X_{t-\tau})$, $\gamma_{XX}(\tau) = E\left(X_t X_{t-\upsilon}\right)$.

But if $\{Y_t\}$ follows (2.1), we can substitute (2.1) in (2.3) to get:

(2.4) $\gamma_{YX}(\tau) = E\left(A(L)X_t X_{t-\tau}\right) + E\left(u_t X_{t-\tau}\right)$

Since $\{u_t\}$ is i.i.d. (0, σ^2), $E(u_t X_{t-\tau}) = 0$. Hence, (2.4) simplifies to

(2.5) $\gamma_{YX}(\tau) = \sum_{j=0}^{\infty} a_j \gamma_{XX}(\tau - j)$.

Equation (2.5) states that the covariance of the endogenous variable (γ_{YX}) depends on the variance of the explanatory variable (γ_{XX}), where $\gamma_{XX}(\tau - j) = E\left(X_t X_{t-\tau_j}\right)$, and on a sequence of parameters a_j from A(L). That is to say, if we interpret (2.1) as an estimated equation, then the cross-covariances between $\{Y_t\}$ and $\{X_t\}$ will all depend on the estimated coefficients of the distributed lag model (2.1). Consequently, if the estimates obtained for coefficients in(2.1) are <u>efficient</u>, then the estimated cross-covariance functions will also be efficient (given knowledge of γ_{XX}), since both functions depend on the same estimators.

The innovation here is that, using estimated coefficients from (2.1) vastly simplifies estimation of the spectra. Generally speaking one of the disadvantages of a direct estimation approach is the large number of observations that would be necessary to carry out the necessary frequency analysis. This may be a particular problem in the case of structural breaks, since the subsamples could be too small for estimating the spectra directly. We now show how we can get round that disadvantage by starting from regression based estimation as follows.

---

[6] where the moduli of the eigenvalues of A(L) are less than one in absolute value.

We can always write the *cross spectral density* ($g_{YX}(z)$) of the exogenous variable as being proportional to the Fourier transform of the lag coefficients (*Nerlove et al.*, 1995). That is to say

$$(2.6) \quad g_{YX}(z) = \sum_{\tau=-\infty}^{\infty} \sum_{j=0}^{\infty} a_j \gamma_{XX}(\tau - j) z^{\tau} = A(z) g_{xx}(z)$$

where $A(z)$ is called the *frequency response function*, and $|A(z)|^2$ is called the *transfer function* of the filter $A(L)$. But equation (2.6) can also be written in terms of the spectra involved. By multiplying both sides of (2.6) with $\dfrac{1}{2\pi}$ we find that the cross-spectrum of the dependent variable (g_{YX}) is depending on the spectrum of the explanatory variable (g_{XX}): i.e.

$$(2.7) \quad f_{YX}(\omega) \equiv \frac{1}{2\pi} g_{YX}(z)$$

and

$$(2.8) \quad f_{XX}(\omega) \equiv \frac{1}{2\pi} g_{XX}(z). \text{ From here we get the cross spectrum } f_{YX}(\omega) \text{ as}$$

$$(2.9) \quad f_{YX}(\omega) = A(z) f_{XX}(\omega)$$

where $A(z)$ is the Fourier transform of the weights $\{a_j\}_{j=-\infty}^{\infty}$. In this paper we are particularly interested in the gain, which is – loosely speaking – the Fourier transform. To explain our technique, consider the following example. We are interested in $A(z)$ because $A(z)$ transforms the X-process into the Y-process. This is important, since it implies that, even if the X-process exhibits a lot of volatility, then $A(z)$ might transform this high volatility into lower volatility and vice versa. So, $A(z)$ plays a crucial role, as demonstrated in the following diagrams:

Figure 2.1: Example of A(z)   Figure 2.2: Example Spectrum of X

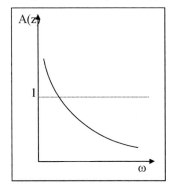
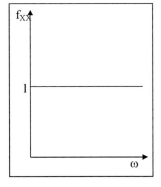

Figure 2.2 shows the spectrum of the X-process. For the sake of the argument, we have assumed that all frequencies (ω) have the same weight. In that case the X-series would look like a white noise process with a given (fixed) variance. That is because the spectrum of a time series is nothing more than a decomposition of its variance. But, the question we now need to answer is, what cycles determine the observed variance of the Y-process? If one keeps in mind that high frequencies are equivalent to small cycles and vice versa[7], the answer is shown by the gain function A(z) for Y_t, given in figure 2.1 and derived from (1.9).

However, the Fourier transformation in (1.9) shows that A(z) is essentially a spectrum as well. In this case, the shape of A(z) shows that longer cycles are more important than shorter cycles. Thus, in contrast to diagram 2.2, the observed time series for $\{Y_t\}$ would look like a long (business) cycle with a small degree of volatility of intermediate frequencies. The implication of A(z) is therefore that, regardless of the X-process, A(z) would always transform the X-process so that long cycles gain weight and small cycles lose importance.

Nevertheless, that said, we have not yet shown how to calculate A(z) from time series data on $\{Y_t\}$ and $\{X_t\}$. Returning to (2.9) we see that

$$(2.10)\quad A(z) = \frac{f_{YX}(\omega)}{f_{XX}(\omega)}$$

Since the cross spectrum is (defined to be) positive while the Fourier Transform is not necessarily positive, the absolute value of the Fourier Transform is taken:

$$(2.11)\quad |A(z)| = \frac{|f_{YX}(\omega)|}{f_{XX}(\omega)}$$

The function $|A(\omega)|$ is sometimes called the *gain*. This gain is equivalent to the regression coefficient for each frequency value ω. It measures the amplification of each frequency component in the X-process, which is needed to obtain the corresponding components of the Y-process. However, it is often more convenient to express the gain in terms of a complex scalar $z = e^{-i\omega}$, so that $|A(\omega)| = |A(z)|$. Equation (2.11) then becomes

$$(2.12)\quad |A(z)| = \sqrt{|A(z)|^2} = \sqrt{A(z)A(\bar{z})}$$

where $\bar{z} = e^{i\omega}$ is the complex conjugate of z. Thus, to calculate the gain, all we have to know is the sequence of the coefficients $\{a_j\}$ from (2.1). Section 2.2 below shows how to do that in practice. But before we do that, we need to introduce another cross-spectrum feature, which is very useful in the analysis of financial markets.

---

[7] The period "p" is defined as $p \equiv 2\Pi/\omega$.

We can rewrite $f_{YX}(\omega)$ from (2.9) in terms of its real and complex components:

(2.13) $f_{YX}(\omega) = C_{YX}(\omega) - iQ_{YX}(\omega)$

where $C_{YX}(\omega)$ is the *cospectrum* and $Q_{YX}(\omega)$ is the *quadrature spectrum*. We can then define the *phase angle*, $\varphi(\omega)$, between Y_t and X_t in terms of their co-spectrum and quadrature spectrum:

(2.14) $\varphi(\omega) = \tan^{-1} \dfrac{-Q_{YX}(\omega)}{C_{YX}(\omega)}$

In practice, the *cospectrum* $C_{YX}(\omega)$ is usually defined as[8]:

(2.15) $C_{YX}(\omega) = f_{XX}(\omega) \displaystyle\sum_{j=0}^{\infty} a_j \cos \omega j$;

whereas the *quadrature spectrum* $Q_{YX}(\omega)$ is defined as

(2.16) $Q_{YX}(\omega) = -f_{XX} \displaystyle\sum_{j=0}^{\infty} a_j \sin \omega j$.

The phase angle is therefore calculated using (2.15) and (2.16), as

(2.17) $\varphi(\omega) = \tan^{-1} \left(\dfrac{\displaystyle\sum_{j=0}^{\infty} a_j \sin \omega j}{\displaystyle\sum_{j=0}^{\infty} a_j \cos \omega j} \right)$

The result, once again, is that all we need to know in order to calculate the phase angle are the coefficients a_j. In this paper, however, we have actually used a "standardised" phase angle, or *phase shift*:

(2.18) $\tau(\omega) = \dfrac{\varphi(\omega)}{\omega}$

This phase shift measures the lead-lag relationship between two variables. As an example, please look at the following figure:

---

[8] *Wolters* (1980).

Figure 2.3: Assumed Shape of a Phase Shift

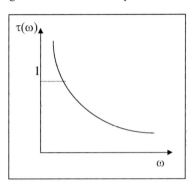

The phase shift shows the lead-lag relationship between two variables. In the above diagram, $\varphi(\omega)$ indicates one time series is following the other one at long cycles with a delay of 1 month, then, if one time series is on the peak of the long cycle, the other time series needs one month to be on the peak of its long cycle. For smaller cycles the delay will be shorter if the $\tau(\omega)$ value is smaller at that value of ω. The reason why we are looking at the phase shift is that it tells us how rapidly news is being processed in financial markets. If the market in question is efficient, the prices of different assets should follow each other very closely. In our case, the yields on short term bonds should follow those of the base rate (and vice versa) since agents should be able to incorporate any new information into bond prices almost immediately.

Finally, we also present a test whether the gain or the phase shift changes over time. We use confidence intervals for this test, like in the time domain approach. In order to calculate these confidence intervals, we have to know the coherence and the spectra of the individual time series. The coherence is nothing else than the R^2 of the time domain. The coherence measures for each frequency the degree of fit between X and Y: or the R^2 between each of the cyclical components in X and Y. Assuming the spectra are known (see below), the coherence is[9]

$$(2.19)\ K_{12}^2(\omega) = \frac{1}{1 + f_{YY}(\omega)/|A(z)|f_{xx}(\omega)}$$

The $100(1-\alpha)\%$ confidence intervals for gain are then

$$(2.20)\ |A(z)| \pm |A(z)| \sqrt{\frac{2}{v-2} f_{2,v-2}(1-\alpha)\left(\frac{1-K_{12}^2(\omega)}{K_{12}^2(\omega)}\right)}$$

---

[9] *Jenkins/Watts* (1968).

where v is the number of degrees of freedom associated with the esti-mated/calculated output spectrum[10], and $f_{2,v-2}(1-\alpha)$ is the upper $100(1-\alpha)\%$ point of the $F_{2,v-2}$ distribution. Similarly, the $100(1-\alpha)\%$ confidence interval for the phase shift is

$$(2.21) \quad \tau(\omega) \pm \arcsin \sqrt{\frac{2}{v-2} f_{2,v-2}(1-\alpha) \left(\frac{1-K_{12}^2(\omega)}{K_{12}^2(\omega)} \right)}.$$

2.2 Indirect Estimation

In order to calculate the sequence of coefficients $\{a_j\}$ from (2.1), we have to analyse the lag structure of the underlying economic model. In order to do this, we start from a general linear model of distributed lags:

$$(2.22) \quad V(L)Y_t = U(L)X_t + \varepsilon_t$$

where

$$V(L) = \sum_{s=0}^{p} v_s L^s, \quad v_0 = 1, \text{ and } U(L) = \sum_{r=0}^{q} u_r L^r.$$

Thus, as long as all eigenvalues of the characteristic equation of $V(L)$ are less than one, as they will be if Y_t is stationary, we can write

$$(2.23) \quad Y_t = \frac{U(L)}{V(L)} X_t + \frac{1}{V(L)} \varepsilon_t$$

We are particularly interested in the first ratio of eq. (2.23) in order to derive the gain of the variable X_t. Let

$$(2.24) \quad \frac{U(L)}{V(L)} = W(L)$$

where $W(L) = \sum_{j=0}^{k} w_j L^j$ is the weighting function[11] from (2.23). The sequence $\{w_j; j = 0, 1, ..., k\}$ defines the model's lag structure. The coefficients show the impact which results from a change of the explanatory variable j periods ago. In particular, w_0 is the instantaneous reaction coefficient. In order to achieve a sensible economic interpretation, it is required that if $X_t = X_{t-1} = ... = X$, i.e. in equilibrium, then the dependant variable Y should also be constant (and finite). Hence, it is required that

---

[10] The value of v is equal to "k", the minimum number of lags needed to compute the weighting function in (2.20) below. Once, k was chosen, it was the same for all points in time to make the gains comparable.

[11] k may tend to infinity, but does not have to, in order to generate an infinite history for Y_t.

(2.25) $\sum_{j=0}^{k} w_j = W(1) = \dfrac{U(1)}{V(1)} = w$, where $0 < |w| < \infty$ and $0 \le w_j \le 1$.

In order to calculate w_j in terms of u_r and v_s, we make use of the following relationship (*Hendry*, 1995; *Laven/Shi*, 1993):

(2.26) $\left(\sum_{j=0}^{k} w_j L^j \right) \left(\sum_{s=0}^{p} v_s L^s \right) = \sum_{r=0}^{q} u_r L^r$

Equating the powers of L on the two sides of (2.26), and noting that $v_0 = 1$, we get the following recursive equations:

$w_0 = u_0$;

$w_1 + w_0 v_1 = u_1$;

$w_2 + w_1 v_1 + w_0 v_2 = u_2 \ldots$

Solving for the unknown coefficients w_j, we have

$w_0 = u_0$;

$w_1 = u_1 - u_0 v_1$;

$w_2 = u_2 - \left(u_1 - u_0 v_1 \right) v_1 - u_0 v_2$; and so on.

Finally, if all the w_j coefficients have the same sign we are able to generate a normalised distributed lag model[12]:

(2.27) $H(L) = \dfrac{W(L)}{W(1)} = \dfrac{U(L) V(1)}{V(L) U(1)} = \sum_{j=0}^{k} h_j L^j$, where

$h_j = \dfrac{w_j}{w}$, and $w = \sum_{j=0}^{k} w_j$. Consequently

$0 \le h_j \le 1$, $\sum_{j=0}^{k} h_j = H(1) = 1$,

and the normalised parameters h_j correspond to a mapping of discrete probability weights. In particular, the *mean* lag is:

(2.28) $\mu = \sum_{j=0}^{k} j h_j = H'(1) = \dfrac{W'(1)}{W(1)} = \dfrac{U'(1)}{U(1)} - \dfrac{V'(1)}{V(1)}$ (where ' denotes the first derivative).

This mean lag comprises everything which has not happened immediately. The lag variance is:

(2.29) $Var = H''(1) + H'(1) - \left\{ H'(1) \right\}^2$.

---

[12] If the coefficients w_j do not have the same sign then the lag distribution has changing signs, so it is not defined.

Given the lag structure in (2.26), we are now able to generate the gain according to (2.12):

$$(2.30) \quad r(z) = \sqrt{\sum_{j=0}^{k} w_j z \sum_{j=0}^{k} w_j z^{-1}}$$

where $z = e^{-i\omega}$, and the phase angle by (2.17)

$$(2.31) \quad p(\omega) = \tan^{-1}\left(\frac{\sum_{j=0}^{k} w_j \sin \omega j}{\sum_{J00}^{k} w_j \cos \omega j} \right)$$

For $\omega = 0$, it can be seen from (2.30) that

$$r(1) = \sum_{j=0}^{k} w_j = w$$

Hence, for $\omega = 0$, r becomes the long-run coefficient value from the regression result in the time domain.

3   Econometric Implementation: a Time-Varying Approach to the Term Structure of Interest Rates

So far we have described the case of time-invariant parameters only. We now look at the case where the parameters are time-varying, i.e. (2.22) changes to

$$(3.1) \quad V(L)_t Y_t = U(L)_t X_t + \varepsilon_t$$

In what follows, we have estimated (3.1) using Kalman filter techniques. We have used the Kalman filter because we need to test certain hypotheses about the time-varying nature of underlying parameters, which we discuss in this section. The starting point of our argument is that it is entirely possible that the agents in the financial markets will change their behaviour, and hence the way in which interest rates are determined in those markets, depending on which policy regime or information regime they face (see also: *Barberis et al.*, 1998, 1999; *Daniel et al.*, 1998; *Shleifer*, 2000; *Shefrin*, 1999; *Thaler*, 1994). The Lucas critique in other words: if we change the way in which monetary policy is set, the way agents determine the relevant short and long term interest rates (and risk premia) will also change.

We apply these estimation techniques to analyse the behaviour of British and German short term interest rates over the period 1982 - 1998. That period includes the era of soft (adjustable) EMS exchange rates, the "hard" EMS regime, the collapse to ERM wide bands, and the introduction of inflation targeting in the UK, but the progression to EMU in Germany. It is important that we should be able to take the consequences of all these regime changes into account in our model of interest rate determination. The advantage of the Kalman filter algorithm is that it assumes a behavioural way of how agents form expectations:

agents form one-period ahead forecasts. These forecasts are then compared with each new observation. According to the Kalman gain, the coefficients are systematically updated in order to minimise the one period ahead forecast error. That property makes the Kalman filter convenient for modelling updating behaviour (see also *Hall/Garrat*, 1997a, b): it incorporates rational learning behaviour by market participants, in terms of minimising short-run forecast errors. Hence we estimated the following state space model:

$$(3.2) \quad i_t = D_t X_t + \varepsilon_{1,t}$$

where (3.2) is the measurement equation, and

$$(3.3) \quad D_t = D_{t-1} + \varepsilon_{2,t}, \text{ with } \varepsilon_{a,t} \sim \text{i.i.d.} (0, \ \sigma^2_{\varepsilon_a}) \text{ for a} = 1, 2.$$

is the state equation. In eq. (3.2) i_t is the British two year interest rate, X_t is a set of exogenous determining variables (which also includes lags of the endogenous variable), such as the British base rate (the monetary instrument), the German two year interest rate (to represent ERM influences in the British case), the British ten year interest rate, and the US two year interest rate (to represent world markets). D_t is a matrix of estimated parameters, including a time-varying constant term which if (3.2) is correctly specified, represents a time-varying country-specific risk premium. The rationale of (3.3) is that agents only update the parameters of the model once an unforeseen shock occurs (*Lucas*, 1976).

The question is now how the parameters of (3.2) may be updated to reflect learning. *Wells* (1996) shows that, in the case of an exogenous shock, the parameters are updated as

$$(3.4) \quad d_{t|t} = d_{t|t-1} + K_t \left(i_t - X_t d_{t|t-1} \right)$$

where $d_{t|s}$ denotes the estimate of the state d at time t conditional on the information available at time s. The interesting part of (3.4) is the term in brackets. It shows the forecast error. Hence, the current parameters are updated according to the forecast error resulting from an estimated parameter which did not contain the additional information revealed in the current period. This forecast error in turn affects the Kalman gain. Thus the Kalman gain may be calculated according to

$$(3.5) \quad K_t = P_{t|t-1} X_t' \left(X_t P_{t|t-1} X_t' + \Xi \right)^{-1}$$

where $P_{t|s}$ is the variance of the forecast error at time t conditioned on the system at time s and Ξ is the covariance matrix of $\varepsilon_{2,t}$. In other words, the updating process depends on the one period forecast error <u>and</u> its distribution in the past.

As it stands, the measurement equation, (3.2), allows us to test the expectations hypothesis, as well as testing for uncovered interest parity, time varying risk premia, and the efficiency of the markets in question.

To estimate our term structure model, (3.2) and (3.3), we used monthly data from the Bank of England, Federal Reserve, and the Bundesbank. The sample runs from 1982:1 to 1998:10. In the following section, we analyse the effects of one (significant) shock, namely the collapse of the ERM in 1992. We investigate the parameter changes before the shock, during the shock, after the shock (in 1992:10); and then compare them with the parameters at the end of the sample (1998:10). These different empirical results then allow us to infer the changes in the gain and phase shift over different periods of time.

4 Derivation of the Theoretical Model and Results in the Time Domain

4.1 Specification

In this section we derive the theoretical model and show how we constructed the test for uncovered interest parity. We are interested in investigating the relationship between the German, British, and US interest rate. As a testable approach, our model basically states that (see *Hallwood/MacDonald*, 1994)

$$(4.1) \quad i_{t,m} = \varphi_1 i_{t,m}^1 + \Delta e_{1,t}^e + \varepsilon_{2,t}, \text{ and}$$

$$(4.2) \quad i_{t,m} = \varphi_2 i_{t,m}^2 + \Delta e_{2,t}^e + \varepsilon_{3,t},$$

where $i_{t,m}$ and $i_{t,m}^k$ are respectively the home and foreign interest rates ($k = 1 =$ US and $k = 2 =$ Germany in the British case); $\Delta e_{k,t}^e$ is the change of the exchange rate expectation at time t. In the case that agents act perfectly rational, and if all bonds are perfect substitutes, φ_1 and φ_2 are supposed to be one. If all bonds are perfect substitutes then agents are generally indifferent with respect to the issuing country (given exchange rate expectations). So, if there are arbitrage opportunities then agents will exploit these opportunities. Otherwise they would lose profitable opportunities. However, in *Richter* (2001), we show that the British and the German term structure are not compatible. In particular, the outcome of the (generated) British term structure is a hypothetical zero coupon bond while the German term structure represents an "average" (federal government) bond which is not well defined in terms of its characteristics. Moreover, both bond markets are different with respect to the existing stock of bonds. It is therefore unlikely that these yields do really represent bonds which are perfect substitutes. Furthermore, the assumption that agents can exploit even small arbitrage opportunities neglects transaction costs - meaning information costs and capacity restrictions here. Capacity restrictions occur because agents might only have limited access to funds. Information cost occur because agents have to compare yields of different bonds. Taking everything together, there are a number of reasons why φ_1 and φ_2 will in fact be different from unity.

On the other hand, neglecting one or all of these assumptions leads to models where bond prices and yields might under- or overreact to shocks. Recent research in finance has demonstrated that proposition (see for example *Daniel et al.*, 1998). That implies that φ_1 and φ_2 should actually be greater or equal to zero. In any event, the possibility of under- or overreaction would mean the coefficients φ_1 and φ_2 should deviate significantly from one.

Furthermore, eq. (4.1) and (4.2) suggest a way to estimate the changes in the expected exchange rate. We assume that the observed interest rate is depending on the monetary instrument (in accordance with *Estrella/Mishkin*, 1995, 1997), i.e. that

$$(4.3)\ i_{t,m} = \beta_1 CB_t + \varepsilon_{4,t}, \beta_1 \geq 0$$

where CB is the central bank rate. If monetary policy is completely successful, we would expect to see $\beta_1 = 1$[13]. However, agents might over- or underestimate the effects of monetary policies, so that β_1 is bigger or less than one (*Barberis et al.*, 1998; *Daniel et al.*, 1998).

The observed interest rate also depends on a long-term interest rate ($i_{t,10}$). If the long term interest rate increases, then agents will take that as an indicator for future higher yields. Since agents are (at least to a certain degree) indifferent to longer terms to maturity, agents will demand more longer-term bonds in order to obtain those higher yields, increasing the yield on short-term bonds. This is also true if agents prefer shorter terms to maturity to longer ones, which would imply the yield of short-term bonds is less than that of long-term bonds. Hence β_2 in the following equation should be greater than zero, but does not have to be greater than one,

$$(4.4)\ i_{t,m} = -\gamma + \beta_2 i_{t,10} + \varepsilon_{6,t}.\ \beta_2 > 0$$

In eq. (4.4) γ can be interpreted as the liquidity preference. In our case we are assuming that agents are risk averse. The interesting question is whether γ is indeed positive.

Finally, a natural assumption here would be to have β_2 equal to one. That would make the spread between long- and short-term yields constant. However, as *Lowe* (1992) and *Frankel/Lown* (1991) point out, a constant spread is only likely under very restrictive assumptions. So, we only assume that β_2 is positive (or at least nonnegative) and leave its precise value to empirical quantification. To return to the rest of the story, adding up eq. (4.1) to (4.4) yields:

$$(4.5)\ 4i_{t,m} = -\gamma + \varphi_1 i_{t,m}^1 + \varphi_2 i_{t,m}^2 + \beta_1 CB_t + \beta_2 i_{t,10} + \Delta e_1^e + \Delta e_2^e + \varepsilon_{1,t} + \varepsilon_{2,t} + \varepsilon_{3,t} + \varepsilon_{4,t}$$

where $\varepsilon_{i,t}$, i = 1..4, is i.i.d.(0, $\sigma_{\varepsilon_i}^2$). It is assumed that each error series $\{\varepsilon_i\}$ is white noise (integrated of order 0, I(0)) so that their sum is also stationary (see *Engle/Granger*, 1991). That yields

---

[13] However, *Lowe* (1992) and *Estrella/Mishkin* (1995, 1997) argue that this is only true for the short end of the term structure. Longer term interest rates should depend less on the central bank rate than short-term rates, since they are reflecting more long-term inflation expectations, so that β_1 should be decreasing with increasing term to maturity (m).

(4.6) $\sum_{i=1}^{4}\{\epsilon_i\} = \{\zeta\}$.

Now setting

(4.7) $-\gamma + \Delta e_{1,t}^e + \Delta e_{2,t}^e = \eta_t$

and substituting (4.7) and (4.6) into (4.5) yields

(4.8) $4i_{t,m} = \eta_t + \varphi_1 i_{t,m}^1 + \varphi_2 i_{t,m}^2 + \beta_1 CB_t + \beta_2 i_{t,10} + \zeta_t$

Hence, we have

(4.9) $i_{t,m} = \frac{1}{4}\eta_t + \frac{1}{4}\varphi_1 i_{t,m}^1 + \frac{1}{4}\varphi_2 i_{t,m}^2 + \frac{1}{4}\beta_1 CB_t + \frac{1}{4}\beta_2 i_{t,10} + \frac{1}{4}\zeta_t$

where

$\zeta_t \sim \text{i.i.d.}\left(0, \sigma_\zeta^2\right)$

There are several implications to be taken from (4.9). Firstly, even if we assume constant risk premia, the inclusion of unknown exchange rate expectations automatically makes the risk premium (η_t) time-varying[14]. The risk premium in (4.9) is, in that case, only stable if exchange rate expectations are stable too or – in the case of time-varying risk premia – if the changes in the risk premia are equal to the changes of the exchange rate expectations. Furthermore, the risk premium can now be positive or negative. That is in line with *Modigliani/Sutch* (1966).

Secondly, even in the case of perfect capital markets, the immediate effect of an increase of a foreign interest rate is reduced to one-quarter of its previous value. So, when testing (4.9) we would expect relatively small coefficient for the foreign interest rates, if uncovered interest parity actually holds. In fact, the co-efficients would be even smaller if foreign bonds are also not perfect substitutes to domestic bonds. However, the coefficient might be bigger if agents tend to overreact to disturbances or foreign events in the market.

On the other hand, eq. (4.9) does not say anything about how agents learn. In order to do so, the coefficients in eq. (4.9) should be allowed to vary over time. As *Sheffrin* (1996) points out it is not enough to expand (4.9) by creating additional lags in order to model the learning process. There is a difference between "stable deterministic systems" and "stable stochastic systems". As long as the solution of characteristic equation of a deterministic system, i.e. eq. (4.9) including lags, does not contain roots bigger or equal to one, the system will always converge (after a certain time). In contrast, stochastic systems may react to

---

[14] Other authors come to the same conclusion: *Driffill* (1990) finds that the expectations hypothesis cannot be rejected once an autoregressive risk premium is introduced. Furthermore, there are theoretical models which suggest time-varying risk premia even in the case of (unbounded) rationality. Namely, if the current behaviour of agents is affected by their losses in the past, for example (see *Barberis et al.*, 1999, 1998). Hence, if other variables are relevant which determine the behaviour of the agents then that results in a time-varying risk premium.

shocks by changing coefficients. Stochastic systems may or may not settle down to a particular state, therefore. In this framework, eq. (4.9) is interpreted as the (long-run) equilibrium of the stochastic system (if η_t is stable as well). In our implementation we will allow for lags and determine the best lag-length by using the Akaike criterion[15].

In this paper, we are particularly interested in the parameter values which held during and after the ERM crisis in 1992. We want to investigate whether the ERM crisis led to a change of the gain and the phase shift. The gain relates the spectrum of the explanatory variable to the spectrum of the endogenous variable. If that relationship changes, then it says something about the underlying volatility of the observed time series. The phase shift, meanwhile, tells us how the lead-lag relationship between the endogenous and exogenous changed. So a change in that relationship tells us something about the speed of reaction, i.e. how fast can agents process new information. The faster they can do that, the more instantaneous will the lead-lag relationship be and the more efficient will the market be in that regard.

4.2   Parameter Estimates

The measurement equation (3.2) for Britain has now the following form for all periods:

$$(4.10) \quad i_{t,2}^{brit} = \alpha_{1,t} + \alpha_{2,t}\text{Base Rate}_t + \alpha_{3,t}i_{t,2}^{ger} + \alpha_{4,t}i_{t,10}^{brit} + \alpha_{5,t}i_{t,2}^{US} + \alpha_{6,t}\text{Base Rate}_{t-1}\partial$$
$$+ \alpha_{7,t}i_{t-1,2}^{brit} + \alpha_{8,t}i_{t-1,2}^{US} + \alpha_{9,t}i_{t-1,10}^{brit} + \varepsilon_t$$

where $i_{t,m}^{a}$ is the interest rate of country a (Britain, Germany, US) at time t with a term to maturity of m years. The following table gives the estimated parameter values at different points in time. We are particularly interested in the parameters α_1 (the risk premium), α_3 (the impact of the German interest rate), and $\alpha_{4,5}$ (the impact of the US rate). We analyse the question how interest parity was affected due to the ERM crisis. The following table shows the parameter values for before, during, and after the ERM crisis. From eq. (4.1) and (4.2), we would expect that φ_1 and φ_2 are equal to 1 in case of efficient capital markets. In other words, the estimated long run parameter value of the German and US rate should be ¼.

Table 4.1: Parameter Values for the British Regression for Different Points in Time

TIME	α_1	α_2	α_3	α_4	α_5	α_6	α_7	α_8	α_9
1992:08	0.585	0.433	0.038	0.449	0.572	-0.271	0.673	-0.341	-0.261
1992:10	0.576	0.435	0.036	0.405	0.590	-0.274	0.666	-0.321	-0.257
1993:01	0.570	0.441	0.036	0.392	0.596	-0.268	0.669	-0.327	-0.261
1998:10	0.481	0.422	0.030	0.408	0.599	-0.290	0.689	-0.332	-0.280

[15] All tests can be found in *Richter* (2001).

We can now use the parameter values of Table 4.1 to calculate the long run parameter values for different points in time. Table 4.2 therefore shows the long run parameter values for different points in time for the German and US interest rates as calculated from above.

Table 4.2: Long Run Parameter Values of the German and US Rates

TIME	GERMANY	AVG LAG	VAR LAG	US	AVG LAG	VAR LAG
1992:08	0.116	2.058	1.133	0.706	0.582	1.237
1992:10	0.107	1.994	1.435	0.805	0.801	1.536
1993:01	0.109	2.021	1.400	0.813	0.806	1.217
1998:10	0.097	2.215	1.018	0.858	0.972	1.655

Table 4.2 shows that the long run parameter values are far away from being ¼ for each country. Interestingly, the long run parameter for Germany is less than half of ¼ and the long run parameter values of the US rates are sometimes more than 3 times of ¼. This result is surprising because we can assume that near perfect capital mobility does exist in between these markets. Yet, the results indicate an underreaction in the first case and an overreaction in the latter case. Hence, neither case is really compatible with rational or efficient markets. Moreover, we also found that the parameter values are stable at the end of the sample period (for the last ten months). So, we would conclude that some kind of equilibrium has been reached. The interesting point here is that parameter stability has been reached, although the parameters are from being close to the UIP values. Hence, inefficient capital markets do not necessarily imply that they are unstable. This point is obvious when we look at the lag distribution for Germany. The average lag did not change due to the ERM crisis. It seems that the variance of the lag distribution changed. The cross spectral analysis of section four provides us with a tool to check this. For example from figure 5.3 we can see that the gain never leaves the confidence bands at all frequencies. As will be seen the gain is derived from the regression in the time domain. From the time domain, we derive the lag-structure as well. In the frequency domain, we have an indirect test, whether they differ from each other. Since the gain did not significantly change over time, we would not expect the lag-structure to change, so that the lag-distribution remains constant. Hence, we can argue that the change of the variance is not significant. Therefore, the long run equilibrium values did not change either.

In the case of the US, the long-run value of the coefficient increased after the shock by 0.1 or 0.15 towards the end of the sample (Table 4.2). Hence the question is again whether this is a significant change of the long-run coefficient. From figure 5.3 we can see that the long-run parameter values lie within the confidence bands. Although the gain moved to the upper band, it did not cross it. Hence, the change of the long-run coefficient is not significant. Furthermore, we can also conclude that the lag structure and also the lag-distribution did not change over time. However, we can conclude that in both cases the long run parameter values are not included in the confidence bands. Hence, they are significantly different. So the capital markets do not fulfil the UIP condition. But we can conclude that British markets need on average two periods (i.e. two months) to react on changes of the German interest rate while to react on changes in the US the market only needs only half a month. That is quite a difference. Furthermore, this difference is also relatively stable. That means, increasing samples do not lead to a reduction of the time period agents need to process new information.

If markets were fully efficient we would expect an instantaneous adjustment after a shock occurs. Since we have established that the market is not efficient, the question is, how long does it take for the market to return to the equilibrium and whether this adjustment process has changed over time. We start again with Germany.

Figure 4.1: Lag Structure of the Impact of the German Interest Rate

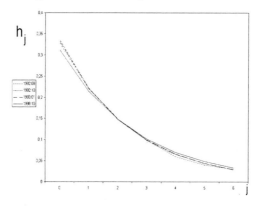

Figure 4.1 shows the lag structure of the German interest rate. It makes the point clear that the differences of the lag structures are very small. In all cases, about 30% of the impact is incorporated into the two year interest rate after one period. After six periods only 3% of the original shock remain. If markets were efficient, we would expect a faster assimilation of the shock.. The next diagram will make this point clear.

Figure 4.2: Accumulated Lag Structure

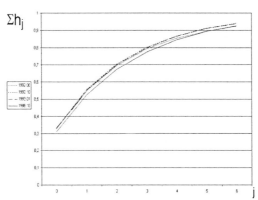

Figure 4.2 shows the same coefficients but added up. It shows that it takes about five periods until 90% of the shock are processed. This long adjustment period may cause problems, because it can well be that within this adjustment period another shock occurs. Hence, we would end up with several layers of adjustment processes at the same time. This may be the reason, why an equilibrium might not be reached although it does exist. It also shows that the differences of the lag structures at different points in time are very small. Even shocks like the ERM crisis did not lead to a substantial change of the relationship of the German interest rate to the British one.

We are now looking at the impact of the US interest rate. The following diagram shows the lag structure of the US rate.

Figure 4.3: Lag Structure of the US Rate

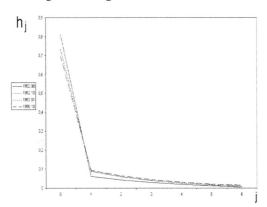

From the above diagram, we can see that the lag structures are basically the same. In all cases about 80% of the impact is processed immediately. The first period carries only about 10%. The interesting point is that although we stated above that agents are overreacting concerning US bonds, that does not imply that all information is immediately processed. However adjustment towards equilibrium is much faster than in the German. That will become obvious in the next diagram.

Figure 4.4: Accumulated Lag Structure for US Rates

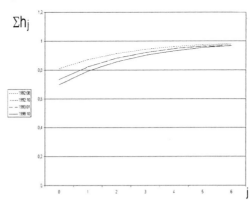

From the above figure we can see that almost the entire adjustment has taken place within six months. This property has not changed due to the ERM crisis. Hence the relationship between US and British interest rates is stable, although this relationship is also characterised by inefficient markets. Therefore, neither over- nor underreaction of market participants causes unstable market relationships. Suprisingly, even in the case of overreaction, it takes half a year until the impact of a shock is processed. We would have expected a somewhat shorter adjustment period. Still most of the adjustment is done in the first period. The question is whether this is a stabilising property. On the one hand, the observed values are closer to the equilibrium values. On the other hand, that might be the reason, why a time series looks volatile since a shock might require a drastic adjustment which would largely take place immediately.

To summarise, we find that agents in financial markets do not behave as the UIP condition would suggest. In particular, adjustment to the equilibrium takes longer than expected. We also find only one equilibrium for the interest rate relationships. The question is how shocks are absorbed In particular what causes the volatility of the observed time series. In order to answer this question, we look at cross spectral analysis. In particular, the "gain" tells us how agents react, once a shock occurs.

5   Cross Spectral Analysis

5.1 The Impact of German Monetary Policy on the UK

Market participants in the UK may have correctly anticipated the significance of German interest rates, but in order to determine the cyclical consequences of the ERM crisis, but they do not rely on German monetary policy to help them determine interest rates (Table 4.1 and Table 4.2). Although there is a significant impact, it is relatively small. Looking at the gain confirms that point. The gain is close to zero at all frequencies in each time period (figure 5.1). If anything, the German interest rate causes long term cycles. But even that impact is quite small. In other words, British short term interest rates are close to being independent of changes in the German two year interest rate. As we could see in the last section that relationship is relatively stable on that level.

The conclusion therefore has to be that British monetary policy had been operating more or less independently both before and after the pound left the ERM, i.e. British capital markets are not as much affected by changes of German interest rates as we would expect them to be. That is going to make it very hard to operate one single monetary policy which is going to be effective in both the UK and Germany, using one common set of market based policy instruments. This may seen to be a surprising result since the uncovered interest parity theorem would predict equal interest rates (at least in the absence of changes in the exchange rate expectation, that is in 1992:08, if not thereafter).

Although capital mobility existed within Europe at that time, British and German bonds are obviously nothing like perfect substitutes at any or all maturities. The difference between them could perhaps be explained in terms of risk premia (see below). But, whatever the explanation may be, it is clear from these results that the bond characteristics are quite different in the two countries (see also *Richter*, 2001). That means the bond markets would have to be harmonised before a common monetary policy could be implemented (that also holds for all other countries within EMU). In order to make open market policies more efficient, government bonds of different countries should have the same characteristics, so that they are directly comparable. That would eliminate one element of the risk premium. Another question is whether agents ask for a risk premium for some countries (for example, if one country faces an institutional crisis like Italy recently). That could cause different transmission mechanisms which would undermine common monetary policy.

Figure 5.1: Gains for Different Points in Time of the German Rate on the British Rate

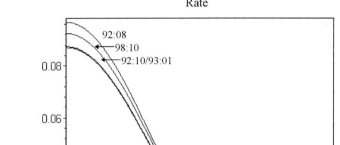

Figure 5.2 shows the coherence. The coherence is equivalent to R^2 in the frequency domain. For each frequency, i.e. period, it shows how much of the cyclical movement of the first series can be explained by the second. It makes the point, once again, that both series are not really correlated with each other[16]. At longer cycles, the German interest rate explains 24% at most of the cyclical movement of the British interest rate. For small cycles the German interest rate explains 3% of the British interest rate. That means the German interest is not responsible for short term volatility of the British interest rate. This is in line with our analysis of the lag structure: the immediate adjustment was relatively small. Hence, changes of the German interest rate have largely long term effects. That in turn implies that the German interest rate is stabilising the British interest rate. This result is surprising since the UIP does not hold (as we saw in the last section). But it is also true that the "weak" link between these two capital markets is probably not as stabilising as it could be. It also shows that interest rate spill over effects cannot be used in the short tem to stabilise the British interest rate. At least in the short term, both markets are quite separated from each other. as can be seen in figure 5.2 below.

---

[16] We plotted only the coherence for 1992:8 only in figure 5.2. Since the gain does not change significantly, the coherence is constant as well.

Figure 5.2: Coherence between the British and the German Interest Rate

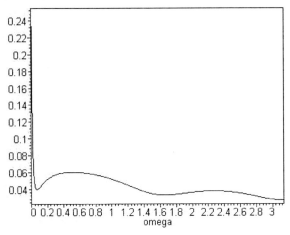

Figure 5.3: Confidence Intervals and the gains

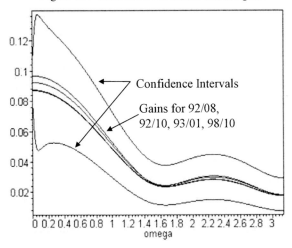

Figure 5.3 shows the gain of the German interest rate and its confidence intervals. As can be seen the long run values of the gain, i.e. zero frequency, are the same as the long run values in Table 4.2 (although there are some small deviations due to rounding errors). This link is not a coincidence. Laven and Shi (1993) and Nerlove et al. (1995) show that this has to be the case. Hence the gain shows the impact of the explanatory variable on the dependent variable for all cycles. What is interesting though is that the confidence bands are at no frequency near the UIP value (0.25). Hence, the cross spectral analysis extends our

analysis to short term reactions as well. And, cross spectral analysis enables us to analyse this impact continuously over all periods. The confidence bands also give us a continuous picture of which values could be reached by the estimated parameters. This is very convenient since we do not have to calculate (hypothetical) variance-covariance matrices.

We now turn our attention to the phase shift. The phase shift shows for all frequencies how many periods is one time series leading or lagging the other series. The interpretation of the phase shift is therefore different to the adjustment of a series to the equilibrium.

As with the gain, the phase shift also remains more or less constant over time. For short periodicities, both series move in phase; while for longer periodicities the German interest rate is leading (anticipating) any changes in the two year interest rate, with a lead of one month ahead.

Figure 5.4: Phase Shifts between the British and German Two Year Interest Rate at Different Points of Time

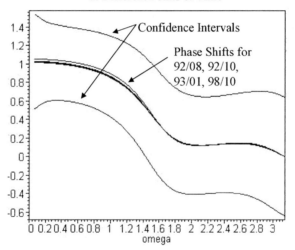

5.2   The Impact of US Monetary Policy on the UK

Figure 5.5 shows that the impact of the two year US rate on the British two year interest rate is higher at each frequency than the German one. Hence, US bonds are regarded as closer substitutes for British bonds, than German bonds are for British bonds. That too suggests a common monetary policy would cause problems because of the differences in the monetary transmissions implied. Indeed, since the ERM crisis was a purely European problem, it is interesting to see how the impact of the US monetary policies on British interest rates changed through the 1990s. In general, the gain for the US interest rate variable increases over time; i.e. the weight of the latter in determining British rates at the longer cycles increased. That in turn reduced volatility of British short term interest rates. In other words, US interest rates actually helped stabilise British interest rates during and after the crisis. On the other hand, the next diagram shows that these changes are well within their confidence interval. There is a tendency to move towards the upper limit of the confidence band as time passes. It gets close to the top of its bands, but the gain for 1998:10 is still within the limits. Hence, learning did not lead to significant changes in the frequency domain behaviour (in contrast to the aggregated time domain behaviour). That indicates quite a stable economy as far as the cycles caused by policy changes are concerned.

Figure 5.5: Confidence Intervals for the Gain on the US Rate

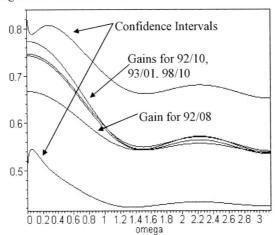

As in the German case, figure 5.5 shows that the UIP value is not included in the 95% confidence interval at all frequencies. But in difference to the German case, we can observe an overshooting behaviour here. As said above this overshooting behaviour is stable over all cycles.

Moving to the phase shift diagram, although, the US rates may have helped to stabilise the British interest rate, the lead of the US rate increased from 7.5 days to 12 days for the longer cycles. For shorter cycles both series are in phase, beginning with those 4 months in length or less. Since at the same time, the dependence on US rates has gone up, this result suggests that agents learnt it was to their advantage to align UK short term rates more closely with those in the US after the ERM crisis.

Figure 5.6: Confidence Interval for the Phase Shift of the US Rate

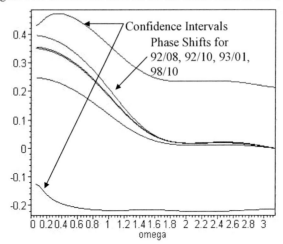

On the other hand, the above diagram also shows that these changes in the phase shift were again insignificant. Even if there is a tendency to move towards the upper limit, the phase shift has not (yet) reached the upper confidence bound. Thus, although the US rate has a bigger impact on UK interest rates than do German rates, those changes in financial behaviour have also turned out to be statistically insignificant overall. But the interesting point is that in the US case we have an overshooting behaviour and in the German case an undershooting behaviour. Not only is in both cases UIP not fulfilled, both deviations are in opposite directions.

5.3 The Risk Premium on the UK Interest Rate

Finally, the risk premium can be modelled as the time-varying constant in equation (4.7). In this formulation, the risk premium contains liquidity preferences as well as uncertainty about changes of the expected exchange rate. Hence, the risk premium may be time varying due to changing preferences, or changing expectations, or both.

Figure 5.7: Impact of the Risk Premium on British Rates at Different Points in Time

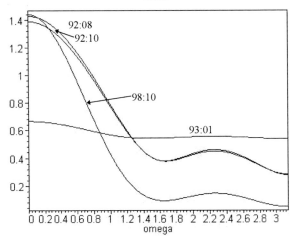

From figure 5.7 we can see that, at the beginning of the sample, the effect of the risk premium is mainly stabilising, but has (as one might expect) a stronger impact on the longer cycles than on the shorter cycles. This is still the case during the ERM crisis. However, an adjustment at that point led to a more evenly spread impact over the entire band by 93:01 – especially after the pound had left the ERM system altogether. Later on, the gain gradually returned to its previous shape. Although, the impact on longer cycles is now substantially less than before, and decreasing, the risk premium remains more stabilising in the short term since the impact on shorter cycles has been reduced.

Finally, figure 5.8 shows that by 1998 the risk premium term had moved outside its lower confidence band for values of $\omega \geq 0.6$. That implies a statistically significant and permanent reduction in short and medium term risk in the British financial markets. Before that, i.e. by 1993 but after the onset of the ERM crisis, there had been a significant, but temporary, reduction in the long term risk (i.e. for 1993 and $\omega < 0.9$) – the crisis having made the financial markets focus on the short term implications of any changes in monetary policy, to the neglect of the long term consequences. Later, as learning begins to be effective, we move to the reductions in short term risk revealed in the 1998 results, with no increase in long term risk.

The interesting finding here is that the risk premium is the only variable whose changes were big enough for them to leave their confidence interval entirely. This was particularly obvious for 1993:01. And although the risk premium moved back into the interval in 98:10, it is still outside the confidence interval for frequencies higher than 0.6 (i.e. for cycles of 10 months or less).

From this we can conclude that, in Britain, adjustments to the ERM crisis took place through changes in the risk premium. The risk premium/liquidity preference variable is the only variable which changed significantly during the ERM crisis. It acted to absorb the volatility or uncertainty effects of that crisis, and allowed the underlying interest rates to remain constant.

Figure 5.8: Confidence Intervals for the British Risk Premium

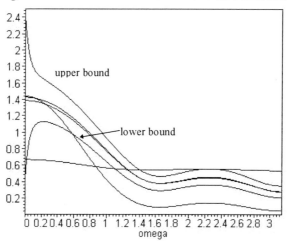

In the context of our model, that means agents in the British markets learnt rather rapidly how the new monetary regime was going to work, and how to adapt their behaviour to fit.

6   Conclusions

Contrary to conventional wisdom perhaps, conditions in the UK financial markets were remarkably stable - from a frequency domain point of view - through the tensions of the 1990s and the collapse of the ERM exchange rate system. Learning and "activist adjustment" by market participants meant that most of the volatility was absorbed through changes in risk premia or liquidity preferences - leaving the underlying relationships which determine interest rates and the term structure unchanged. This result is surprising because the UIP relationship is not fulfilled. And that, contrary to most theoretical analyses, implies that inefficient financial markets are not necessarily unstable in their relationships. Moreover, we could also show that inefficient markets do not cause higher volatility. This is even true for undershooting and overshooting behaviour. The difference though lies in the speed of adjustment towards the equilibrium. Obviously undershooting behaviour implies a longer period to reach the equilibrium than overshooting behaviour.

Like many other studies (for example, *Bong-Soo*, 1989; *Engle et al.*, 1987; *Engle/Ng*, 1993; *MacDonald/Macmillan*, 1994) before, we find that behavioural changes are reflected in the (time-varying) risk premium. The risk premium therefore plays a crucial role in the behavioural process of agents. This makes especially sense, when the risk premium is considered to reflect all uncertainties resulting from market activity. The question is then whether there are any differences in between markets. *Hughes Hallett/Richter* (2001) compare the German market with the British one and find some interesting differences in the behaviour of agents in those countries. They find that, the German risk premium is more stable than the British one.

We also find that larger samples do not reduce the adjustment period. On the contrary, it also happened that the variance increased, i.e. the adjustment period could also increase with increasing sample sizes. If that is true then the question arises what information is really contained in observable yields/prices. We cannot answer the question here, but our results suggest that observable yields/prices do not contain all information available. Otherwise, one could not explain why it takes so long for agents to adjust to shocks.

Finally, these results could not have been obtained without a technique that can disentangle the different layers of the agents' dynamic behaviour, as represented by different frequency bands and cross spectral components in a time-varying spectral analysis.

References

Barberis, N. / Huang, M. / Santos, T. (1999): Prospect Theory and Asset Prices. mimeo.

Barberis, N. / Shleifer, A. / Vishny, R. (1998): A Model of Investor Sentiment, mimeo.

Baumol, W. J. (1957): Speculation, Profitability and Stability. Review of Economics and Statistics, pp. 263 - 271.

Black, F. (1989): Noise. Journal of Finance, Volume 48, pp. 540-555.

Bong-Soo, L. (1989): A Nonlinear Expectations Model of the Term Structure of Interest Rates with Time-Varying Risk Premia. Journal of Money, Credit, and Banking, 1989, Volume 21, pp. 348-367.

Daniel, K. / Hirshleifer, D. / Subrahmanyam, A. (1998): A Theory of Overconfidence, Self-Attribution, and Security Market Under- and Overreactions. mimeo.

Driffill, J. (1990): The Term Structure of Interest Rates: Structural Stability and Macroeconomic Policy Changes in the UK. Centre for Economic Policy Research, Discussion Paper no 430, London.

Easley, D. / O'Hara, M. (1992): Adverse Selection and Large Trade Volume: The Implications for Market Efficiency. Journal of Financial and Quantitative Analysis, Volume 27, pp. 185-208.

Engle, R.F. / Granger, C.W.J. (1991): Long-Run Economic Relationships. Oxford University Press.

Engle, R.F. / Lilien, D.M. / Robins, R.P. (1987): Estimating Time Varying Risk Premia in the Term Structure: The ARCH-M Model. Econometrica, 1987, Volume 55, (2), pp. 391-407.

Engle, R.F. / Ng, V.K. (1993): Time-Varying Volatility and the Dynamic Behavior of the Term Structure. Journal of Money, Credit, and Banking, 1993, Volume 25, pp. 336-349.

Estrella, A. / Mishkin, F.S. (1997): The Predictive Power of the Term Structure of Interest Rates in Europe and the United States: Implications for the European Central Bank. European Economic Review, Volume 41, pp. 1375 - 1401.

Estrella, A. / Mishkin, F.S. (1995): The Term Structure of Interest Rates and its Role in Monetary Policy for the European Central Bank. NBER Working Paper no. 5279, Massachusetts.

Frankel, J.A. / Lown, C.S. (1991): An Indicator of Future Inflation Extracted from the Steepness of the Interest Rate Yield Curve Along its Entire Length. NBER Working Paper no. 3551.

Frydman, R. (1983): A Distinction between the Unconditional Expectational Equilibrium and the Rational Expectations Equilibrium. *Frydman, R.* and *Phelps, E.S.* (eds.): Individual Forecasting and Aggregate Outcomes, pp. 139-146, Cambridge University Press.

Garratt, A. / Hall, S.G. (1997a): E-equilibria and Adaptive Expectations: Output and Inflation in the LBS Model. Journal of Economic Dynamics and Control, Volume 21, pp. 1149 - 1171.

Garratt, A. / Hall, S.G. (1997b): The Stability of Expectational Equilibria in the LBS Model, in: *Allen, C.* and *Hall, S.* (eds.): Macroeconomic Modelling in a Changing World, pp. 217 - 246, Wiley.

Gençay, R. / Selçuk, F. / Whitcher, B. (2002): An Introduction to Wavelets and Other Filtering Methods in Finance and Economics, Academic Press, San Diego.

Hallwood, C. P. / MacDonald, R. (1994): International Money and Finance, 2nd ed., Oxford.

Hamilton, J. (1994): Time Series Analysis, Princeton University Press.

Hendry, D.F. (1995): Dynamic Econometrics, Oxford University Press.

Hughes Hallett, A. / Richter, C. (2004): Spectral Analysis as a Tool for Financial Policy: An Analysis of the Short End of the British Term Structure. Journal of Computational Economics, Volume 23, pp. 271 - 288.

Hughes Hallett, A. / Richter, C. (2002): Are Capital Markets Efficient? Evidence from the Term Structure of Interest Rates in Europe. Economic and Social Review, Volume 33, no. 3, pp. 333 – 56.

Hughes Hallett, A. / Richter, C. (2001): Are Capital Markets Efficient? Evidence from the Term Structure of Interest Rates in Europe, Ludwig Boltzmann Institute Working Paper no 2001.22, December 2001.

Jenkins, G.M. / Watts, D.G. (1968): Spectral Analysis and its Applications, Holden-Day, San Francisco.

Kaldor, N. (1939): Speculation and Economic Stability. Review of Economic Studies, 1939, pp. 1-27.

Laven, G. / Shi, G. (1993): Zur Interpretation von Lagverteilungen, University of Mainz discussion paper, no. 41.

Lowe, P. (1992): The Term Structure of Interest Rates, Real Activity and Inflation. Research Discussion Paper 9204, Reserve Bank of Australia.

Lucas, R.E. (1976): Econometric Policy Evaluation: A Critique. Brunner, K. and Meltzer, A. (eds.): The Phillips Curve and Labor Markets, pp. 19-46, North-Holland, Amsterdam.

MacDonald, R. / Macmillan, P. (1994): On the Expectations View of the Term Structure, Term Premia and Survey-Based Expectations. The Economic Journal, Volume 104, 1070-1086.

Modigliani, F. / Sutch, R. (1966): Innovations in Interest Rate Policy. American Economic Review, 1966, Volume 56, pp. 178 – 197.

Nerlove, M. / Grether, D.M. / Carvalho, J. L. (1995): Analysis of Economic Time Series Academic Press, New York.

Percival, D.B. / Walden, A.T. (2000): Wavelet Methods for Time Series Analysis, Cambridge University Press, Cambridge, UK.

Perron, P. (1989): The great crash, the oils price shock and the unit root Hypothesis. Econometrica, Volume 57, pp. 1361-1401.

Richter, C. (2001): Learning and the Term Structure of Interest Rates in Britain and Germany, PhD thesis, University of Strathclyde, Glasgow.

Shefrin, H. (1999): Beyond Greed and Fear: Understanding Bahvioral Finance and the Psychology of Investing, Harvard Business School Press.

Sheffrin, S. (1996): Rational Expectations, 2nd ed. Cambridge Surveys of   Literature.

Shleifer, A. (2000): Inefficient Markets, Oxford University Press.

Stock, J.H. / Watson, M.W. (1991): Variable Trends in Economic Time Series, in: Engle, R.F. and Granger, C.W.J. (eds.): Long-Run Economic Relationships, pp. 17-49, Oxford University Press.

Thaler, R.H. (1994): Quasi Rational Economics, Russell Sage Foundation.

Wells, K. (1996): The Kalman Filter in Finance, Kluwer Academic Publishers, London.

Wolters, J. (1980): Stochastic Dynamic Properties of Linear Econometric Models, Springer-Verlag, Berlin.

Heterogeneous and Imperfect Information in an Experimental Asset Market

Simone Alfarano, Iván Barreda-Tarrazona and Eva Camacho-Cuena

1 Introduction

Financial markets have traditionally been analyzed under the theoretical framework of the Efficient Market Hypothesis (EMH, hereafter)(*Fama* 1970). Within this framework asset markets are viewed as efficient economic institutions in aggregating information. Nevertheless, only indirect implications of the EMH have been investigated so far, since by its nature private information is not observable. Recently, two main approaches have been used to overcome this problem: controlled economic experiments (e.g., *Sunder* 1995) and computer simulations of artificial financial markets(e.g., *Arthur et al.* 1997). In this paper we focus on the experimental approach. We analyze the behavior of a pool of heterogeneously informed traders who can allocate their portfolio between a risky and a riskless asset. In our experiment, the degree of heterogeneity of the information is not limited to two levels, as it is typically done in the experimental literature, but it involves (potentially) a higher number of levels. *Huber et al.* (2004) were the first authors to introduce a heterogeneous information structure with more than two information levels in an experimental asset market. In their experimental setting, the market participants with information level I_j know the future j dividends given by the asset. The dividend process is a gaussian random walk. The system of *cumulative* and *exogenously* given information structure is common knowledge among the market participants. This peculiar information structure allows the analysis of the impact that an additional piece of information has on the net returns of the traders. They found a non monotonic relationship between the information level and the net returns of the traders ("J" shaped returns, *Huber* 2006).

Our experimental setting can be considered a variant of the Huber original experiment. In the asset market here designed, the subjects can decide whether to invest their money in a risky asset, paying a random dividend, or keep it in a bank account with a constant risk-free interest rate. The evolution of the dividend follows a random walk, which implies that the different trading periods are strongly correlated. Parallel to the asset trading, we introduce an information market where the traders can buy an imperfect prediction of the future value of the dividend with a maximum anticipation of 4 periods ahead. The accuracy of the prediction decreases with the chosen time horizon, whereas its price remains constant. The structure of our market adds a further element of complexity to the existent literature on asymmetric information (e.g., *Sunder* 1992; *Hey and Morone* 2004, among others), namely higher heterogeneity in the information levels. In particular, via the possibility to buy costly information, we *endogenize* the information structure, contrary to other contributions in the literature (e.g., *Huber* 2006; *Huber et al.* 2004, 2006a,b; *Kirchler* and *Huber* 2006a,b). In our approach, in fact, every trader could in principle decide to buy information about the value of future dividends. The information is noisy with decreasing precision when the time horizon increases, and heterogeneous, since every trader gets an idiosyncratic signal. In comparison to previous approaches, we loose control over the distribution of information among the traders and we are faced with an increased complexity of the emerging informational structures. However, might observe the emergence of 'self-selected' insiders and we might analyse their ability to exploit their information. In the following section we explain the experimental market designed and the procedure followed in order to conduct the experiments. Section 3 discusses the observed results and Section 4 concludes.

2 Experimental Model and Procedure
2.1 Market Model

The market is conducted for T trading periods. At the beginning of the session each trader is endowed with a portfolio consisting of an initial working capital (cash) and a number of shares. At the end of each trading period $t = 1,...,T$, the cash held in their portfolios pays a fixed interest rate, r, and each share of the asset pays a common dividend d_t to the holder. The underlying dividend process is modeled as a geometric random walk in the following form:

(2.1) $\ln(d_t) = \ln(d_{t-1}) + \sigma_d \varepsilon_t$,

where ε_t follows a normal distribution with mean zero and standard deviation of 1.

The present value of the asset at time t is equal to the sum of the expected future cash flows discounted at the proper interest rate, r. Besides, at the end of period T, we include a buy-back option, since a per-unit terminal value is paid to the holders of the assets. This value is

(2.2) $P_T = \dfrac{d_T}{r}$,

which is the fundamental price of one asset that pays a constant dividend d_T forever. [1]

Therefore, the payment received by the traders per unit of asset hold at the end of period T will be the corresponding dividend, d_T, plus the buy-back value described in Eq.(2.2):

(2.3) $D_T = d_T + \dfrac{d_T}{r}$,

Hence, the present value of an asset at time t is given in our model as:

---

[1] It is not usual in the literature on experimental asset markets to include a buy-back option. Two examples are *Noussair et al.* (2001) and *Smith et al.* (1988). However, if the final buy-back option is not included the fundamental value declines linearly with the age of the asset.

$$(2.4) \quad P_t = \sum_{k=t+1}^{T} \frac{E_t[d_k]}{(1+r)^k} + \frac{E_t[d_T]}{r(1+r)^{T-t}},$$

where we show explicitly the expected discounted value including the buy-back option. Given that the dividend follows a geometric random walk as appears in equation (2.1) and applying the properties of the Lognormal distribution, we have that:

$$(2.5) \quad E_t[d_k] = d_t \quad \forall k > t.$$

Plugging equation (2.5) into the expression for the fundamental value provided in Eq.(2.4) we obtain that the fundamental value at the end of period t is given by the following expression:

$$(2.6) \quad P_t = \frac{d_t}{r}.$$

An additional feature of our experimental design is the possibility in some treatments to buy information about the future value of the dividend. At any time during each period, every trader has the possibility of purchasing, at most, one piece of information. In our setting the information refers to a prediction, in period t, of the future value of the dividend at the end of period $t+n$, where $n \in 0,1,2,3$ accounts for the time horizon of the information. That is, any trader could buy information about the future dividends with a maximum foresight of four periods, including the end of period t.

The price of the information, P_t, is fixed independently of the time horizon, whereas the quality of the information is inversely related to the time horizon. If we consider quality as the accuracy of the prediction purchased in period t for the end of period $t+n$, the longer is the horizon, n, the less accurate is the prediction. Therefore, all traders who decide in period t to purchase information on the value of the dividend in period $t+n$, receive a prediction based on the true value of the dividend in the following way:

$$(2.7) \quad \hat{d}_{t,n}^i = d_{t+n} + \sigma_I \sqrt{n+1} \varepsilon_i,$$

where $\hat{d}_{t,n}^i$ is the information given to trader i in period t about the value of the dividend in the period $t+n$, d_{t+n} denotes the real dividend at the end of period $t+n$, σ_I denotes the standard deviation of the information and ε_i is a noise term normally distributed with $N(0,1)$. Note that the second term in equation (2.7) represents the accuracy of the prediction provided as information that decreases as the time horizon n increases.

2.2 Experimental Procedure

Our experiment was conducted at the Laboratori d'Economia Experimental (LEE) at the University Jaume I of Castellón (Spain) in May 2005. Participants were 216 volunteers recruited among Business Administration students from the same University. Earnings and dividends during the experiments were designated in experimental units (EUs) and converted into € at the end of the experiment, using an exchange rate of 1€=3,000 EUs. A total of 24 markets were conducted in six sessions lasting about 120 minutes each, with average earnings of about 18€.

At the beginning of the session participants received a set of instructions.[2] Instructions were afterwards explained aloud using a short Powerpoint presentation to make subjects familiar with the basic trading mechanism as well as with the computer interface.[3] The experiment was programmed using Z-tree software developed by *Fischbacher* (1999).

Each subject was endowed with a portfolio consisting of 20 units of some asset and 10,000EUs as initial working capital. We had nine traders per market. Each market consisted of 25 trading periods ($T = 25$) of 120 seconds each.[4] As mentioned in section 2.1, at the end of each trading period, the cash held in their portfolios pays a fixed interest rate $r = 1\%$, and each asset pays a common dividend d_t to the holder. However, the dividend at the end of each period is uncertain and, according to equation (1), it is determined as a function on the dividend of the previous period. Therefore, the traders in our experimental setting were informed that the dividend paid in period 0 was 20 EUs per asset hold and $\sigma_d = 0.15$.[5]

Regarding the trading process, we used a single-unit double auction in which the traders were free both to place their bids and asks for assets or directly accept any outstanding bid or ask. In every bid, ask, or transaction only one asset was involved and every trader was allowed to place any number of orders (bid/ask) or trade as much as desired in a period of 120 seconds. However, no short sale was allowed and some price boundaries were embedded into the program.[6]

At the end of each trading period the true value of the dividend was announced and paid to the traders as well as the interest from their working capital. Note that both, the assets and cash held by each trader carried from one period to the next. Moreover, a chart with the history of the dividends was constantly displayed in the room using a beamer, so that subjects could keep track of the past

---

[2] The instructions are provided in Appendix A.

[3] A summary of the script used in the presentation of the computer interface is provided in Appendix B.

[4] Except for session 1 in the information treatment where only 24 periods were conducted.

[5] The value chosen for the standard deviation is slightly higher than the values observed in real markets. We wanted to introduce more variability in the dividends to give a better chance for the decrease in uncertainty produced by the information bought being relevant.

[6] A minimum price of 0 and a maximum of 10,000 EUs.

evolution of the dividend. Two different dividend series (see figure 2.1) were used in the different sessions per treatment.

Figure 2.1: Dividend series

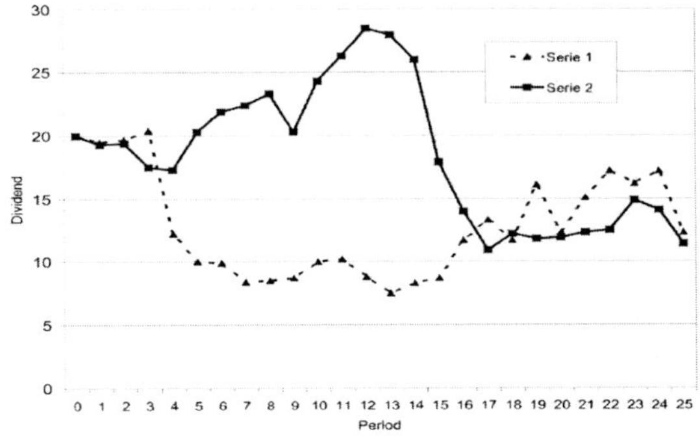

In order to study how the availability of private information affects the market performance, we implemented two different treatments which differ in terms of the availability of private information. In the "no information" treatment no additional private information was available to the traders, while in the "information" treatment they had every period the possibility to buy, at a fixed price $P_I = 100$ EUs, at most one piece of private information about the future value of the dividend in the form of an imperfect signal. Recall that one of the main characteristics of the information in our experiment is that the trader has the possibility to decide the time horizon of the signal, that is, n in equation (2.7). In our experimental setting we consider $n \in 0,1,2,3$ and $\sigma_I = 0.07$. This means that any trader can get an imperfect signal about the true value of the dividend at the end of the same period or up to 3 periods ahead at the same price. However, a trader who buys information about the value of the dividend at the end of the same period ($n = 0$) reduces significantly the uncertainty faced by the uninformed traders, since the value of σ_d is 0.15. While the uncertainty associated to a prediction for 3 periods ahead ($n = 3$) is higher, the information is valid for a longer time period.

At the end of period 25, their earnings in EUs were computed according to the value of their portfolio at this moment, that is, the cash in their accounts plus the value of their assets. Recall that the assets held were purchased by the experimenter at a price according to equation (2). Then, the EUs were converted into €, and the subjects were paid in cash.

3 Experimental Results

From the six sessions we obtained the following data (See Table 1) on contracts (bids and asks) and trades:

Table 1: Data obtained on bids and asks, transactions, mean and variance of the observed prices

	Series 1 Info	Series 1 no Info	Series 2 Info	Series 2 no Info
Contracts	14,485	10,268	10,469	10,465
Traded	3,341	2678	3172	2069
Average	1,230.2	1,495.5	1,654.7	1,239.8
Std. Dev.	1,035.2	1,428.4	828.2	910.2
Markets	8	4	8	4

If our markets were efficient, we should observe a match between the market prices and those implied by the fundamental value, or at least a convergence. But from direct observation of the data plots it was easily observed that market prices in our experiment never match closely the prices implied by the fundamental value. See as an illustration Figure (3.1) were this typical phenomenon is clearly seen.

Figure 3.1: Behaviour of bids, asks, transaction prices and fundamental price of market is4m3 with the possibility of buying information

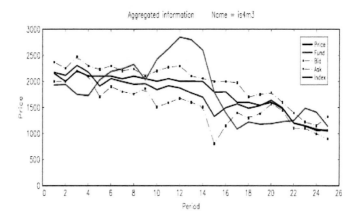

Some markets are more efficient than others, both in information and no information treatment. Normally the trends in the prices go on for some periods before adjusting even if the trend in the fundamental value has already changed. This happens until the last periods when observed prices usually converge to the fundamental price due to the buy-back option, but there are also a minority of markets where convergence never occurs.

Result 1: *Our experimental asset markets were not efficient, that is, the observed transaction prices did not match those implied by the fundamental value of the shares.*

We have made an aggregate statistical analysis of the above data. We calculate first the deviations between observed prices and fundamental value. Then we calculate a median for each market in order to obtain independent observations (12 for each of the two dividend series used) and we check that there are no significant differences between the data obtained under the two dividend series used each day (A battery of Mann-Whitney U tests on volumes and median prices of bids, asks and trades did not signal significant differences). So we proceed then to compare if there are differences between the two treatments: with information and without information (16 and 8 independent observations respectively).

We wanted to test if the existence of self selected insiders would make the market more efficient. However, the data obtained did not show any significant difference in the median of the transaction price deviations from the fundamental price. So our experimental markets are always inefficient to some extent and the existence or not of informed traders does not seem to produce in principle a differently efficient aggregate market behaviour.

Result 2: *The existence of informed traders did not reduce the overall price inefficiency of our experimental asset markets.*

Another evidence against efficiency in our markets is that informed traders in the information treatment are able to obtain slightly higher final profits than non informed. The null hypothesis of lower final profits from traders buying some information is rejected against the unilateral alternative that informed traders earn more. Mann-Whitney U=-1.7, p=0.0445 and Kolmogorov-Smirnov Z=1.341, p=0.028.

Result 3: *Informed traders were able to earn more at the end of the experiment than non-informed traders.*

Figure 3.2: Average net profit depending on the information purchased per subject

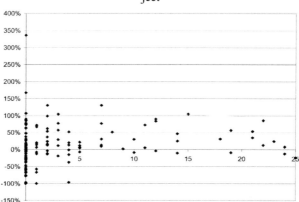

Although the informed traders obtain higher profits that the non informed ones, when we compare the profits within the informed traders our results do not confirm a strictly positive relation between the pieces of information purchased by a trader and the net profit obtained. In fact, those traders acquiring *at least 7* predictions or information signals significantly reduce the probability of obtaining negative net profit.

Result 4: *Although Figure 3.2 confirms a non strictly monotonic relationship between the information level and the net returns of the traders, our results do not reproduce the "J" shaped returns reported in Hurber (2006).*

The little evidence favouring the EMH in our markets is that even if the presence of insiders in the market does not avoid departure of the prices from the fundamental value, it significantly reduces the variance of these departures. Using a mean based Levene-Test we obtain a statistic of 4.748, rejecting the null of equal variance with p=0.04. So we obtain that the variance of the median deviation between fundamental and transaction prices is greater without information.

Result 5: *The more information in the market, the less volatility around the fundamental value was observed.*

Also using a Mann-Whitney U test we find significant differences in the number of Contracts, Asks, Bids and Trades (Mann-Whitney U of -2.939, -3.001, -2.327 and -2.206 respectively, all significant at the 0.05 level): volume is always greater when there is no possibility of buying information. It seems that more information in the market also means less heterogeneous expectations, so less chances to trade.

Result 6: *The more information in the market, the less trading was observed.*

Putting all these results together it seems that the presence of "self selected insiders", that is, traders who decided to buy information some periods when they had the possibility to do so, has some influence on the market.

The increase in information is translated into less variable pricing and less trading volume, but there is a failure in the market to transmit to all the traders the information about the true fundamental value.

There can be several reasons for that: One reason is that there are few informed traders (70 out of 144 who played in the information treatment). According to a questionnaire that the subjects responded after the experiment, many of them found information too costly in terms of experimental units or time to analyze it, or simply they did not trust it. Even from the few informed traders only a small fraction were effectively trying to use the private information they had. The information bought was mainly short term: for the end of the current period or for the next (see figure 3.3). And the main concern for the information buyers seemed to be the last period of the market, when the shares in their portfolios where bought back (see figure 3.4).

Figure 3.3: Distribution of the information per time horizon

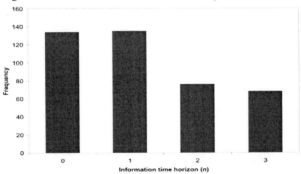

Figure 3.4: Distribution of information regarding each period

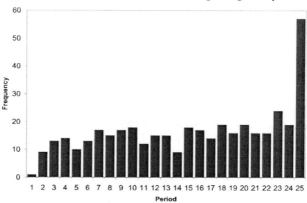

Another reason is that having private information and being able to exploit it is not the same thing. All traders in the markets where it was possible to buy information knew that there could be traders with better information trading in their market, but they had no way to distinguish them from noise traders. So they did not really know if they were following a bubble initiated by a noisy chartist or the price signal of an informed fundamentalist.

All this can be illustrated having a look at some of our graphs. See for instance figure 3.5 which presents a market where it was possible for the traders to buy information. We observe that the asks, bids and transaction prices lie quite apart from the fundamentals.

Figure 3.5: Aggregated behaviour in market is2m1

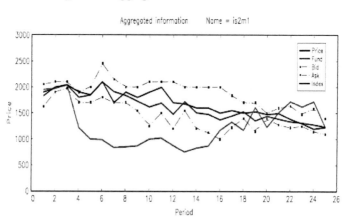

If we look at the behaviour from the uninformed Trader 11 in Market 1 in Session 2 from the information treatment (portrayed by figure 3.6) we see that his bids, asks and trades follow mainly the market average transaction prices, and not the fundamentals. In the treatment where the traders did not have the possibility to buy information their behavior was also usually similar to this pattern. Sometimes, when the market prices come close to the fundamentals it is very difficult to tell apart which of them are the subjects following. Besides, when they diverge we can observe both approximately chartist or fundamentalist behaviour by our subjects. There is nearly always a mixture which creates quite a lot of noise in every market.

Figure 3.6: Individual behaviour of subject 11 in market is2m1

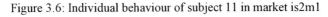

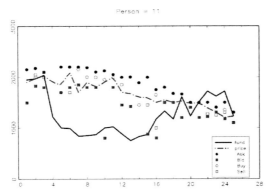

Then if we look at the behaviour of an informed trader of the same session, such as subject 17, who bought information regularly every four periods, we observe in figure 3.7 how he tried to take advantage of the information he possessed, which he also realized the market was not reflecting. We see that the bids follow quite closely the fundamentals, while the asks lie over the market prices and much higher than the fundamentals. So he tried to extract all the possible gains from trade. However he was unsuccessful, given that if we observe the transaction prices which he closed, they match closely the market averages and not his desired bids and asks. Even if he tried to find counterparts for low bids close to the fundamental value and high asks above the market price, nobody wanted to follow him, and the only way to trade some shares was bidding and asking around the existing market prices. Hence, the price signals about the fundamentals he was emitting with his low bids were completely ignored by the majority of the traders in the market.

Figure 3.7: Individual behaviour of subject 17 in market is2m1

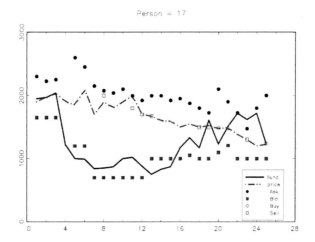

To try to control for this effect of the homogeneity-heterogeneity of information we are currently conducting a treatment in which all the traders have the same information about the future value of the dividend at the end of the next period, so that everybody has the same information about the fundamentals, however we think that the expectations built by each trader will again be very different.

4 Conclusions and Future Work

We carried out an asset market experiment where, in the experimental treatment, we offered the traders the possibility of buying information about the future value of time evolving uncertain dividends. We are able to observe the informational structure of the market, apart from the trading, so we can analyze some questions related with the Efficient Market Hypothesis.

Aggregate analysis of the results indicates that our experimental asset markets are not efficient in transmitting information about the fundamental value of the shares. Observed transaction prices always deviate from those implied by the fundamentals. Besides, those traders who buy and use information about the dividends obtain higher payoffs at the end of the experiment than the other traders, this indicating that they are able to exploit their private information. And in the markets with informed traders the observed transaction prices were not closer in average to those implied by the fundamental value.

However, the presence of more information in the market has some effects: in the treatment with traders buying information significantly less trading was observed, as if more common expectations about the true values had been induced. Consistently, less variance of the trading prices around those implied by the fundamental value was observed, even if, as already commented, on average they did not coincide.

Only 50% of the traders in the information treatment bought some information, and even less traders tried to use it. Also trying to use it and being able to do so were not the same, given that the uninformed traders had no way to tell apart the price signals from the informed traders. Information bought was mainly short term, that is, for the end of the current period or for the next period, and much more frequent concerning the value of the dividend in the last period of the market.

As we did not get conclusive evidence for or against the EMH with the analysis of the data carried out so far we will continue analysing the connection between microscopic behaviour of the traders and their aggregate behaviour, which affects the market efficiency. We will also analyze the role of risk aversion using our risk-test data and the role of gender differences. The experiments of an additional treatment in which all traders have homogeneous information about the prediction of the dividend for the end of the current period are currently under way. As a last step we contemplate the use of computational models for the simulation of the experiment (genetic programming or algorithm methodology) to overcome some limitation of the experimental method (number of subjects, limited time of the experiments).

Acknowledgements

The paper benefitted a lot from suggestions by anonymous referees, and also from comments by Otwin Becker, Aurora García-Gallego, Nikolaos Georgantzís, Eva Haase, Maximilian Jung, Ulrike Leopold-Wildburger, Luisa Nieto-Soria, Tibor Neugebauer, John Thanassoulis and other participants at INFER 2006. We also want to thank the collaboration of our colleagues in the Laboratory of Experimental Economics (LEE) and in the Finance and Accounting Department of the University Jaume I of Castellón which greatly facilitated the experiment. Excellent research support by Raquel Barreda, Adriana Breaban and Ainhoa Jaramillo is also gratefully acknowledged. Iván Barreda wants to acknowledge financial support by Fundació Caixa Castelló – Bancaixa (P11A2006-13 and Mobility Grants). All remaining errors are the authors' responsibility alone.

Appendix A: Instructions

We reproduce the instructions for the information treatment. In the no-information treatment, the instructions were exactly the same but for the section on private information, and the cost of information, which was also removed from the earnings section.

Instructions (Info Treatment)

Welcome. This is an experiment in the economics of financial market decision-making. The instructions are simple and if you follow them carefully you might earn a considerable amount of money. Your earnings will be paid out to you in cash at the end of the experiment. Your data will be treated confidentially and they will not be used for any purposes alien to this experiment. Do not reveal your choices to any other participant during the experimental session. Unauthorized communication with other subjects will result in the immediate termination of the experiment without any gain for any participant who has infringed this rule.

At the beginning of the experiment you will randomly be assigned to a market composed by eight to ten people. You will remain in this market for the rest of this experiment. However, you will not be told each other identities.

The currency used in the market is experimental units (EUs). All trading and earnings will be in terms of EUs. At the end of the experiment, the EUs that you have accumulated will be converted to euros at the exchange rate of 1 euro for each 3,000 EUs and you will be paid in euros. The more EUs you earn, the more euros you get.

The Asset Market

At the beginning of the experiment you will be given a **starting-portfolio**, which consists of **20 assets and 10.000 EUs as cash balance**. Every participant has the same starting-portfolio.

The experiment consists of 25 trading periods, lasting 2 minutes each. In each trading period you, and the other participants in the experiment, will have the opportunity to buy and sell units of an asset in a market.

You can buy and sell as many units of your portfolio as you want but each bid or ask is limited to only one unit of the asset.

The Interest Rate and the Dividends

At the end of every period, each component of your portfolio generates a profit for you:

• **For each EU of cash** in your current account you will get an **interest rate of 1%**. Remember that the interest rate will remain fixed all 25 periods.

• **Each unit of asset** in your inventory at the end of each trading period pays a **dividend** to you. The exact value of the dividend per unit will be announced at the end of each trading period and it is the same for every participant.

However, it is common knowledge that the dividend evolves in the following manner:

The dividend at the end of period $t+1$, d_{t+1}, depends on the dividend at the end of the previous period, d_t, in the following way:

• with a 70% probability: $d_t - 0.15d_t \leq d_{t+1} \leq d_t + 0.15d_t$

• with a 99% probability: $d_t - 0.45d_t \leq d_{t+1} \leq d_t + 0.45d_t$

For example, if the dividend in period 1 was 20 EUs per asset, the dividend in period 2 will be:

• with a 70% probability, between 23 [20+(20·0.15)] and 17 [20−(20·0.15)] EUs per asset.
• with a 99% probability, between 29 [20+(20·0.45)] and 11 [20−(20·0.45)] EUs per asset.

Remember that your inventory of assets and cash carries over from one trading period to the next.

The Information on the Evolution of the Dividends
    Public Information
    During all the experiment you, and the other participants, will have information on screen about the dividend in the previous period. Additionally, a graph showing the dynamics of the dividend will be continuously displayed in the room. The graph will be updated at the end of every trading period.

At the beginning of period 1, the information that you and the other traders in the market have is that the dividend in period 0 was 20 EUs.

    Besides, you should take into account that technically the assets are valued on the basis of the actual discounted value of the infinite current of future dividends. In this market this value, even if unknown for any given period, can be approximated as the dividend at the end of the last period divided by the interest rate. Consequently, the approximate value of each asset at the beginning of period 1 is 2,000 EUs ($20/0.01$, or equivalently $20 \cdot 100$).

Private Information
    Each participant in the market can also buy in any moment during each trading period private information about the future value of the dividend. Each piece of information consists of a prediction on the future value of the dividend at the end of the current period, or for 1, 2, or 3 periods ahead.
    The cost of each piece of information is 100 EUs and this cost is independent on the time horizon. However, the quality of the information, in terms of precision, decreases with the time horizon. Therefore, when you buy information, you will receive a number drawn from the following interval around the real dividend in the future:

• End of current period: information $\in [d_t + 0.07 \cdot d_t, d_t - 0.07 \cdot d_t]$
• 1 period ahead: information $\in [d_{t+1} + 0.10 \cdot d_{t+1}, d_{t+1} - 0.10 \cdot d_{t+1}]$
• 2 periods ahead: information $\in [d_{t+2} + 0.12 \cdot d_{t+2}, d_{t+2} - 0.12 \cdot d_{t+2}]$
• 3 periods ahead: information $\in [d_{t+3} + 0.14 \cdot d_{t+3}, d_{t+3} - 0.14 \cdot d_{t+3}]$

    Observe that the interval around the true value increases with the time horizon for which you buy information. For example, consider that the true future dividend at the end of period 4 were 20 EUs per asset. The estimated number that you would receive if you bought information would be drawn from the following interval:

• buying in period 4 (same period) it will be between 21.4 $[20+20\cdot0.07]$ and 18.6 $[20-20\cdot0.07]$.
  • buying in period 3 (1 period before) it will be between 22 $[20+20\cdot0.10]$ and 18 $[20-20\cdot0.10]$.
• buying in period 2 (2 periods before) it will be between 22.4 $[20+20\cdot0.12]$ and 17.6 $[20-20\cdot0.12]$.
• buying in period 1 (3 periods before) it will be between 22.8 $[20+20\cdot0.14]$ and 17.2 $[20-20\cdot0.14]$.

Each trader buying information will receive a different information from the corresponding interval. The number of traders buying information at each period and the type of information bought will not be revealed during the experiment.

Your Earnings
        Periods before the last
        Your earnings at the end of every period are equal to:
• Your cash balance at the beginning of the period
• + 1% over your cash balance at the end of the period
• + dividend received per unit of asset hold at the end of the period times the number of assets you hold
    • + price received for the assets sold
    • - price paid for the assets bought
    • - price paid for the information bought in the period (100 EUs)

Final Earnings
        And your earnings, in EUs, for the entire experiment will be equal to:
• your cash balance at the end of period 25
• Repurchase value of your assets. That is, at the end of period 25, each asset that you hold in this moment will be bought from you at a price equal to its estimated value.
        Value of assets $=100\cdot$ *dividend in period* $25\cdot$ *number of assets*
        If at any moment you have any doubt or problem do not hesitate to address the experimentalist. Remember that it is important that you understand correctly the functioning of the market, given that your profit depends both on your decisions and those made by the other participants in your market.
Thank you for your participation.

Appendix B: Graphical User Interface
        The experiments were programmed in Z-Tree v.2.1.3. The interface used by the participants in the treatment with the possibility of buying private information can be found on figure A.1.
        Traders had information about the number of periods already played and the time left at the current period. In the information treatment there was a box which the participants could use to buy information about the expected dividend

at the end of the current period (t), 1, 2 or 3 periods ahead. In case information was bought, a dividend prediction for the selected period appeared on the information column and 100 EUs were subtracted from the current account. Once information has been bought by a person for a given period, there is no possibility of this person buying more information until the following period. All information bought is private and it remains at the subject's disposal in the information column until the end of the experiment.

Traders could see in real time the stand of their asset portfolio and current account. Furthermore they were remembered of the interest rate and the dividend paid at the end of the preceding period.

The five columns for the double auction market can be found in the central area of the screen:

• The first of them from left to right can be used to place asks, that is, to name a price at which a participant wishes to sell one asset. Once the offer was confirmed there was no possibility of canceling it.

• In the second column current asks appeared ordered decreasingly by price. The cheapest ask was automatically selected if a trader pressed the buy button.

• The central column was a list of the prices at which each transaction had closed in the market.

• The fourth column showed all the current bids ordered from the cheapest to the more expensive, which was automatically selected if the sell button was pressed.

• The fifth column acted in quite the same way as the first, but it was used when a participant wanted to make a bid.

Contrary to the private information column which kept record of every information bought, the five central columns were reset at the end of every trading period.

Figure A.1: Graphical User Interface

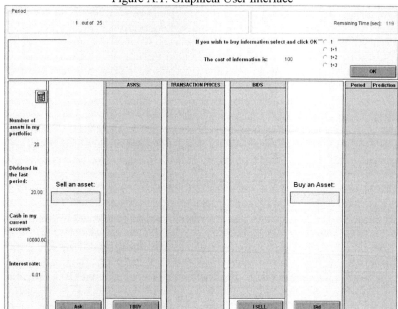

References

Arthur, B. / Holland, J. / Lebaron, B. / Palmer, R. / Tayler, P. (1997): Asset Pricing Under Endogenous Expectations in an Artificial Stock Market. In The Economy as an Evolving Complex System II, Eds.: W. Brian Arthur, Steven N. Durlauf, David A. Lane, Westview Pr., Boulder, Colorado.

Fama, E. (1970): Efficient Capital Markets: A Review of Theory and Empirical Work, Journal of Finance, Volume 25, pp. 383-417.

Fischbacher, U. (1999): Z-tree: Zurich Toolbox for Readymade Economic Experiments. Working Paper No. 21, Institute for Empirical Research in Economics, University of Zurich.

Hey, J. / Morone, A. (2004): Do Markets Drive Out Lemmings-or Vice Versa?, Economica, Volume 71, pp. 637-659.

Huber, J. / Kirchler, M. / Sutter, M. (2004): On the Benefit of Information in Markets with Heterogeneously Informed Traders: An Experimental Study. In Nonlinear Dynamics and Heterogeneous Interacting Agent, Eds.: *Lux, T. / Reitz, S.* (eds), Springer-Verlag, Heidelberg, pp. 41-54.

Huber, J. (2006): J-shaped returns to timing advantage in access to information - Experimental evidence and a tentative explanation. Journal of Economic Dynamics and Control, forthcoming.

Huber, J. / Kirchler, M. / Sutter, M. (2006): Is more information always better? Experimental financial markets with cumulative information, Journal of Economic Behavior and Organization, forthcoming.

Huber, J. / Kirchler, M. / Sutter, M. (2007): Does the level of information matter for traders? On the usefulness of information in experimental asset markets. In The experimental economics week in honour of Dr Vernon L. Smith, Ed.: Oda, S. Springer-Verlag, Heidelberg, forthcoming.

Kirchler, M. / Huber, J. (2007): Fat tails and volatility clustering in experimental asset markets, Journal of Economic Dynamics and Control, forthcoming.

Kirchler, M. / Huber, J. (2006): Underreaction to new information and stylized facts in an experimenal asset market. Working paper.

Noussair, C. / Robin, S. / Ruffieux, B. (2001): Price Bubbles in Experimental Asset Markets with Constant Fundamental Values, Experimental Economics, Volume 4, pp: 87-105.

Smith, V. / Suchaneck, C. / Williams, A. (1988): Bubbles, Crashes and Endogenous Expectations in Experimental Asset Spot Markets, Econometrica, Volume 56, pp. 1119-1151.

Sunder, S. (1992): Market for Information: Experimental Evidence, Econometrica, Volume 60, pp. 667-695.

Sunder, S. (1995): "Experimental Asset Markets: A Survey". In Handbook of Experimental Economics, Eds.: *Kagel* and *Roth*, Princeton University Press, Princeton, pp. 445-500.

Investor Reactions, Trading Volume and EPS surprise: The Case of Profit Warnings

Ioannis Krassas[1]

1 Introduction

This paper examines the association between abnormal trading volume and the magnitude of a profit warning induced earnings per share (EPS) surprise. Most trading volume theories support the argument that belief revisions and differential interpretations of common news lead to trading volume. The informational content of an earnings' related announcement as well as the level of the surprise caused by this is associated with the level of disagreement, magnitude of differential belief revisions and scale of differential interpretations of the common news presented by the announcement. Therefore theoretically, the magnitude of the earnings surprise caused by an announcement is positively associated with abnormal trading volume.

The above theoretical proposition is tested empirically using data for approximately 2000 U.S. firms covering a period between February 1998 and October 2000. For the purposes of this empirical testing a regression model is utilized that contains the main EPS surprise variable. This main variable is constructed by comparing the profit warning provided EPS value to the latest mean EPS estimate available by the analysts before the warning. In contrast, related studies compare analysts' EPS estimates to actual audited quarterly or annual EPS announcements. In addition to the main variable, three more control variables are used in the model to control for market wide effects, firm size and past abnormal trading activity effects. With respect to earnings surprise magnitude, four different specifications are used in respective models with the same control variables across the models. These four EPS surprise magnitude variable specifications are:

- Absolute percentage change of earnings per share
- Absolute price-weighted change of earnings per share
- Absolute percentage change of EPS using Damodaran's method

The estimation results provided by these models are then interpreted and associated with theories from related financial and behavioural literature. These theories include: "differential beliefs revisions", "differential interpretations of common news" and "cognitive dissonance" as well as a comparison of the results and the "no trading theorem". The first two theories and reasons that cause trading volume formed the theoretical argument described earlier. Cognitive dissonance explains how a profit warning announcement can result in abnormal

---

[1] I would like to thank Prof. G.Bulkley, Dr.D.Balkenborg, Dr.T.Kaplan, Prof. J.Davidson and the School of Business and Economics at Exeter University for their invaluable support and guidance that led to this paper throughout my studies as a PhD student at Exeter.

trading response by the investors. Furthermore this behavioural bias can also explain how the magnitude of the surprise can be positively associated with abnormal trading volume.

The rest of the paper is organized as follows. The next section covers a literature review on EPS announcements and investor reactions, different measures of disagreement, trading volume responses and profit warnings research. Following the literature review, in section 2 the dataset is analyzed in detail, while section 3 provides details on the conceptual and mathematical construction of the main and control variables used in the regression models as well as methodological comments. Section 4 provides the hypotheses tested by the regression models and section 5 provides the relevant estimation results and brief comments on them. Section 6 discusses the results and interprets them by using relevant theories. Finally the paper concludes with a summary and closing remarks and comments in section 7.

2 Literature review

The vast majority of the literature with respect to volume reactions to announcements has focused on quarterly earnings announcements or voluntary corporate disclosures. Very little research has focused on profit warnings announcements. One potential reason for this can be traced to the fact that profit warnings were rarely issued by firms before the late 1990s. It is worth noting that available data for profit warnings in the U.S. appear from 1998 onwards (money.cnn.com and briefing.com). Quarterly EPS announcements are audited and provide "solid" earnings values, whereas voluntary corporate disclosures provide an "estimated" value of EPS which shares similarities in nature with profit warnings announcements.

Topics in the literature included testing for the informational content and responses to information, as well as more detailed examinations of reactions to news under the scope of disagreement amongst investors. Furthermore the various measures and sources of disagreement were also studied. *Foster* (1973) finds evidence on both volume and price reactions to such events. He refers to volume as the reaction of the individual agents in the market whereas price as the aggregate reaction of the market to these EPS estimates announcements. He also reports that investors' heterogeneous expectations and different attitude towards risk are potential causes of abnormal trading volume.

Morse (1981) finds that the most significant price changes and excess (abnormal) trading volume occur at the day prior to and the day of the announcements on the WSJ. Morse argues that the trading volume that follows such announcements could be due to different interpretations of the signals released through these announcements. One of the most important studies in the field of volume reactions to information, by *Kim/ Verrecchia* (KV) (1991), finds a relationship between trading volume and earnings surprise that is consistent with the profit warning results of this paper. This result stems from the verification of KV's 1st proposition that is as follows:

> *"The price reaction to a public announcement is proportional to the importance of the announced information relative to the average posterior beliefs of traders and the surprise contained in the announced information plus noise."*

Furthermore they argue that for a volume analysis, volume is proportional to the absolute price change (reaction). Thus by combining these two propositions, it can be argued that trading volume is related to the importance of the announced information and the surprise element of it. In the case of profit warnings, this argument was an inspiration in order to formulate the first and main hypothesis of this study, which associates earnings surprise magnitude with trading volume reactions. *Bamber* (1987) in an empirical study hypothesized that unexpected earnings and firm size are related to both the magnitude and the duration of trading volume reaction around quarterly earnings announcements whereas, *Kandel/Pearson* (1995) argue that volume and price reactions can be independent.

There have been studies that examined trading volume as a result of tax-incentives, overconfidence and not as a result of "reactions" to information. *Odean* (1999) who is concerned with trading volume being excessive in securities markets, attributes this "excessiveness" to particular groups of investors (those with discount brokerage accounts), and their display of overconfidence. *Lakonishok/Smidt* (1986) associate trading volume with tax incentives and the rebalancing of non-fully diversified portfolios. *Ryan/Taffler* (2004) argue that most of the economically significant trading volume and stock returns are driven by firm specific news releases.

2.1 Trading volume and disagreement

There has been considerable difficulty in interpreting trading volume reactions to releases of public information due to the lack of theories that link information and trading volume. *Verrecchia* (1981) argues that this is the case when this information is distributed symmetrically among investors. He also argues that intuitively there must be some explanation for the existence of abnormal volume around earnings reports. The results of Verrecchia establish that the absence of volume reactions to an informational event is associated with a total consensus among investors. *Verrecchia/Holthausen* (1990) continue to investigate the "volume puzzle", by testing the effects of informedness and consensus on price and volume behaviour around informational events. The two most important findings of this study are that:

> *"An increase in consensus results to an increase in the variance of price changes and a decrease in trading volume"*, and *"...both price and volume studies are equally relevant means of assessing the information content of an earnings announcement."*

The second implication/finding is supporting the significance of trading volume studies with respect to reactions to information, and renders them of equal explanatory power to price studies.

Ziebart (1990) empirically investigates the association between changes in the level of consensus of beliefs in the market and abnormal trading volume. Additionally he associates abnormal trading volume reactions to changes in aggregate beliefs. He finds that trading volume is positively associated to both the changes in the level of consensus about earnings expectations (proxy for individual beliefs) and to the absolute value of the change in the mean earnings forecast (which proxies for changes in aggregate beliefs). *Ajinkya/Atiase* and *Gift* (1991) support similar hypotheses to *Ziebart* (1990) with respect to forecast dispersion (or consensus) and forecast mean revisions, but instead of testing around specific accounting disclosures they use an almost continuous flow of information which is used by analysts themselves in order to perform their periodic revisions of earnings forecasts. Their findings support the theoretical positive association between dispersion of beliefs and abnormal trading volume activity. Similarly *Barron* (1995) by using analysts' forecast revision data correlates abnormal trading volume to differential belief revisions. In addition to this correlation, Barron associated abnormal trading volume to prior dispersion of beliefs. It is worth mentioning that prior dispersion of beliefs and differential belief revisions are considered both as measures of disagreement (that cause trading). *Bamber/Barron* and *Stober* (1997) by focusing around quarterly earnings announcements, test for the explanatory power and association with abnormal trading volume, of three measures of disagreement among investors. BBS find positive association between trading volume and the three different measures of disagreement.

Morse et al. (1991) focus on the dispersion analysts forecasts subject to earnings announcements and the associated earnings surprise that can be induced by such announcements. Further support to the link between trading volume and differences in opinion or differential interpretations of common signals, is provided by *Harris/Raviv* (1993). By using a model of speculative trading volume and price dynamics, they establish that:

> "*trading volume is generated by differences of opinion among traders regarding the value of the asset being traded. These differences of opinion result from different interpretations of public information announcements.*"

An important element of their model is that although every investor is rational, some investors view others as non-rational. Among their results, trading volume is positively related to absolute changes in the mean forecasts (of payoffs). The mention of "irrationality" led to the addition of "behavioural" elements in the paper presented here, whereas the trading volume result is consistent with the empirical findings of this paper, if "payoffs" are substituted by earnings per share estimates.

Kandel/Pearson (KP) (1995) agree with Harris and Raviv by continuing the research in "trade in speculative markets". They criticize the general assumption that agents (in speculative markets) interpret information identically. In their model they incorporate trade around public announcements that incorporates differential interpretations. They find that investors do interpret common public signal differently as a result of differential interpretations. KP attribute this disagreement over the common signal as a result of using different models to assess the information or different likelihood functions. KP finally argue that time and effort is required for an investor to fully understand new information and compare it with his prior beliefs. This final point, in association with the two-day[2] event window that is used in this paper can imply that investors disagree based on differential speed of information processing and the resulting trading decisions. This differential speed argument can be easily pictured by assuming the following example. Assume two traders that differ with respect to their ability to process information fast. The "fast" trader can make in a certain "X" assessment in "x" time. The "slow" trader need more than "x" time to reach the same assessment, and in "less than x" time reaches to a "Y" assessment. "Y" and "X" are different, therefore trade occurs. One can argue that subject to no further information disclosures, the "slow" investor will reach to the same assessment of the situation. However as KP argued this takes time and effort to do, and time is constrained by the two-day event window that is used in this thesis.

Bamber/Barron and *Stober* (BBS) (1999) combined speculative trading, abnormal trading volume activity and differential interpretations of common public signals. The main argument examined is whether differential interpretations of public information have significant explanatory power with respect to the presence of abnormal trading volume. BBS argue that there are two conditions under which differential interpretations have a significant explanatory power over the presence of abnormal trading volume. The first condition is linked with the empirical results provided by *Kandel/Pearson* (1995) and associates the presence of abnormal trading volume with differential interpretations, subject to minimal price changes following informational events. BBS provide empirical results based on regression models that verify this hypothesis. The most important element of the results provided by BBS lies in the second condition with regards to the differential interpretations and abnormal trading volume. This condition links the differential interpretations and abnormal volume association with the presence of abnormal trading volume following quarterly earnings announcements. BBS similarly to the setup of this thesis, determine as abnormal the firm specific trading volume for the announcement period that is significantly higher than the non-announcement period average firm specific trading volume.

BBS argue very successfully that differential interpretations are a cause for trading where abnormal trading activity is evident, since situations where

---

[2] This two-day event window (instead of a longer one), helps capturing the immediate reaction of investors.

abnormal volume is observed, provide an ideal opportunity for informed traders to camouflage their movements and informational advantages (differential interpretations) among liquidity traders. Arguably, insiders could also take advantage of this situation and take trading positions covered by the unexpectedly high volume. These insiders based on their informational advantage will trade subject to the EPS announcement since they will interpret the news differently to non-insiders and non-informed traders. BBS used quarterly earnings announcements as a focal point for their study, whereas profit warnings announcements are used for the purposes of this paper. Furthermore BBS use similar control variables such as firm size and market wide abnormal volume in similar fashion to the models presented here later, as well as similar statistical methodologies (log-values). Finally the most importance difference is that BBS use pre and post announcement analysts' forecasts, whereas in a similar methodological manner, the EPS surprise magnitude variable used in this paper uses pre-announcement analysts' EPS forecast and profit warnings announcement EPS (firm issued) forecast. The earliest argument over the debate on the existence of trading activity in absence of significant price movements can be attributed to *Louis Bachelier's* published PhD thesis (1900). This study, although 106 years old is widely considered as a pioneer study in mathematical finance. While the thesis' most widely acknowledged contribution lies in the fact that Brownian motion was modeled for the first time, *Bamber/Barron* and *Stober* (1999) find evidence in favor of differential interpretations by quoting an abstract from Bachelier that states:

> *"Past, present and even discounted future events are reflected in market price, but often show no apparent relation to price changes… Contradictory opinions concerning these changes diverge so much that at the same instant buyers believe in a price increase and sellers in a price decrease."*

2.2 Profit warnings related research

Profit warnings literature is very limited comparatively to studies that used quarterly or annual earnings announcements as informational events. *Jackson/Madura* (JM) (2003) have explicitly focused on profit warnings announcements for U.S. firms, in their study, and found that profit warnings have significant negative valuation effects to the issuing companies. *Collet* (2004) examines trading volume reactions to company trading statement announcements for the first time by using U.K. data. His analysis results with respect to trading volume reactions (albeit for U.K and not U.S data), has displayed a strong abnormal trading volume presence for the day of the profit warning announcement and the following day, which is in direct accordance to the results presented later for U.S firms.

2.3 Profit warnings' definition and details

Definitions: Profit warnings are defined as a public announcement/statement issued by a firm in order to revise and correct shareholders' expectations with respect to earnings per shares, when these expectations are not going to be achieved. Shareholders have formed expectations based on earnings forecasts either provided by analysts or by the firm itself at a previous point in time in the form of an earnings' guidance or earlier issued preliminary profit warning. Profit warnings are a specific sub-class of earnings related disclosures. In the case were a firm obtains a forecast that implies a forthcoming negative earnings surprise based on what the market/analysts/investors expect and what the actual quarterly EPS announcement is likely to be, then a profit warning is issued. In the opposite case where a positive earnings surprise is expected by the firm, a profit update is issued. To summarize, a profit warning is issued when "bad" news are expected by the firm, whereas a profit update is issued when "good" news are expected. Profit warnings were also described as voluntary corporate disclosures (if they were EPS related), earnings guidance, earnings warnings, and company trading statements (U.K. see *Collet* 2004). With respect to the importance of warnings, *Kasznik/Lev* (1995) stated that:

> *"While warnings are typically limited to the forthcoming earnings announcement, they may raise investor concerns about the long-term competitiveness and economic viability, contributing to large price declines".*

1.d Reasons to warn: Litigation, Reputation, Valuation: The main reasons for a firm to issue a profit warning, apart from the aforementioned expectations' correction, are to reduce possible litigation risks and associated costs (*Kasznik/Lev* 1995), to improve managers' reputation (*Hirst/Koonce* and *Miller* 1999) and market valuation reasons (*Jackson/Madura* 2000).

1.e Profit warnings' mechanism: Intuitively the mechanism for deciding to issue a profit warning is as follows: Investors have formed expectations based on analysts' forecasts or firm's earnings guidance with respect to a forthcoming quarterly (or annual) earnings announcement. The firm based on newer (not previously available) information, estimates that the investors' and analysts' consensus on the expected earnings to be announced in the forthcoming formal EPS announcement will deviate (downwards) significantly from the actual figure. In order to eliminate this informational asymmetry and the associated negative earnings' surprise, the firm then informs investors of the new revised EPS estimate by issuing a profit warning.

3 Data

The original dataset is comprised by approximately 3000 profit announcements that range from March 1998 to October 2000 which were issued by US companies. These profit announcements include both profit warnings and profit updates. As described earlier, the profit updates represent announcements concerning an upward or breakeven earnings estimate revision. The profit warnings represent announcements that correspond to downward earnings per share estimate revisions. Therefore, profit updates were filtered out of the sample and the remaining profit warning announcements sum up to 2634 announcements. The announcements used in this study were characterized as profit warnings by the CNN site www.cnn.com/markets/IRC/warnings.html . The CNN "profit warnings" database acquires it's data from briefing.com and the earliest point of briefing's dataset is February 1998. These 2634 profit warnings as a dataset include company names, associated tickers, date of the warning issue, financial quarter to which the profit warning corresponds, the pre-warning earnings per share estimate and the actual profit warning earnings per share revision. A sample of the dataset as described above can be seen in the table below.

Table 1: Sample of Profit Warnings Dataset

Date of Issue	Company Name	Ticker	Qrt	Pre-estimate	Profit Warning
5-June-98	DII Group	DIIG	Q2	$0.40	$0.23-0.25
5-June-98	H.B. Fuller	FULL	Q2	$0.86	Below $0.78
5-June-98	Rouge Industries	ROU	Q2	$0.33	Below estimate
8-June-98	Advisory Board Co.	ABCO	Q2	$0.86	$0.65

The table above shows that the actual profit warnings can take various forms with respect to the level of precision of the earnings revision whereas the pre-estimate is always of the same form which is a point estimate. This led as described in the paper that corresponds to "profit warnings and precision", to classify and split the profit warning announcements to four main classes depending on form and precision of the announcement. These four classes are:

- Point Estimate profit warning announcements: e.g. *0.5$*
- Closed Range profit warning announcements: e.g. *0.4 - 0,6$*
- Open Range profit warning announcements: e.g. *Less than 0.5$*
- Qualitative profit warning announcements: e.g. *Less than expected*

In order to test for the effects of the size of the surprise to trading volume, a numerical estimate in the profit warning announcement is required. This requirement stems from the nature of the variable that is used in this study for measuring the size of the earnings surprise. This variable which will be described in detail later on, is based on the difference between the "new" earnings per share (profit warning) and the pre-announcement "old" earnings per share estimate. A "new" EPS value can only be derived from the "point estimate", "closed range" and "open range" classes of warnings. Thus, the "qualitative" class of profit warnings was also filtered out from the dataset, which resulted to a final sample of 2015 profit warning announcements, all of which contained the required numerical element in the warning's content.

The resulting sample of 2015 profit warnings showed variability with respect to the number of profit warnings per calendar month. As it can be seen in the graph below, the number of profit warnings per month follows a periodic pattern based on financial quarters, something that is expected from the fact that profit warnings correspond to audited quarterly earnings announcements. Furthermore there is a spike in the number of profit warnings for September and October 2000, which can be linked to new "stricter" disclosure legislation[3] which was introduced in August 2000, as well as to the stock markets' crashes worldwide.

Figure 3.1: Distribution of Profit Warnings February 1998 – October 2000

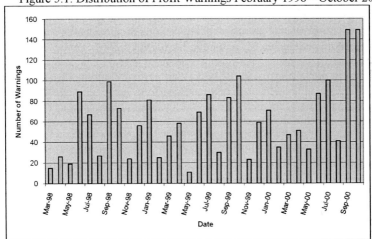

After sorting out and filtering the profit warnings dataset, the next step involved attaching to it, data from the CRSP and Datastream databases. More specifically the data used from CRSP using both the monthly and daily databases were:

- Daily Trading volume data for warning firms
- Daily Returns data for warning firms
- Monthly Trading Volume data for warning firms

---

[3] Quoting from the CNNMoney website: *"Adopted by the U.S. Securities and Exchange Commission on August 10th, the rule, Regulation FD (Fair Disclosure), requires companies to disclose profit warnings, earnings reports and any other information it issues to analysts simultaneously to the public via press releases or other notifications."* The difference of this legislation comparatively to the previous one is the element of simultaneity on informing both the public and the analysts at the same time, whereas previous legislation obliged firms to disclose the profit warning but not simultaneously to analysts and the public.

- Monthly Stock price data for warning firms
- Number of shares outstanding for warning firms

4 Main model and variables used

4.1 Using Trading Volume

It is evident from earlier studies in the field that financial news induce reactions in financial markets. This reaction can be either reflected by changes in stock prices and returns and by changes in trading volume. This study chooses to test trading volume reactions depending on the scale/magnitude of the news' surprise. The choice of trading volume instead of stock returns is due to the fact that trading volume captures the individual investor reactions to financial news. In comparison stock returns capture the aggregate market's reaction to such news (*Foster*, 1973).

By using trading volume as the main variable for testing, it is feasible to link the results to theories of trading. Most notably, on why investors decide to trade given the fact that they receive common information in the form of a common profit warning announcement that is public information available to every investor. Theoretically, common news to every investor should result in no reason to trade if the investors receive the same information and revise their beliefs homogenously. As it will be discussed later on, this is clearly not the case. Investors receive common information in the form of the profit warning and have common pre-announcement information in the form of "pre-announcement estimate" as described in the data section earlier. Even with common news and common priors, there is evident trading volume reaction to profit warnings which can be either attributed to differential levels of private information (*Kim/Verrecchia*, 1991) or by differential interpretations of the common news by investors (*Harris/Raviv*, 1993). In order to measure the trading volume reactions to profit warnings, abnormal trading volume is used, which as analyzed in the variables description section is a ratio comparing announcement period trading volume to non-announcement period trading volume.

4.2 Model and methodology

After calculating and creating the variables that would be used in this study, the main model was developed. Abnormal trading volume for the day of the announcement and the following day is the dependant variable. The main independent variable that is the focal point of this study is the "magnitude of earnings surprise" variable that measures the size of the profit warnings' earnings surprise. This is denoted in equation 1 that follows by *SURPRISE*. This main variable is complemented by three other control variables that capture market wide, past trading activity and firm size effects. These control variables are: "Firm's abnormal trading volume one day before the profit warning", "Firm size" and "Market wide abnormal trading volume for the day of the profit warning and the next". These variables constitute the main model used for estimation of "magnitude of surprise" effects that is represented by the following equation:

$$(4.1) \quad LABV_{i,t,t+1} = a_0 + a_1 LABV_{i,t-1} + a_2 LSIZE_{i,t} + a_3 LABVNYSE_{t,t+1} + a_4 SURPRISE_i + \varepsilon_i$$

The model represented by equation (1) above is using a generalized surprise variable denoted by $SURPRISE_i$. This surprise variable is going to be replaced by three specific earnings' surprise variables that will be presented in detail. This results into three surprise-variable specific models that are represented by the following equations:

$$(4.2) \quad LABV_{i,t,t+1} = a_0 + a_1 LABV_{i,t-1} + a_2 LSIZE_i + a_3 LABV_{NYSE,t,t+1} + a_4 L\Delta EPS_{i,ABS} + \varepsilon_i$$

$$(4.3) \quad LABV_{i,t,t+1} = a_0 + a_1 LABV_{i,t-1} + a_2 LSIZE_i + a_3 LABV_{NYSE,t,t+1} + a_4 L\Delta EPS_{i,DnP} + \varepsilon_i$$

$$(4.4) \quad LABV_{i,t,t+1} = a_0 + a_1 LABV_{i,t-1} + a_2 LSIZE_i + a_3 LABV_{NYSE,t,t+1} + a_4 L\Delta EPS_{i,DAM} + \varepsilon_i$$

4.3 Descriptions of the variables and Definitions of Earnings' surprise

4.3.1 $ABV_{t,t+1}$ Firm's abnormal trading volume

Abnormal trading volume for the firm over the announcement period is calculated as a ratio between daily trading volume and a six month's average trading volume. More specifically, the event window chosen here is the day in which the profit warning is issued and the following one. Therefore daily trading volume is an average of the trading volume for the day of the warning (time t) and the following day (time $t+1$). The reason for using a two day event window $(t,t+1)$ instead of just the "day of the announcement" is that some warnings are issued very close to the market's closure and some are issued after the market's closure but in the same day date-wise. In those two occasions it is obvious that the investors' trading reaction will take place during the next trading day $(t+1)$. Unfortunately the profit warnings dataset did not include intra-daily data in order to provide a refined solution to capturing this effect. Therefore it was decided to use the average value for those two dates in order to capture this effect. *Damodaran* (1989) also supports the setup described above. He argues that firms choose to issue "good" news early in the trading day, whereas they follow the inverse strategy when they issue "bad" news by issuing these news very late in the day and often after the market closure. This two day daily trading volume was then divided by the average trading volume of the past six months before the issue of the profit warning. For example if a warning was issued in January 2000, the average trading volume was calculated by using the monthly trading volume data from July 1999 to December 1999. A mathematical representation of the above method for calculating firms' abnormal volume which is the dependent variable in the model can be seen below:

$$ABV_{t,t+1} = \frac{\dfrac{V_t + V_{t+1}}{2}}{\dfrac{\bar{V}_6}{1}} = \frac{V_t + V_{t+1}}{2\bar{V}_6} \quad , \quad \text{where} \quad \bar{V}_6 = \sum_{t=k-1}^{k-7} V_{t,monthly}$$

k: month of announcement

4.3.2 $SURPRISE_i$ Magnitude / Scale of the news surprise

This is the main regressor in the model used to test the effects of the scale of the earnings surprise on trading volume. The profit warnings dataset as described earlier provides values for the pre-announcement earnings per share estimate and the profit warning's new earnings per share estimate for each announcement. The old EPS estimate is represented by *"O"* whereas the new estimate by *"N"*. The magnitude of news surprise variable $SURPRISE_i$ is constructed by using three different specifications:

- $L\Delta EPS_{i,ABS}$: Absolute percentage change of EPS
- $L\Delta EPS_{i,DivP}$: Absolute price weighted change of EPS
- $L\Delta EPS_{i,DAM}$: Absolute percentage change of EPS using Damodaran's method of outliers' modification.

The absolute percentage change of EPS is the natural logarithm of the absolute value of the rate of change between the new EPS estimate (N) and the old EPS estimate (O). The Damodaran method of outliers' modification essentially changes any values of the absolute percentage change of EPS that are above 100% to be equal to 100%. Such a method controls for outliers that can distort the relevant statistical results (see *Damodaran*, 1989 for more details). The absolute price weighted difference of EPS is the absolute value of the difference between (N) and (O) divided by the average monthly stock price for the month during which the profit warning was issued.

4.3.3 $SIZE = SHROUT \cdot \bar{P}_{month}$ Firm's size

The size control variable is represented by the product of number of shares outstanding and the average stock price for the month of the announcement. This product essentially provides the firms' market capitalization and is was strongly suggested to be used as a control variable by *Atiase* (1985) where he argues that:

> *"A basic implication of the results is that future empirical research designs requiring control for (private) predisclosure information should control for the capitalized value of the sampled firms. This is particularly important for studies aimed at testing the "economic consequence" and/or "effectiveness" of new public information disclosure rules."*

This control variable captures the "richness" of the informational environments for firms. Large firms have a larger analyst following comparatively to smaller firms. This implies that a profit warning announcement from a smaller firm corresponds to a much bigger piece of the firm's "informational pie". Source: *CRSP monthly database.*

4.3.4 $ABV_{t-1} = \dfrac{V_{t-1}}{\overline{V}_6}$ Firm's abnormal trading volume one day before the warning

This control variable captures the serial correlation of trading volume with lagged values. It is constructed similarly with the firm's abnormal trading volume for the event window of t, $t+1$. Daily trading volume for the day before the announcement is divided by the average trading volume for the past six months before the announcement. Source: *CRSP daily/monthly database.*

4.3.5 $ABV_{NYSE,t,t+1} = \dfrac{V_{NYSE,t} + V_{NYSE,t+1}}{2\overline{V}_{NYSE,6}}$ Market wide abnormal trading volume

This control variable captures any macro-effects that can affect the individual firm's trading volume in addition to the firm-specific information that is issued by the profit warning. The construction of this variable is identical to the firm's abnormal volume for the day of the warning and the following one, and the only difference is in the data used which are taken for the market as a whole for the trading volume figures. Source: *Datastream.*

5 Hypotheses development

H1: *The level of the abnormal volume following a profit warning announcement is positively associated with the level of the earnings surprise induced by the profit warning. / The size of the difference between the new earnings per share estimate and the previous is positively related to firm's event-period level of abnormal trading volume.*

H1 is the main and core hypothesis tested in this paper. Several studies have focused on the effects of the scale of news on trading volume and stock returns (*Bamber et al.*, 1986). It is worth noting in this hypothesis that investors have common prior estimates for the EPS as represented by the "old" (*O*) estimate and common new estimates given by the profit warnings by the "new" (*N*) estimate.

Therefore, if: the "new" and the "old" estimates are common to every investor concerned. There are no informational asymmetries between the investors, for example differential levels of private information (*Kim/Verrecchia*, 1991)

Investors interpret news in the same manner, or more formally the have homogenous beliefs and news interpretation.

One would expect that there shouldn't be any abnormal trading volume following a profit warning announcement, since such an announcement would "level" the informational playing field among investors. Additionally, according to *Aumann* (1976), the investors who possess the same priors and posteriors should not agree to disagree and therefore they should not trade. It is evident though from the descriptive statistics provided later on the results section that abnormal volume is present following a profit warning, and the main focus is to test if the "size" of the earnings surprise represented by either the difference or weighted difference between the "old" and "new" EPS estimates has an impact on this trading volume.

H2: *Abnormal trading volume measured one day before the profit warning announcement is positively related to event period abnormal trading volume.*

This is the first control variables' hypothesis and was formed based on *Harris* (1993), who cites a previous study (*Harris*, 1987) where he found a positive correlation between the number of transactions in a day and the number in the previous day.

H3: *Firm's size is inversely related to abnormal trading volume following a profit warning.*

This control variable hypothesis was formed based on the arguments provided by the "description of the variables" section of this paper. To summarize briefly, these include facts such as that larger firms have a larger analyst following; profit warnings constitute a larger piece of information for smaller firms; smaller firms have less information leaks before a profit warning, therefore trading volume reaction to news should be more pronounced (*Jackson/Madura*, 2003). It must be noted however that profit warnings are by nature unexpected informational events in sharp contrast to formal (audited) quarterly EPS or Dividend announcements. Therefore, one would expect that, unless there are significant "leakages" of information from insiders/analysts to investors, firm size and the relevant analyst following might not influence the firms' abnormal trading volume for the two day window around the announcement.

H4: *Market wide abnormal trading volume is positively related to firms' abnormal trading volume.*

This hypothesis and the inclusion of the relevant control variable that controls for market factors was inspired by *Morse* (1981), in order to contribute to the isolation of such non firm-specific information effects.

6 Results
6.1 Descriptive statistics

This section will provide all the estimation results for the models discussed earlier as well as descriptive statistics and correlation tests for the main and control variables used. The next table (Table 3.2) provides descriptive statistics of all the variables used in the main regression model. The variables are used in raw non-logged form for the purposes of the following table:

Table 2: Descriptive statistics[4] for all model's variables

	$L\Delta EPS_{i,DnP}$	$LABV_{i,t,t+1}$	$LABV_{i,t-1}$	$LABV_{NYSE,t,t+1}$	$LSIZE_i$
Mean	-4.709	2.682 (25.6)	1.271 (5.8)	0.069 (1.08)	12.855
Median	-4.732	2.641 (14.03)	1.296 (3.67)	0.076 (1.07)	12.606
Maximum	0.658	6.141	5.309	0.545	19.721
Minimum	-8.809	-1.347	-3.279	-0.730	8.690
Std. Dev.	1.324	1.042	0.976	0.149	1.804
Skewness	0.024	0.108	-0.389	-0.473	0.744
Kurtosis	3.225	3.032	4.861	4.334	3.425

By observing the above table it can be noticed that trading volume for the two day event-period is 25.6 times higher on average (median: 14.03) than the non-event period of six months before the announcement. Since pre-announcement and profit warning EPS estimates are common to all the investors, this abnormal trading activity can be either attributed to differential levels of pre-announcement information, differential interpretations of common signals, and speculative trading.

Similarly, the level of trading volume one day before the announcement is on average 5.8 times higher than the non-event period (median: 3.67). This can imply that the profit warning information has either "leaked" to some investors, or that it is anticipated by some investors that have made inferences and formed expectations about a potential profit warning. If one takes into account that a profit warning announcement is an unexpected informational event, then investors are unlikely to "forecast" that a profit warning will appear at a very specific day. Therefore, the "leakage" of information is the most rational explanation for the appearance of abnormal trading volume before the actual profit warning appearance.

It must be noted that Reg.FD legislation that enforces simultaneity of profit warning disclosures to both analysts and the public was introduced in late 2000, so for the sample used here, there is scope for leakage of information based on the at the time existing legislation. The level of trading of the market during the two day event-period is on average the same in comparison to the non-event period. This implies that the market wide trading volume levels are not abnormal.

---

[4] The values provided in table 3.2 are as used in the estimations of the model in logarithmic form. In parentheses (italics) the non-log-form values are provided for the levels of abnormal trading volume.

6.2 Regression results

The regression models in all the equations described earlier were estimated using ordinary least squares. The variables involved in all models (unless otherwise stated) are in log-form in order to correct for any skewness that these exhibit. More importantly, the resulting residuals of the regression estimations using variables in non-log-form appear to be highly non-normal. This issue is rectified using all variables in log-form. Prior to this final model specification that uses all the variables in log-form, various model specifications were tested. These included specifications were only abnormal volume variables were in log-form, none of the variables in log-form, all of the variables except the surprise variable in log-form etc. The estimation results did not vary substantially across specifications. Finally, the t-stats of the O.L.S. estimations are heteroskedasticity consistent using White's method.

6.2.1 Regression results using the absolute percentage change of EPS as a surprise variable

The following table provides regression estimates for the model specification as seen in equation (1), using the absolute price weighted change of earnings per share variable. Panel A provides results using the full sample of 2015 profit warnings. Panels B and C provide results for samples that exclude 5% and 10% of extreme outliers (with respect to the earnings surprise variable). Finally, Panel D provides results of the estimation of a simplified specification of the main model that excludes all the control variables.

The coefficient a_4 of the earnings surprise variable $L\Delta EPS_{i,ABS}$ is positive but not statistically significant using the full sample of 2015 profit warnings (t-stat=1.806). By re-estimating the model using the reduced samples that exclude 5% and 10% of outliers, the statistical significance improves significantly (t-stat=2.946 by excluding 5% of outliers and t-stat=4.320 by excluding 10% of outliers). This leads to accepting hypothesis H1, which states that the earnings surprise is positively associated to abnormal trading volume levels observed during the two day announcement period. The hypothesis is also accepted by estimating the simplified version of the main model that excludes all the control variables in panel D, where the coefficient of the earnings surprise is again positive and statistically significant.

Finally, the hypothesis H2 that concerns the control variable of lagged firm specific abnormal volume is accepted, whereas the hypotheses H3 and H4 that refer to firm size effects and market wide event-period abnormal volume are rejected. The respective coefficients: a_2 and a_3 are statistically insignificant throughout the estimations.

Table 3: Results of estimating the following model[*]:
$$LABV_{i,t,t+1} = a_0 + a_1 LABV_{i,t-1} + a_2 LSIZE_i + a_3 LABV_{NYSE,t,t+1} + a_4 L\Delta EPS_{i,ABS} + \varepsilon_i$$

Panel A: Full sample including outliers

Coefficient	a_1	a_2	a_3	a_4	a_0
Estimate	0.2949	0.0077	0.1338	0.0328	4.3681
t-stat[**]	10.743	0.579	0.873	1.806	15.611
R^2	0.077				
Observations	2015				

Panel B: Reduced sample excluding 5% of outliers[***]

Coefficient	a_1	a_2	a_3	a_4	a_0
Estimate	0.2862	0.0137	0.1288	0.0645	2.2066
t-stat[**]	10.048	1.048	0.814	2.946	12.776
R^2	0.075				
Observations	1915				

Panel C: Reduced sample excluding 10% of outliers

Coefficient	a_1	a_2	a_3	a_4	a_0
Estimate	0.2727	0.0166	0.1010	0.1043	2.2611
t-stat[**]	9.286	1.166	0.628	4.320	12.832
R^2	0.072				
Observations	1815				

Panel D: Results of estimating the following model[*], excluding 5% of outliers:
$$LABV_{i,t,t+1} = a_0 + a_1 L\Delta EPS_{i,ABS} + \varepsilon_i$$

Coefficient	a_1	a_0
Estimate	0.0577	3.4028
t-stat[**]	2.735	98.040
R^2	0.003	
Observations	1915	

A Chow breakpoint-test was performed in order to investigate if there are any structural breaks[5] in the data with respect to earning surprise. An examina-

---

[*] Magnitude of EPS surprise is measured using the logarithm of the absolute percentage change of EPS depicted in the model by the following variable: $\ln(\Delta EPS_{ABS})$, where:
$$\ln(\Delta EPS_{ABS}) = \ln\left(\left|\frac{N-O}{O}\right|\right).$$

[**] White Heteroskedasticity-Consistent Standard Errors and Covariance.
[***] Outliers where eliminated by using the EPS surprise as a reference variable. The sample was ranked according to EPS surprise such as observation #1 is the smallest EPS surprise and observation #2015 the largest.

tion of the results from the previous table shows that the t-stat for the earnings surprise variable improves if we exclude outliers from the estimation sample. The results of the test reveal that there is a potential breakpoint (observation 1912-1913). A further estimation of the main model using absolute percentage change of EPS as a surprise variable leads to similar results (to excluding 5% of outliers) and is provided in panel B of the following table (Table 4). The coefficients and their respective t-stats are identical to panel B from table 4. This is to be expected since the sample sizes are very similar (1912 and 1915). Again hypothesis H1 is accepted as well as the hypotheses for lagged firm specific abnormal volume and market wide abnormal volume.

Table 4: Chow Breakpoint test and re-estimation of the main model

Panel A: Chow Breakpoint test

Observations ($\ln(\Delta EPS_{ABS})$)	p-value
1912 (out of 2015)	0.033
1913 (out of 2015)	0.097

Panel B: Re-estimation of the model excluding outliers beyond the breakpoint.

Coefficient	a_1	a_2	a_3	a_4	a_0
Estimate	0.2861	0.0138	0.1284	0.0659	2.2137
t-stat[**]	10.040	0.988	0.811	3.002	12.815
R^2			0.075		
Observations			1912		

6.2.2 Regression results using the Damodaran modified absolute percentage change of EPS as a surprise variable

The following table (Table 5) provides estimation results for the main model where the earnings surprise variable is the absolute percentage change of EPS using Damodaran's method of outliers' modification. Only one sample estimation is performed when using the Damodaran based surprise variable. Outliers are modified in this case, therefore a re-estimation excluding outliers (which are now controlled for) is redundant when using this surprise variable.

The estimation results with respect to all the hypotheses are consistent with the ones provided earlier using the non Damodaran modified absolute percentage change of EPS in tables 3 and 4. The coefficient a_4 of the earnings surprise variable $L\Delta EPS_{i,DAM}$ is positive and statistically significant (t-stat = 3.866). It is worth noting that the statistical significance of a_4 in Table 5, panel A is

---

[5] I would like to thank an anonymous journal referee for pointing out the idea for performing a Chow-Breakpoint test.
[**] White Heteroskedasticity-Consistent Standard Errors and Covariance.

much greater than the equivalent estimation of table 3, panel A. This is expected since the majority of outliers have been modified to non-extreme values. Therefore, the main hypothesis H1 is again accepted using this surprise specification. Similarly, hypothesis H2 is accepted, whereas hypothesis H3 and H4 that refer to firm size and market wide abnormal volume are rejected.

Testing for the existence of a breakpoint using a Chow test is redundant when the Damodaran based surprise variable is utilized in the model. The outliers are now modified, so no structural breaks are to be expected. Finally, the results provided by panel B again confirm hypothesis H1 without using control variables in the model's estimation.

Table 5: Results of estimating the following model[*]:

Panel A: Full model's estimation

$$LABV_{i,t,t+1} = a_0 + a_1 LABV_{i,t-1} + a_2 LSIZE_i + a_3 LABV_{NYSE,t,t-1} + a_4 L\Delta EPS_{i,DAM} + \varepsilon_i$$

Coefficient	a_1	a_2	a_3	a_4	a_0
Estimate	0.2949	0.0198	0.1241	0.0937	2.1534
t-stat[**]	10.765	1.478	0.811	3.866	13.076
R^2	0.082				
Observations[***]	2015				

Panel B: Simplified model's estimation

$$LABV_{i,t,t+1} = a_0 + a_1 L\Delta EPS_{i,DAM} + \varepsilon_i$$

Coefficient	a_1	a_0
Estimate	0.0506	2.7392
t-stat[**]	2.239	75.192
R^2	0.002	
Observations	2015	

6.2.3 Regression results using the absolute price weighted change of EPS as a surprise variable

---

[*] Magnitude of EPS surprise is measured using the logarithm of the absolute percentage change of EPS depicted in the model by the following variable: $L\Delta EPS_{i,DAM}$

Where: $L\Delta EPS_{i,DAM} = \ln\left(\left|\dfrac{N-O}{O}\right|\right)$, $\forall \left|\dfrac{N-O}{O}\right| < 100\%$

$L\Delta EPS_{i,DAM} = 0$, $\forall \left|\dfrac{N-O}{O}\right| \geq 100\%$

[**] White Heteroskedasticity-Consistent Standard Errors and Covariance.

[***] Only one sample estimation is performed when using the Damodaran based surprise variable. Outliers are modified in this case, therefore a re-estimation excluding outliers is redundant when using this surprise variable.

Similar results were obtained by using the absolute price weighted change of earnings as a surprise variable by estimating the main model. The corresponding surprise variable coefficient a_4 is positive and statistically significant throughout the estimations that appear in Table 6. The statistical significance of the said coefficient is improving with the sequential exclusion of outliers from the sample. The respective t-stats confirm this (1.976, full sample; 2.723, 5% outliers eliminated; 3.224, 10% outliers eliminated). Based on these results, the hypothesis H1 that associates positively earnings surprise to firm specific event-period abnormal volume is accepted. Hypothesis H2 is also accepted based on the results of all panels, while hypothesis H3 and H4 are rejected throughout as in the previous model specifications seen in Tables 3, 4 and 5. Similarly to Table 3.4, a Chow breakpoint test revealed a breakpoint at observations 1949 (p-value = 0.041) and 1950 (p-value = 0.170). Subject to this finding, a further estimation of the model was performed excluding observations between 150 and 2015 (Table 6, panel E). The estimation results were consistent to the ones provided in Table 6.

A comparison of the t-stats improvement subject to outliers' exclusion and the respective Chow tests when using the absolute price weighted EPS difference and the absolute percentage change of EPS as a surprise variable, reveals that the price weighted variable is less sensitive to outliers (breakpoint at 1912 for absolute percentage change and 1949 for price weighted change of EPS). This could imply that the use of a price weighted EPS change as a surprise variable can yield stronger results in similar studies, where the existence of extreme outliers is very pronounced in the estimation sample.

Table 6: Results of estimating the following model[*]:

Panel A: Full sample including outliers

$LABV_{i,t,t+1} = a_0 + a_1 LABV_{i,t-1} + a_2 LSIZE_i + a_3 LABV_{NYSE,t,t+1} + a_4 L\Delta EPS_{i,DwP} + \varepsilon_i$

Coefficient	a_1	a_2	a_3	a_4	a_0
Estimate	0.2942	0.0149	0.1375	0.0402	2.3069
t-stat[**]	10.751	0.972	0.898	1.976	14.674
R^2	0.077				
Observations	2015				

Panel B: Estimation results for sample excluding 5% of outliers.

Coefficient	a_1	a_2	a_3	a_4	a_0
Estimate	0.2817	0.0135	0.0932	0.0617	2.4497
t-stat**	9.958	0.922	0.593	2.723	15.003
R^2	0.070				
Observations***	1915				

---

[*] Magnitude of EPS surprise is measured using the logarithm of the absolute price weighted EPS change depicted in the model by the following variable: $\ln(\Delta EPS_{DwP})$.

[**] White Heteroskedasticity-Consistent Standard Errors and Covariance.

Panel C: Estimation results for sample excluding 10% of outliers.

Coefficient	a_1	a_2	a_3	a_4	a_0
Estimate	0.2767	0.0180	0.0559	0.0766	2.4790
t-stat"	9.436	1.211	0.350	3.224	14.508
R^2	0.069				
Observations	1815				

Panel D: Chow Breakpoint test

Observations ($\ln(\Delta EPS_{DivP})$)	p-value
1944 (out of 2015)	0.035
1945 (out of 2015)	0.073

Panel E: Re-estimation of the model excluding outliers beyond the breakpoint.

Coefficient	a_1	a_2	a_3	a_4	a_0
Estimate	0.2830	0.0132	0.6211	0.0553	4.5155
t-stat"	10.047	0.901	6.218	2.466	15.565
R^2	0.088				
Observations	1944				

7 Discussion of the results and links with financial and behavioural literature

7.1 Agreeing to disagree

Robert Aumann (1976) argued that:

> "If two people have the same priors, and their posteriors for a given event A are common knowledge, then these posteriors must be equal. This is so even though they may base their posteriors on quite different information. In brief, people with the same priors cannot agree to disagree."

Two investors will trade when they agree to disagree with respect to the valuation of shares. Therefore, it is expected that if these two investors share common priors and common posteriors, they will not agree to disagree and therefore they are expected not to trade. In other words, in the presence of common priors and posteriors, there shouldn't be any differences in opinion which result to trading. Any differences in subjective probabilities are exclusively related to informational differences amongst investors. Investors under rationality should not maintain different subjective probabilities if they have been fed with precisely the same information (*Aumann* (1976) by citing *Harsanyi* (1968)). Systematic biases and psychological factors can lead to differential interpretations and trading even if investors share the same priors and posteriors.

In the case of profit warnings based on the setup followed throughout this paper, the main EPS surprise magnitude variable explicitly implies (as a mathematical variable) that "old" pre-profit warning EPS estimate and "new" profit warning EPS estimate are common knowledge to every investor. If the "old" estimate is considered as "priors" and the "new" estimate as "posteriors", then according to the earlier arguments no abnormal trading is to be expected following a profit warning announcement. However, it is clear from the descriptive statistics provided earlier, that there is evident abnormal trading volume for the two day event window surrounding a profit warning announcement. Furthermore, this abnormal trading volume is positively related to the difference between the "old" and "new" estimates based on the regression results provided. A reason for this contrast between the theoretical argument that appears in Aumann's paper and the results in this paper can be found in the behavioural bias of cognitive dissonance which will be described later. In addition to this behavioural bias, abnormal trading volume can be explained by arguments with regards to differential interpretations and disagreement measures, as well as the nature of profit warnings announcements in comparison to "formal" quarterly earnings announcements.

7.2 Differential beliefs revisions and interpretation of common news

The majority of past trading volume studies supports the argument that abnormal trading volume is caused by disagreement across investors and occurs when investors revise their beliefs differentially. Disagreement and differential belief revisions can arise from differences in the precision of investors' pre-disclosure information and/or differential interpretations of the news[6]. *Bamber* (1997) argues that informational events trigger "belief jumbling":

> *"... jumbling refers to information-triggered belief revisions that differ across investors and change an individual's expectation relative to the distribution of expectations held by others."*

Therefore, the abnormal trading volume following profit warnings that is evident from this study's descriptive statistics, can be explained by differential beliefs revision either stemming from differences in pre-announcement information or from differential interpretations of the profit warning's informational content.

The main finding of this study is the positive relationship between the size of the earnings surprise induced by a profit warning and the abnormal trading activity surrounding the announcement. *Bamber* (1987) argues that, based on capital markets and human information processing research, the magnitude of dispersion of beliefs following a corporate disclosure amongst investors is positively related to the level of information induced by such a disclosure. Following this link, a greater level of beliefs' dispersion/heterogeneity is associated with greater levels of disagreement amongst investors and thus more trading volume.

---

[6] differential interpretations of common news represented by a new quarterly EPS announcement or a profit warning (for the purposes of this study)

Furthermore, more surprising/informative announcements are more likely to induce greater dispersion of beliefs and thus more scope for differential interpretations of the common news. To associate this argument with the findings of this study and the relevant EPS surprise magnitude variable: A larger EPS surprise constitutes a more informative/surprising disclosure; therefore, a more pronounced trading response is expected by the investors receiving this disclosure. *Bamber* (1987) confirms this result empirically; however, the results do not refer to profit warnings announcements.

7.3 Trading response: The case and nature of profit warnings

The vast majority of prior studies on trading volume reactions used quarterly earnings per share announcements in order to test the relationship between the magnitude of the EPS surprise and trading volume. The relevant EPS magnitude variable in these studies uses the difference between the "actual" audited quarterly EPS announcement and a pre-estimate value for the EPS that has been actually issued by the said quarterly announcement. In contrast, the EPS surprise magnitude variable used here for the profit warnings, instead of using the difference between an actual and an estimated EPS value, uses the difference between two estimated values. This difference has been highlighted for the purposes of investors' reactions. An investor receiving a profit warning, in order to make a trading decision, has to compare between two estimated values.

As depicted by the regression results, a surprise induced by the difference in estimates, is sufficient to provoke an abnormally high trading volume response by the investor. Furthermore, to an investor, a larger difference between the estimates provided can imply low forecasting power and precision by the firm. Therefore, qualitatively an investor can "loose trust" in the said firm issuing revised estimates that vary greatly from the previously issued estimate and react more to this situation. In short, the difference between the estimates can be attributed (mainly) to economic/financial circumstances that resulted in a revised earnings estimate, but part of this difference could be attributed to "weak"/"poor" forecasting power/skills displayed by the firm. Both these causes of estimate revisions can explain investors' trading reaction based on the level/size of the revision as depicted by the EPS surprise magnitude. The comparison between old-new estimates can be seen as weaker versus a comparison between estimate and actual value. The behavioural bias of cognitive dissonance that follows can create an additional perspective to how an investor reacts to receiving a new estimate that is in contrast to his prior beliefs depicted by the previous estimate.

7.4 Cognitive dissonance and the balancing between estimates

Cognitive dissonance is a behavioural heuristic which corresponds to the situation where an individual is presented with two contrasting pieces of information (cognitions/beliefs). The presence of these two contrasting beliefs requires a balancing process that involves demoting/discarding one of the two cognitions. The weaker belief is the one that is demoted/discarded and the individual continues with the appropriate decision making process (trading) based on this balancing. In the case where the two cognitions are represented by a pre-estimate of EPS and an actual EPS announcement, it is clear that the actual EPS announcement will be the more powerful cognition. Therefore, the investor will discard his prior beliefs represented by the previous EPS estimate. In the case of profit warnings, both cognitions are estimates of EPS. The second EPS estimated issued by the profit warning announcement is a revision to the previous EPS estimate and thus constitutes an improvement over it. As a result, the cognition (new) represented by the profit warning EPS content is the more powerful cognition, and the previous estimated is discarded. Based on the above argument and the theory of cognitive dissonance, abnormal trading volume is to be expected following profit warnings as is expected following quarterly EPS announcements.

With respect to the size of the difference between the two estimates, the new EPS estimate, if it is significantly different to the previous estimate, induces a larger surprise element. This larger surprise element in conjunction with the improved revision qualities displayed by a new EPS estimate constitutes in an even greater disparity between the two contrasting cognitions and an even more pronounced advantage for the new EPS estimate. This can be explained by the fact that the reason for a big difference between the two estimates can be either significant financial/economic/corporate circumstances that have rendered the issue of the new estimate essential, and/or previous weakness/inaccuracies with respect to the previous estimate. Therefore, a bigger difference between old and new estimates results in a stronger informational power for the cognition represented by the profit warning. Thus, the main regression results that associate EPS surprise size with a more pronounced trading volume reaction can be also interpreted by the behavioural bias of cognitive dissonance.

8 Conclusions

This study has examined the effects of the earnings per share surprise size induced by profit warning announcements, on trading volume activity for a two day event window surrounding the announcements. By using abnormal trading volume the individual investors' responses and reactions to profit warnings are examined. Four different specifications of EPS surprise magnitude are used throughout this study. These are the difference between the profit warning EPS estimate and the pre-announcement EPS estimate; the absolute percentage EPS change; the absolute price weighted EPS change and the "Damodaran" modified absolute percentage EPS change.

The main finding of this study by using the aforementioned EPS surprise specifications shows a positive relationship between the EPS surprise size and the abnormal trading volume observed in a two day event window surrounding a profit warning announcement. Therefore investors receiving profit warnings that induce a larger EPS surprise are likely to display a more pronounced trading activity, comparatively to investors receiving a smaller EPS surprise. However since the used EPS surprise specifications imply common priors and posteriors, according to the no-trading theorem, one would expect no statistical significance of the said variables. Furthermore, using symmetric information, rational agents should not trade excessively, arguments to which the results provided here are against to.

The link between profit-warning induced EPS surprise and trading volume, is explained and interpreted qualitatively by theories such as "differential beliefs revision", "cognitive dissonance", and "measures of disagreement". According to these theories, investors can interpret common news differentially even if they share common prior beliefs, therefore they can agree to disagree and trade. Furthermore, in a fully efficient market, abnormal trading volume should not have been observed before an announcement, and investors should homogenously react to information. This would result in no abnormal volume before a profit warning, and to a much less pronounced abnormal trading response to news (since a much pronounced response implies differences in opinion and vast dispersion in beliefs revisions). Therefore the results provided here can be also seen under the scope of criticism against efficient markets.

To conclude, investor reactions to profit warnings by using abnormal trading volume and EPS surprise magnitude as the main variables, provided very similar results to studies that used quarterly EPS announcements as the focal point for event studies such as *Bamber* (1987), *Bamber/Barron* and *Stober* (1997) as well as theoretical papers provided by *Kim/Verrecchia* (1991).

References

Aumann, R.J. (1976): Agreeing to Disagree, Annals of Statistics. Volume 4, pp.1236-1239.

Bamber L. (1987): Unexpected Earnings, Firm Size and Trading Volume Around Quarterly Earnings Announcements. The Accounting Review, Volume 62 (3), pp 510-532.

Bamber L. / Barron O. / Stober T. (1999): Differential Interpretations and Trading Volume. The Journal of Financial and Quantitative Analysis, Volume 34 (3), pp 369-386.

Barron, O. (1995): Trading Volume and Belief Revisions that Differ among Individual Analysts. The Accounting Review, Volume 70 (4), pp. 581-597.

Bulkley G. / Herreiras R. (2003): Stock Returns Following Profit Warnings: Evidence for Behavioral Finance. Working paper.

Collett N. (2004): Reactions of the London Stock Exchange to Company Trade Statement Announcements. Journal of Business Finance & Accounting, Volume 31(1)&(2), pp 3-35.

Damodaran A. (1989): The Weekend Effect in Information Releases : A Study of Earnings and Dividend Announcements. The Review of Financial Studies, Volume 2 (4), pp 607-623.

Diamond, D.W. / Verrecchia, R.E. (1981): Information aggregation in a noisy expectations economy. Journal of Financial Economics, Volume 9, pp.221-235.

Foster G. (1973): Stock Market Reaction to Estimates of Earnings per Share by Company Officials. Journal of Accounting Research, Volume 11 (1), pp 25-37.

Harris L. (1993): Transaction Data Tests of the Mixture of Distributions Hypothesis. Journal of Financial and Quantitative Analysis, Volume 22, pp.127-141.

Harris M. / Raviv A. (1993): Differences of Opinion Make a Horse Race. The Review of Financial Studies, Volume 6 (3), pp. 473-506.

Hirst D. / Koonce D. / Miller J. (1999): The Joint Effect of Management's Prior Forecast Accuracy and the Form of Its Financial Forecasts on Investor Judgment. Journal of Accounting Research, Volume 37.

Holthausen R. / Verrecchia R. (1990): The Effect of Informedness and Consensus on Price and Volume Behavior. The Accounting Review, Volume 65 (1), pp. 191-208.

Jackson D. / Madura J. (2003): "Profit Warnings and Timing. The Financial Review, Volume 38, pp. 497-513.

Kandel, E. /. Pearson, N.D (1995), Differential Interpretation of Public Signals and Trade in Speculative Markets. Journal of Political Economy, Volume 103, pp.831-872.

Kasznik R. / Lev B. (1995): To Warn or Not to Warn: Management Disclosures in the Face of an Earnings Surprise. The Accounting Review. Volume 70 (1), pp. 113-134.

Kim O. / Verrecchia R. (1991): Trading Volume and Price Reactions to Public Announcements. Journal of Accounting Research ,Volume 29 (2), pp. 302-321.

Lakonishok J. / Smidt S. (1986): Capital Gains Taxation and Volume of Trading. The Journal of Finance, Volume 41, pp. 951-974.

Morse D. (1981): Price and Trading Volume Reactions Surrounding Earnings Announcements: A Closer Examination. Journal of Accounting Research, Volume 19 (2), pp. 374-383.

Morse D. / Stephan J. / Stice E. (1991): Earnings Announcements and the Convergence (Or Divergence) of Beliefs. The Accounting Review, Volume 66, pp. 376-388.

Odean, T. (1999): Do Investors Trade Too Much? American Economic Review, Volume 89, pp.1279-1298.

Ryan P. / Taffler R. (2004): Are Economically Significant Stock Returns and Trading Volumes Driven by Firm-specific News Releases? Journal of Business Finance & Accounting, Volume 31 (1)&(2), pp. 49-82.

Wysocki P. (2000): Private Information, Earnings Announcements and Trading Volume or Stock Chat on the Internet: A Public Debate About Private Information. Working paper.

Ziebart D. (1990): The Association between Consensus of Beliefs and Trading Activity Surrounding Earnings Announcements. The Accounting Review, Volume 65 (2), pp. 477-488.

Part II: Bounded Rationality in Industrial Organisations

Strategic Change: Small Is Beautiful, to Research (Especially, But Not Only in Big Firms) [1]

Tom De Schryver

1   Introduction

Whereas before strategic management scholars used to emphasize stability as an indication of organizational success (e.g. *Caves/Porter,* 1977; *Hamel/Prahalad,* 1989; *Hannan/Freeman,* 1984), there is a growing belief that flexibility and dynamic capabilities (e.g. *Eisenhardt/Martin,* 2000) have important strategic value for lasting organizational success.

The increased emphasis on flexibility has important implications for firms as well as for researchers of strategic change. The main consequence for firms is that they no longer wait. Instead managers foster, anticipate and manage change. Organizations are no longer overwhelmed by encompassing organizational change. Instead, I argue that if not the whole organization, at least many parts of the organization support and manage strategic change initiatives.

The strategic preparedness of organizations to take on change proactively also has major implications for the research agenda. I will argue that it has become increasingly important for researchers to make the distinction between different sorts of change. Indeed, a shift over the years in the literature on strategic change can be observed. There is a move from research on large-scale change (e.g. *Tushman/Romanelli,* 1985) to specific strategic changes, such as strategic alliances (e.g. *Baum et al,* 2005), mergers and acquisitions (e.g. *Eisenmann/Bower,* 2000), or even changes that were originally deemed to be uninteresting because of their cosmetic nature, like name changes (e.g. *Chuang/Baum,* 2003), or the adoption of sports facilities (*Washington/Ventresca,* 2004).

Despite the shift, I claim that it remains interesting to review the older literature on strategic change. While a review of the existing literature can reveal dominant models, existing research questions, important antecedents, consequences of strategic change, the purpose of such a review cannot merely be reduced to a listing of the existing models, the dominant research questions and the established relationships. Instead it needs to asses what the remaining value of the existing body is for research on strategic flexibility. Put simply, what can be recycled from models of large-scale change to fit the context of small change? Can we simply copy and paste the models? Or should we start from scratch? Similarly, we need to assess whether the same research questions for large-scale change still remain important. Are the same antecedents equally important for small as well as for large change? Do they have the same performance implications? Finally, what remains difficult about managing small change?

---

[1] Paper presented at Bounded Rationality in Economics and Finance December 1-2, 2006 at Loughborough University, Loughborough, UK. This paper has incorporated some of the comments from the workshop.

In addition to reviewing the old research questions on large-scale strategic change, we need to be aware of new questions that relate specifically to small strategic change. In particular, we need to know which strategic changes will be decided upon when. The new research questions highlight the importance of managerial choice in strategic change. Managerial choice is not only important for explaining when change is implemented. It is also important for explaining when particular kinds of change are initiated.

The outline of the literature review is as follows. The first section will show that mediation is the most important theoretical legacy from older approaches to strategic change. The second section introduces different organizational learning theories that allow us to highlight the intermediate variables clearly. The organizational learning theories are also used to identify constraints so that it can be explained why some organizations fundamentally change and why others do not change but muddle through instead. These two sections create a platform for the third section, where the previously defined constraints are used to determine small strategic change. The third section thus deals with the firms muddling through. These are the firms that are likely to make series of small changes. These firms and these changes need to be reappraised in research. Despite the complexity, I will make a general claim that small changes are never initiated impromptu, because organizational constraints always have to be taken into consideration. Thus since, even cosmetic changes are carefully implemented in the organization, the same intermediate variables are highly relevant for small change. I will make use of tests of non linearity to show how small strategic change occurs.

Finally, in the conclusion, a new view on small strategic changes is put forward. The new view contrasts with deterministic theories that argue that only the core and core changes matter. On the contrary, I argue that what is fundamental cannot be identified a priori. Instead, only in retrospect is it possible to define the strategic value of managerial actions. It is therefore important to find out which changes occur, how frequently and what the performance implications of these changes are.

2   Mediation in research on large-scale change

Strategy is about reaping opportunities and curtailing threats. Opportunities and threats are stimuli for action and change. Yet, it has long been acknowledged that strategic change is not an automatic reaction to stimuli. It entails instead a process of unfreezing the existing strategy, moving and freezing to another strategy (e.g. for an overview *Burnes,* 2004) Organizations continuously face a plethora of situations. Some situations will entail threats and opportunities. These threats and opportunities make decision makers reflect about their actions because they involve urgency, difficulty and high stakes (*Chattopadhyay et al,* 2001). The recognition of threats and opportunities is thus a first step for decision-making. The capability to reap opportunities and the capability to avoid threats is another factor.

As a result, models of strategic change should absorb stimuli, intermediate variables, and different responses. Indeed there exist many stimuli that can start the strategic change process (e.g. *Rajagopalan/Spreitzer*, 1997). There are also different models describing different change processes (e.g. *Poole et al*, 2000). Finally, even for the same stimulus and within the same process, different kind of change can be decided upon (e.g. *Dial/Murphy*, 1994; *Chattopadhyay et al*, 2001). In sum, a step model, with intermediate variables, is sufficient general to cover the variation in strategic decision-making because there are different stimuli to change, different processes to change and different kinds of change to decide upon.

Figure 2.1: Mediation in strategic decision-making and change

In a model of mediation of strategic change, learning and implementation processes channel the pressures for change. It is therefore important to focus in detail on these intermediate variables. It can be assumed that organizations rely on a lot of information for strategic decision making. Therefore boundaries are likely to occur somewhere else in the change process. Boundaries may emerge when novel ideas need to be implemented. Indeed, since organizations are bound by different goals of different stakeholders and may have difficulties of reconciling these interests (*Cyert/March*, 1992), actual decision-making does not always result in optimal usage of this information. Consequently organizations may deliberately leave interesting but risky options out. This proposition is difficult to research. Since the intermediate process behind organizational decisions is largely tacit, finding information on this process in large sample research can be hard. This literature review will forward a research methodology that aims carving out the effect of the organizational boundaries on strategic decision-making.

3   Moderated mediation determines whether strategies change

This section identifies from organizational learning theory (*Cyert/March*, 1992; *Staw et al*, 1981) two mediators between a stimulus and strategic decision-making: organizational learning and organizational capabilities for change. This section shows that when there are boundaries to these intermediate variables, strategic decision-making is contingent upon the specific choices and outcomes of the previous learning processes and the capabilities of the organization to implement new strategies. As a result, when strategic decision-making is studied in a comparative setting between organizations with different learning propensity and implementation capabilities, moderation becomes an interesting technique for explaining why not all organizations do (or do not) change after the same motivation to change. Thus the boundaries may account for important parts of the variation in decision-making.

It is impossible to review all stimuli. For reasons of simplicity, I will focus on a rather universal stimulus for strategic decision-making: performance feedback. Performance feedback implies comparing the actual performance level with an aspired level of performance. The aspiration level (L) is the lowest level of performance that is deemed satisfactory.

3.1   The first mediating variable: Organizational learning

The first mediator questions whether stimuli truly lead to learning and strategic decision-making. Learning from performance feedback is in general limited. When performance is above aspirations, organizations learn that they are doing reasonably well. When performance is below aspirations, organizations learn that something is wrong. However, learning beyond that point is much more problematic. Not surprisingly, organizational learning after disappointing performance has been the subject of severe academic debate (e.g. *Ocasio,* 1993; *Lant/Hurley,* 1999), especially between the Carnegie School and the Threat rigidity Theory. In both theories, it is very likely that negative performance feedback does not result in strategic change. As such, the debate does not reflect differences in outcomes. Instead, the debate is about differences in the process to come to a decision.

On the one hand, the Carnegie School suggests that organizations are willing to explore new ways. According to the Carnegie School there is a managerial preparedness to search and venture out because it is assumed that the resources are under threat. Since the success of learning is limited, the principal reason why some organizations do not change is because they fail to make changes. The main problem identified by the Carnegie School is its capability to change. The likeliness of failure to implement changes increases for changes that are far by.

On the other hand, Threat Rigidity Theory argues that organizations do not try to find new ways after disappointing performance but try to fine-tune previous decisions (*Staw et al,* 1981). In Threat Rigidity Theory, threats lead to a sharp and uncontrolled increase in the number of performance signals, just like falling dominos. This increase in the number of signals indicates that the organization is not prepared. Consequently, organizations refuse to search for changes because they fear loss of control. Consequently, they cannot handle additional risks, they rather constrict control and stall risky changes. Instead, the organization tries to regain control by reducing information complexity. This is achieved by increasing standardization, centralization, formalization and routinization. Organizations therefore focus on the internal organization and resort to resource conserving measures like cost cutting. Consequently, they do not consider making strategic change.

An empirical study that reveals the variation in responses after performance feedback is *McDonald/Westphal* (2003). They have argued that the effect of low performance on strategic change is mediated by the kind of advice seeking of different CEOs. They have first tested if low performance has an effect on advice seeking. Since they found a non-significant effect, they made a distinction between different types of advice seeking. The introduction of moderation has led to significant effects between low performance and specific sorts of advice seeking, which indicates that advice seeking is selective. In particular, CEOs favour advice from other CEOs with similar backgrounds, from CEOs in the same industry and from CEOs with whom they have friendship ties. Moreover, they will leave out advice from outside the industry or from non-friends. The bias in advice seeking suggests that low performance makes CEOs less secure about their past strategy. Consequently, they seek advice to regain confidence. Advice does not serve to find new ways of doing. This threat rigidity hypothesis was subsequently tested by looking at the effect of advice seeking on the likelihood of strategic change. *McDonald/Westphal* (2003) indeed have found that the advice from friends, from people with the same background or from the same industry lowers the likelihood of change. There is thus an indication of an escalation of commitment when people with the same background or from the same industry are consulted. On the contrary, it seems that the search channels that were used less frequently by CEOs, lead to higher probability for strategic change.

In addition to the mediating effect, *McDonald/Westphal* (2003) have also found a direct interaction effect between low performance and type of advice seeking on strategic change. The interaction effect indicates that different sorts of CEOs attach different importance to performance signals. In particular, CEOs who consult managers with similar backgrounds or managers who are friends are a-priori less likely to make strategic changes after low performance, even before the advice is given. On the other hand, CEOs prepared to talk to managers who are not considered friends or who come from dissimilar backgrounds, have an a-priori inclination to make strategy changes even before inquiries are made. In general, *McDonald/Westphal* (2003) have shown that the variation in learning propensity between different CEOs leads to the intensification of specific search channels and in different probabilities of change. This study thus supports the idea of moderated mediation as illustrated in figure 3.1.

Figure 3.1: Moderated mediation in strategic decision-making and change

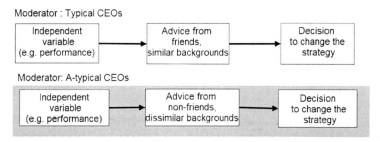

Figure 3.1 also shows that moderation does not replace the mediation process. Rather it supplements the mediation process. Technically speaking, this corresponds with moderated mediation (*James/Brett* 1984) where moderators determine how the mediator relationships between a trigger and strategic change will be shaped.

Another reason to choose for the *McDonald/Westphal* (2003) study was that the highly specific research context. In general, it is hard for empirical quantitative studies to carve out the mediating influence of organizational learning (and capabilities) on organizational decision-making in such fine detail and simultaneously on such a large scale. The problem is that organizational learning is tacit and difficult to measure. This measurement problem confronts researchers with a dilemma. A first possibility is to reduce the number of organizational settings to highlight the mediation process clearly by means of in-depth qualitative research. For example, the strategy as practice stream of research (e.g. *Whittington,* 2006) has the advantage of revealing tacit processes in strategic decision-making. This approach essentially requires case study or process approaches because of its microscopic lens (e.g. *Poole et al,* 2000). Alternatively, a cost efficient possibility for large scale research is to look for relatively easy to collect proxies of the intermediate variables. Attempts to use highly specific forms of learning may be useful in specific contexts. However, they have severe limitations. The first problem is that the proxies never will capture all search activity, assuming that they even capture organizational search. For example, external advice seeking by CEOs (as used in *McDonald/Westphal,* 2003) is learning by individuals in organizations and not truly organizational learning (*Cook/Yanow,* 1993). Secondly, discretionary increases in R&D budgets can be tried out (*Greve,* 2003a, 2003c) but this introduces timing and a bias problems. The timing problem is that organizational search occurs before any commitment is made. Search instead looks for worthy commitments that can be made in the future. Instead, commitments to R&D are commitments of resources with limited knowledge about the value that the commitment will generate in future (*Ranft/Lord,* 2002). They do not overlap. The second problem with an increase in R&D budgets is the introduction of bias. While organizational learning after performance feedback implies a search for innovative as well as non-innovative solutions (e.g. *Ocasio,* 1993), increases in R&D budgets measure only search for innovative solutions.

Since it is from a theoretical point of view important to discriminate between willingness and a failure to make changes, there is thus a lacuna in the research methodology of large scale research where learning is not easy to. I will shortly present how tests of nonlinearity can be used as a third strategy to overcome the measurement problems of the intermediate variables.

3.2   The second mediating variable: Capability to change

The second mediator questions whether organizational learning after a stimulus is at all necessary for change. Rather it is possible that the response to a stimulus is known but not implemented. The change depends on how organizations have anticipated problems and have managed different sorts of uncertainty. This can be shown by highlighting differences in the Carnegie School tradition, where different sources of uncertainty are assumed. The type of environmental uncertainty determines the capabilities of organization to change. In A Behavioral Theory Of The Firm, the organization tries to cope with an environment that is only fraught with price and output volatility (*Cyert/March,* 1992). In this model, the organization does not systematically commit slack resources to learning activities. Consequently, the organization only learns when it is forced to learn. Instead, it uses the slack resources as inducements so that the dominant coalition is prepared to stick to the organization. Clearly, this strategy only pays off as long as the organization generates enough performance.

Thus, once performance is below aspiration, performance feedback draws attention. The resulting performance signal triggers a search for solutions. This search will be directed close to the problem, but it will spread out until a solution has been found. Since solutions can only be implemented as long as organizational members remain in the coalition, the dominant coalition may constrain the implementation of new strategic contents. Since the organization was not set for change, it is possible that organization learns that its aspirations were too ambitious and will respond by lowering its aspirations.

While the prior managerial preparedness for change in the Garbage Can Model (*Cohen et al,* 1972) is as high as in A Behavioral Theory Of The Firm, the managerial capacities to implement change are stronger. The organization is much more focused towards managing technology rather than towards controlling price and output volatility. As a result, the Garbage Can Model assumes more forms of organizational learning. First, the organization responds to the technological uncertainty by systematically dedicating slack resources to search activity (i.e. R&D budgets). To warrant maximum technological flexibility, slack should ideally be spread over diverse projects on competing technologies. However since organizational slack is finite, the technological coverage is not perfect. Second, the Garbage Can Model assumes learning from performance feedback. Performance feedback can reveal that competitors have developed better technology that harms the position of the firm.

Thus, when performance feedback is negative, it signals a problem. However, due to the technological slowness the organization cannot fabricate new solutions easily. Thus quickly searching for new solutions after performance feedback is bound to fail. Instead, it is more successful to consider whether pre-existing solutions match new problems. In the case where a solution can be found within the organization, the organization can roll out an earlier developed technology. As such, the Garbage Can Model helps explaining complete turn-arounds. That way firms who have embarked on solution-rich search strategies, can flourish again. A solution in the model will also trigger changes in the composition of the top management team. Organizational members that advance a solution need to get the authority to implement the strategy. Members that did not advance the solution, accept the change in authority and remain in the organization as long as they can continue their search efforts. Their search efforts are valuable to the organization because of ongoing technological uncertainty. While these search efforts might be pet projects in the short run, these projects can turn out to be crucial in the long run. Alternatively, when the scan of existing solutions does not pay off, the organization as a whole is worse off. The misfit simply persists and the organization muddles through. No new strategic content can be implemented until a technological solution can be found.

Table 3.1: The behavioural differences between different organizational learning theories

Steps in the change process	Carnegie School models		Threat Rigidity Theory
	A Behavioral Theory Of The Firm	Garbage Can Model	
Stimulus: The organization reacts to	price and output volatility	technological volatility	any threat
Mediator I: Organizational Search	widens	stays the same in the short run	is internal
Mediator II: Organizational capabilities to implement change	limited because there is a fixed coalition	are high because there is fluid participation	lower because of increased control
The mediation process is prone to	errors of commission	errors of commission	errors of omission
Probability (Strategic Change after negative performance feedback)	increased	increased	decreased
Directionality of response	internal or cosmetic external	cosmetic external	internal

Table 3.1 summarizes the impact of the two mediating variables of the three different learning theories described above. The difference between Threat Rigidity Theory and The Carnegie School is about differences in search propensity. Differences within the Carnegie School theories can be attributed to differences in organizational capacity to implement changes. These theoretical differences in framing and differences in capability should not be forcefully reconciled. Rather it is possible that the different mechanisms coexist (e.g. *Lant/Hurley,* 1999). Thus the differences in organizational learning theory reflect the idea that the processes triggered by the same stimuli can vary.

Still, there is room for theory advancement. These theories simplify the context of decision-making in the sense that it is assumed that firms always react to specific stimuli in similar ways. Firms do not always feel threatened with an increase in performance signals. It is more plausible that organizations have anticipated some signals and are surprised by other signals. More recent contributions of organizational learning theory indeed suggest that it is possible that sometimes firms are prepared to make changes from performance feedback while in other circumstances they are not (e.g. *March/Shapira,* 1992). Similarly, it is unlikely that firms willing to make changes react always in the same way.

Instead, it is quite plausible that the kind of reaction depends on the situation. This is elaborated more in the following section.

4   Moderated mediation determines what is changed

Whereas the previous section has focused on the processes that determine whether stimuli lead to strategic decision-making, this section allows more variation in the outcome of the actual decision-making. There is more variation to explain when it is acknowledged that firms can decide to make specific changes. Especially threats can lead to a myriad of responses. More than opportunities, threats can lead to truly new changes as well as to discontinuations of past decisions so that the threat is being cut away. This becomes clear when bearing in mind different sorts of learning after performance feedback. When there is a performance problem, *Argyris* (1977) has pointed out that performance feedback can to single loop learning as well as double loop learning. Single loop learning involves actions to restore the performance to aspiration levels. Double loop actions lead to actions that imply a fundamentally new way of doing.

4.1   A theoretical perspective

Also the intermediation of capabilities introduces variation in the kind of strategic decision-making. Different learning theories have predicted that when organizations are confronted with problems, they will make changes where they can (*Ocasio*, 1993). Likely alternatives for change are 1) changes near the symptom because it is there where the organization is loosing money (*Cyert/March,* 1992), or 2) changes in parts of the organizations with low power because it does not affect vested interests (*Pettigrew*, 1987), or 3) changes where they used to make changes because this is also easy (e.g. *Haleblian et al*, 2006), or 4) imitations of institutional practices (e. g *Wezel/Saka-Helmhout*, 2005). In other words, organizational learning theories predict that firms in distress are unlikely to change core technology, to make changes that affect strong units or in areas where neither they nor their peers have experience.

While these are competing theories, they may all be true in the sense that these are the areas where an organization is capable of changes, depending on the organizational circumstances (*Ocasio*, 1993; *Greve*, 2003c, p.178). More than creating new theory there is need for empirical evidence to disentangle between different strategic responses. There is however need for a research methodology that allows us to test the effect of intermediating variables on the directionality of change. I have chosen to review whether tests of nonlinearity are any good as tests of mediation. There is a good chance because non-linearity expresses the idea that the effect of performance feedback varies in strength and direction over time between opposing intermediate variables. Since non-linearity mainly focuses on the outcomes of the mediation process, it may circumvent measuring tacit variables without fully ignoring them. Therefore, it may be a cost efficient test appropriate for large scale research on organizational decision-making.

While non-linearity is a common element in complexity theory (e.g. *Stacey*, 2003), I will review Performance Feedback Theory of *Greve* (2003c) because of its strong ties with organizational learning theory. The ties are crucial for explaining and understanding the non-linear effects. This is the main reason why I have chosen not to elaborate on complexity theory. Literature reviews on complexity theory argue that it ignores the human element in explaining change in organizational change, is that it cannot pinpoint these forces and demands (e.g. *Houchin/Maclean*, 2005; *Stacey*, 2003; *Burnes*, 2005). I will show that the explicit treatment of human capacity and organizational constraints in Performance Feedback Theory helps in showing and explaining the emergence of nonlinear patterns between a stimulus and actual decision-making. The strength of the non-linearity in Performance Feedback Theory is thus its explicit focus on the deliberation process after performance feedback.

The specific shape of the relationship between performance and strategic change is only understood through intermediate effects. The mediation process of Performance Feedback Theory assumes that organizations will first reflect upon the performance signal and subsequently will deliberate about the cost of implementing possible solutions. The role of the performance signal is restricted to a moment where organizations might consider making changes. Thereafter, decision-makers are confronted with a new question which is likely to take more time and energy than the question before. Especially in the case of threats, when it has been acknowledged that something needs to be done, organizations may deliberate more about which solutions to the problem to choose from. This deliberation is not straightforward, even when there are multiple strategies to resolve the performance problem.

Mainly drawing on *Cyert/March* (1992), Performance Feedback Theory argues that at this point organizational constraints come to the fore. For a solution to be decided upon, Performance Feedback Theory predicts that two conditions need to be met. First, the organization should agree that the change has an expected non-negative impact on future performance and second, the organization should accept the consequences of implementing the change on the existing organization. The second criteria thus will filter solutions for which the organizational implications are minor.

In most cases, the attention shifts from the first criterion to the second criterion. Only in rare cases, will there be no shift from problem solving to constraints. The shift suggests that the outcome of the deliberation is not likely to be spectacular. It makes no sense to put a lot of effort into changes with high strategy implementation costs, when the only thing performance feedback learns is that the current strategy does not deliver the performance aspired to. The reason for the shift is that managers realize that the estimated performance effects of new solutions may not be realized. Uncertainty leads to different views on the desirability to change. Negative performance feedback provides arguments for those in favour of change as well for those who are against. *George* (2006) has argued that decision-makers, who fear a loss of resources, will argue that there is nothing more to lose and will argue that new things should be tried out, and will favour change; while decision-makers, who fear a loss of control, will argue that it is not the time to venture out into something new and that control needs to be reinstalled. Also *Pettigrew* (1987, p.667) has reported that finding support for difficult strategic change may require patience and perseverance. When faced with threats, patience is scarce. There is a lack of time (*Chattopadhyay et al, 2001*)

Thus, in most cases the decision-makers against change will win the debate. Therefore it makes sense to assume that managers will resort to more secure strategic responses after substandard performance. It is easier to prefer those alternatives that can be easily implemented without a major impact on the organization. Moreover, according to this logic there is no guarantee that the performance effects of the more secure opportunities are any worse. In sum, Performance Feedback Theory foresees two scenarios after substandard performance: 1) organizations will prefer making changes with low implementation costs or make no changes at all; 2) organizations will in most cases stall strategic changes that imply large implementation costs.

Figure 4.1: Linear and non-linear relationships in Performance Feedback Theory

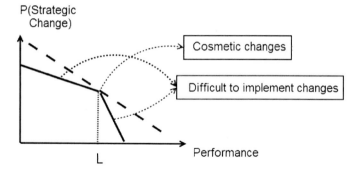

These two scenarios lead to differences in the relationship between performance and the probability of strategic change, as illustrated in Figure 4.1. In the most easy case, where decision-making is straightforward, there are truly cosmetic changes which are revealed by a negative and linear relationship between performance and the likelihood of strategic change. The linearity expresses that above standard performance stalls strategic change as much as substandard performance triggers strategic change. The relationship is negative because it becomes more tempting to institute changes as performance lowers. Performance Feedback Theory assumes that as performance goes down, managers will pick up the performance signal and be motivated to do something about it. On the right hand side of aspirations where performance is high, performance feedback provides no extra motivation by to institute this particular kind of change.

When responses are more difficult to find or when it is likely that they are difficult to be implemented, Performance Feedback Theory no longer assumes a linear relationship. Instead, the relationship breaks up at aspiration level. On the right hand side of aspirations, the relationship is steep because high strategy implementation costs make organizations stall this kind of strategic change. There is no motivation, from positive performance feedback, for difficult-to-implement change. On the left hand side of aspiration the picture is completely different. Although problematic search increases the need for change, the increase in probability is modest because interesting alternatives with less strategy implementation costs will receive priority. However, perhaps, that is 1) once easy alternatives have failed, or 2) once there is enough support for difficult-to-manage change, or 3) in the case that aspirations cannot be lowered, difficult-to-implement change may occur. Therefore the relationship between performance and strategic change is negative but flatter than it is on the left hand side.

The introduction of non-linear relationships reveals new lights on the debate between the Carnegie School and Threat Rigidity Theory. As stated earlier, the main differences between the theories are about willingness versus a capability to implement new initiatives. Performance Feedback Theory can easily display the difference between willingness and ability. To illustrate this, I need to point out that the Carnegie School and Threat Rigidity Theory are multi-period theories, in the sense that they assume that there is time to devise a strategic response. Both theories assume that organizations have time to receive multiple signals and to derive a strategy from it. In A Behavioral Theory Of The Firm, organizations use the time to widen their search. In Threat Rigidity Theory, firms ultimately react by restricting control as the number of signals increases. Thus, since both theories focus on threats, only the relationship to the left hand side of aspirations needs to be explained. In Performance Feedback Theory, the relationship between performance and the probability of strategic change is linear on both sides of the aspirations. To explain how Performance Feedback Theory can map the two views, it therefore suffices to assume that there are two rounds of decision-making because only two time points are needed to draw lines. It is fair to assume that in the first time point, the behavioural differences between A Behavioral Theory Of The Firm and Threat Rigidity Theory are not salient. The first solution after the first performance signals will reflect some rigidity in response as problematic search will be low and cosmetic responses to adversity are most likely to be decided upon (*Ocasio*, 1993, pp.23-24). I assume that the implementation of the first solution at the first time point did not pay off. Consequently, the organizational performance worsens. The second round leads to a new performance signal that is deliberated upon. Now the differences in response will be more salient because different processes are instigated.

In A Behavioral Theory Of The Firm, the deliberation leads to widened search. Accordingly, it becomes more likely that a solution with large strategic implementation costs will be tried out. Therefore the relationship between performance and this kind of strategic change is negative. Just as Performance Feedback Theory predicts, there is a non-linear negative relationship between performance and difficult-to-implement change, which indicates that the changes will only be installed when it is really necessary and possible. Alternatively, Threat Rigidity Theory argues that the second round of deliberation lowers the likelihood of strategic change because it is time to regain control. The constriction of control results in expected strategy implementation costs of strategic changes that are considered to be too high. Consequently, they increasingly favour the status quo. Therefore, the relationship between performance and strategic changes with high implementation costs will be positive when performance feedback is negative. In Threat Rigidity Theory, the most likely reaction for difficult-to-implement and external changes happens when the turmoil started, not when the organization is trying to regain control. Therefore, when performance feedback is negative, a positive relationship between performance and strategic change can be attributed to an unwillingness to change. Thus nonlinearity may reveal different mediation processes. To illustrate the usefulness of this test of mediation, I will turn to reviewing some empirical studies in detail, which were able to depict interesting behavioural responses after threats and opportunities (*Greve, 1998, 2002, 2003a, b, c; Baum et al, 2005; Audia/Greve, 2006*).

4.2 An empirical perspective

First, *Greve* (1998) has used the methodology in the radio broadcasting industry, an industry which consists of rather small companies. This industry was chosen because radio stations rely heavily on performance feedback. In particular, radio stations scrutinize market share figures because market share largely determines future organizational performance. Market share determines the likelihood of new ads being placed. When market shares are too low, radio stations may reflect on how to position themselves better within their market. Indeed, *Greve* (1998) has found a monotonic negative, non-linear relationship between performance and business strategy changes, which indicates that business changes are not instituted light-heartedly. The shape of the curve indicates that positive performance feedback stalls strategic change faster than negative performance feedback triggers strategic change. This result is not very surprising. It is counterintuitive for radio stations to change winning business strategies which are the cornerstones of their achieved performance (*Baum et al, 2005,* p.542).

It is more interesting to know what precisely radio stations change when performance disappoints. Therefore, *Greve* (1998) analyzed single strategic decisions separately. There are three strategic alternatives for radio stations: making changes in the broadcasting format (format changes), investing in satellite emission (satellite changes) and making changes in the production of radio programs (program changes). To identify which of the changes are easier to implement, *Greve* (1998) considered that changes should not put future ads at risk. In other words, changes that entail a change in the customer base will be stalled. On the contrary, satellite changes and production changes were assumed to have low risk since no new customers are targeted. Instead, they are more internally oriented.

For satellite changes, *Greve* (1998) has found as predicted, a linear effect between performance and the likelihood of satellite changes. This result indicates a low resistance to change when there is a clear motivation for change. In other words, it is only when performance deteriorates, that investing in satellite changes becomes more likely. The picture is different for format changes. *Greve* (1998) has found a non-linear relationship between performance and format changes. In particular, when performance is above standard, format changes are more likely to be stalled as performance gets better. On the contrary, when performance is substandard, the effect of performance on format changes is much weaker. This relationship indicates that organizations do not like to make format changes even when performance is severely deteriorating. Finally, contrary to Greve's initial expectations, a non-linear relationship between performance and program changes has been found, which indicates that radio stations are not very receptive to program changes even when performance was deteriorating. In hindsight, *Greve* (1998) explains that program changes are stalled because they imply serious conversion and other learning costs for the program makers which lead to strong resistance in the organization. In summary, the separate analysis of different actions in the business strategy reveals important departures from the picture drawn by the overall analysis of the business strategy. The variation can be attributed to differences in strategy implementation costs. The nonlinear relationships in the radio broadcasting industry also slightly depart from relations expected from the review of the different organizational learning theories. It is not important whether actions are oriented to the outside or inside the organization that determine the shape of the relationship. Rather it is the differences in learning costs and strategy implementation costs that determine the shape of the relationship.

Subsequently Performance Feedback Theory has been applied to the Japanese shipbuilding industry where capital investment decisions and innovations were studied. Capital investments in the shipbuilding industry are not easily taken because the performance effects of investments are highly uncertain. On the one hand, they often involve sunk costs that cannot be recuperated easily when economic downturns indicate excess capacity. On the other hand, they can lead to efficiency gains, knowledge and less capacity constraints that allow shipbuilders to quickly react to economic boosts (*Audia/Greve*, 2006; *Greve*, 2003c, p.105). To test whether performance feedback triggers investment decisions, different operationalizations for investment decisions have been tried out. The study on the effect of performance feedback on investment decisions has lead to only one general result and many fragmented views. The general result is that benchmarking performance has no effect on investment decisions in the Japanese shipbuilding industry. On the contrary, comparing performance with historical performance triggers various responses vis-à-vis investment decisions. Thus historical comparison is an important piece of information. Yet, the picture is complex for the effect of historical comparison matters on how investment decisions are measured.

First, *Greve* (2003b, c) has made use of two indirect measures for investment decisions: asset growth and machinery growth in book values. The difference is that machinery growth is believed to match investment decisions because it excludes slow adjusting assets like buildings. When asset growth is used, only a significant negative effect of performance feedback for above standard performance was found, which indicates that shipbuilders get no extra motivation from performance feedback to make additional investments when performance is good and gets better. Deteriorating performance, when performance was already substandard, does not trigger any change in shipbuilders investment strategies. In case of machinery growth, *Greve* (2003b) has found a non-monotone relationship between performance and machinery growth as in Treat Rigidity Theory, which indicates that 1) shipbuilders are less willing to make new investments as substandard performance deteriorates and that 2) shipbuilders are less willing to make new investments as above performance increases.

Interestingly, when *Audia/Greve* (2006) use a measurement that matches investment behaviour more closely, the threat rigidity response prevails again. Deteriorating performance when performance is already substandard, stalls investment behaviour. Also, improving performance when performance is already above standard, stalls factory expansion. Moreover, they have found that size moderates the relationship, which indicates that it is especially the small shipbuilder in distress who decreases investments and not the large firm in distress.

Thus small shipbuilders most likely make investments when performance is around aspirations. This does not necessarily imply that shipbuilders stay inert all the rest of the time. In fact, shipbuilders can resort to other responses. *Greve* (2003a, c) has also studied whether performance feedback triggers innovative behaviour. This research has separated the decisions to increase the R&D budget from decisions to launch innovations because of time lags between R&D commitments and commercial outcomes of research and development. In terms of the commitments to the R&D budget, *Greve* (2003a) has found no indications of increases in the R&D budget when substandard performance worsens. In addition, he has found that performance above aspiration loosens the discipline of shipbuilders to commit resources to research as performance gets better. The combined result indicates that only opportunity seeking behaviour remains high when performance disappoints.

Further, *Greve* (2003a, c) has used two models testing the effect of performance feedback on launching innovations. There is a model testing whether innovations are launched (*Greve*, 2003c) and a model on the number of innovations. *Greve* (2003a, c) has found that Japanese shipbuilders postpone launching innovations when performance is satisficing. These innovations are more likely to be launched when performance is substandard. Yet the effect of performance feedback is not strong enough to speed up launches when substandard performance worsens.

In summary, a rather detailed view of the decision-making by shipbuilders after performance feedback was made. It appears that performance feedback has the strongest effect when performance is above aspirations, indicating that performance feedback stalls difficult decisions. More importantly is that shipbuilders in distress are selective in their responses. On the left hand side of aspirations it has only become clear that small shipbuilders cut back on investments when substandard performance worsens. In most cases, however, substandard performance that worsens does not bring about many new commitments. And again, it does not matter whether they are internally or externally oriented responses.

This research setting thus again, assumes that only solutions with low implementation costs to the firm are interesting strategic responses when firms are faced with opportunities or with threats. Also the third research setting in the literature is in corroboration of this emerging hypothesis. *Baum et al* (2005) have studied whether network extensions to non-local ties in the relational banking industry were considered after performance feedback. While the use of networks is a common part of the business strategy for banks, extensions of the network are risky decisions. Banks prefer to rely on networks for large financing projects so that the risk is spread. The reason why firms tend to rely in particular on the same network is that changes in the network are costly and risky. On the one hand, adding new ties implies search costs for reliable peers and may lead to negative spillovers if a member of the network defaults. On the other hand, extending to new ties can have positive performance effects because it increases possibilities for new financing opportunities and may bring along new expertise and new customers. Because of the uncertain net benefits, it is assumed that banks tend to stick to their known network. Therefore, it is interesting to see whether performance feedback can alter the network strategy of the firm.

Baum et al (2005) have found a new non-linear relationship between performance and strategic change. The V-shaped relationship between performance and strategic change indicates that extensions to the network are increasingly considered as performance is further from both sides of aspirations. Thus, when the already satisficing market share of banks increases further and when disappointing market share worsens, banks are more likely to extend their network with non-local ties. Clearly, the most surprising result is on the right hand side of aspirations because it counters the empirical regularity that firms never change winning strategies (*Greve*, 1998, 2003a, b, c; *Audia/Greve*, 2006). This is the first time in Performance Feedback Theory that successful firms are found to change winning strategies. This result suggests that the expected organizational threats of extending network ties are only minor for highly successful banks.

5   Tests of nonlinearity and organizational boundaries

The theoretical perspective and the empirical studies allow us to present the strengths and weaknesses of the test of non-linearity in Performance Feed-

back Theory. Two caveats prevail. The first is that only one stimulus for decision-making is being considered. It may be more difficult to apply the test of
non-linearity because the choice of breaking points for the other stimuli may be
less evident. For performance feedback, the choice was easy as the aspiration
level is a logical breaking point.

A second caveat is that is that the results of the tests in many empirical
studies are highly sensitive. The effect of performance feedback on a particular
point of change can differ over slight variations of the chosen performance indicator, the construction and combination of aspiration levels, the measure of the
dependent variable and even the model. This poses two problems. First, there is
need for accompanying theories to select hypothetical relationships between performance indicators, aspirations and particular types of change. Second, it is difficult to draw general conclusions from highly sensitive results. Notwithstanding
these caveats, the tests of nonlinearity in Performance Feedback Theory were
able to show that:
a) organizations have the choice to make decisions after performance feedback.
b) organizational constraints play an important role in strategic decision-making,
in the case of opportunities and as well as in the case of threats.
c) Strategic decisions will lead to commitments that have as least as possible
disruptive effects on the organization. Within these boundaries, strategic responses are highly variable. When organizations decide to change, change has to
be manageable.

Figure 5.1: The debate between the Carnegie School and Threat Rigidity Theory
mapped on Performance Feedback Theory

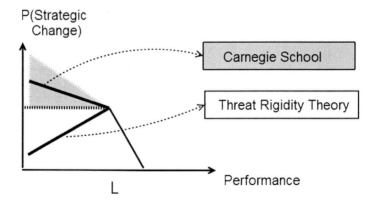

A test of non linearity implies a simultaneous focus on threats and opportunities, which yields richer interpretations. The benefit was most clearly in the
Japanese shipbuilders industry where negative performance feedback makes

sure that the commitment to R&D and innovations remain relatively high. The effect is not stronger than that. Performance feedback creates an atmosphere of alertness but does not seem to be the key factor in final decision-making. Other factors, organizational constraints, have more power to determine the exact timing of risky commitments. Therefore the sign between performance and difficult to implement strategic change is likely to be insignificant when performance feedback is negative. Thus, despite the statistical insignificant effect of negative performance feedback, is Performance Feedback Theory able to draw some conclusions from it when the effect of positive performance feedback is significant. Thus, by taking into account the complete picture of performance feedback, does it become clear that negative performance feedback has some influence on decision-making.

From a theoretical perspective, the non significant effect at the right hand side of aspirations is not a very surprising result. The Japanese research setting has elucidated the theoretical debate between the Carnegie School and Threat Rigidity well: the non-significant effects on the left hand sight of aspirations clearly indicate that horizontal relationship between performance and strategic change when performance is substandard is the demarcation line in this debate, as indicated in figure 5.1. When processes to regain control overrule, a positive relationship should be observed. When processes to try-things-out prevail, a negative relationship should be observed. When the processes are kept in balance, then a non-significant result is most likely.

In general, the strong focus on managerial choice and deliberation in Performance Feedback Theory pays off. The test of non-linearity is especially valuable in quantitative, longitudinal research settings where it may be tempting to ignore the strategy change process (*Rajagopalan/Spreitzer*, 1997). Performance Feedback Theory presents a better alternative. It provides a no-nonsense test of mediation that can be applied when learning and strategy implementation are too fuzzy to be measured.

6   Conclusion

This literature review has shown that the research agenda on strategic change calls for revision. While old questions concerning strategic change - questions traditionally about the antecedents, the processes and the consequences of strategic change – still remain important, they need to be embedded in a new context of strategic flexibility. Since strategic flexibility implies that some parts of the organization's strategy are subject to change while other parts will not change, the new research questions should consider what remains stable and what is changed, for what reason, and on what occasion. These questions highlight strategic choice as an important dimension of strategic change. The literature review has shown that organizations respond to threats and opportunities by making small strategic changes because the impact on the organization is key in the decision- making process. Organizations are especially bound in their attempts to reconcile different stakes within the organization and make changes where they can.

Research on small change is different from past research. According to the old approach, organizational size is an important determinant for reorientations because strategic reorientations coincide with complete organizational replacements. Since it requires more efforts to turn around large firms, organizational size is assumed to stall strategic change (e.g. *Hannan/Freeman*, 1984; *Donaldson*, 2001). Research on small change departs from the old view because it decouples strategic change from organizational turnaround. Therefore organizational size on its own cannot be an important variable for explaining strategic change.

There is no reason why large firms cannot change partially. In a competitive environment, firms do not get the freedom to outgrow and to become outdated (*Barnett/Hanssen*, 1996; *Barnett/Sorenson*, 2002). Especially large, visible firms, who are in contact with many stakeholders, cannot stay put. While some stakeholders may be prepared to give firms some time, when things get out of hand, some stakeholders will apply the brakes: financial markets correct, governments warn, LBOs happen, firms restructure, downscope and downsize. Moreover, because product life cycles have shortened significantly, firms can no longer stick to one successful strategy any more. Thus, forced change is not rare, threats need to be managed and small strategic changes are not necessarily immaterial to organizational performance.

I use a metaphor to highlight the difference in views. The old view assumes that adaptive changes to the core are rare because they are too difficult to be managed. According to the old view, lucky firms can thus become large and old in very much the way they used to. Large firms repeat their practices even long after that the environment has changed. Once firms are big they can weather a storm, or even two and more (*Gersick*, 1991). As such, large firms become dinosaurs who keep on repeating the same old way of doing things. This is bound to go wrong and eventually, when the environment is completely transformed and slack has been eaten, the misfit has become so big that there is no way back and so that the dinosaurs are selected out.

In the new view small changes are no longer downplayed as immaterial. There is no place for dinosaurs. Instead I think that it is more appropriate to compare flexible firms with chameleons. Unlike dinosaurs, these reptiles undergo two changes. First they mature in an evolutionary way like dinosaurs. Secondly, they have an inbuilt capacity to change the colour of their skin when faced with new stimuli. According to a 2002 National Geographic article, chameleons change colour in response to light, temperature, and mood. Similarly, firms undergo these two sorts of changes. Evolutionary changes in the organizations happen because of natural employee turnover, reorganizations etc. In addition, firms can also respond to threats and opportunities by deliberate changes. The metaphor of firms as chameleons is in tune with the main conclusion of this literature review. Firstly, just as chameleons change colour, organizations make visible changes in response to threats and opportunities.

Secondly, just like chameleons change colour in only seconds, most strategic changes happen smoothly because disruptive impact on the existing organizational behaviour is avoided. Finally, it is clear that it does not suffice to make cosmetic changes. While the chameleon decides to change colour depending on his mood, the changes may not always worth the effort. What is the value of changing colour when the chameleon quickly changes into green when it had to change into blue? Similarly, cosmetic changes may have different performance questions. Some cosmetic changes will have beneficial performance consequences and others will have detrimental performance consequences. Research on the performance consequences of cosmetic changes is needed if we want to know whether change really matter. This uncertainty is however an important difference with the old view where small changes are seen a-priori as immaterial. Nor do not swing to the other extreme by saying that fine feathers always make fine birds. I only propound that if an organization disregards every signal, then the organization will look worn out, and will not be able to capitalize on its once accumulated competences.

Metaphors should be taken with a pinch of salt. They can make things clear but there will never be a perfect match. The difference is that chameleons are likely to react in the same way over and over again to the same stimuli.

Thus, although chameleons can change colours, they are – probably- unable to learn. Only appropriate theory and empirical testing will adequately answer the full process of small change. The challenge for small change research is to have appropriate methodological tools.

I therefore have put forward organizational learning theory. This theory shows that what an organization changes depends on 1) its preparedness to learn, 2) what it learns, and 3) how it is able to implement changes. The organizational constraints for change therefore drive the change process. They are in general tacit and difficult to measure, especially in large scale, quantitative research. Tests of non-linearity may be a satisfactory tool to measure the decision-making process because non-linearity reveals differences in strength and direction over time because of opposing forces and demands.

Despite the usefulness of organizational learning theory to strategic change, I do not claim that the learning lens is the only lens to study small strategic change. The strategy as practice stream of research (e.g. *Whittington*, 2006) has the advantage of revealing tacit processes in strategic decision-making. This approach essentially requires case study or process approaches because of its microscopic lens (e.g. *Poole et al,* 2000). On the contrary, when no information on the mediation process can be obtained, researchers can resort to learning theory and complexity theory. While distinct, complexity theory has communalities with organizational learning theory, especially with respect to its emphasis in non-linearity. In this literature review, I decided to review an organizational learning test above complexity theory because the explicit treatment of human capacity and organizational constraints in organizational learning theory is a competitive advantage.

References

Argyris, C. (1977): Double loop learning in organizations. Harvard Business Review, Volume 55 (5), pp. 115-125.

Audia, P.G. / Greve, H.R. (2006): Less likely to fail: low performance, firm size, and factory expansion in the shipbuilding industry. Management Science, Volume 52 (1), pp. 83-94.

Barnett, W.P. / Hansen, M.T. (1996): The red queen in organizational evolution. Strategic Management Journal, Volume 17, pp. 139-157.

Barnett, W.P. / Sorenson, O. (2002): The red queen in organizational creation and development. Industrial and Corporate Change, Volume 11 (2), pp. 289-325.

Baum, J.A.C ./ Rowley, T. J ./ Shipilov, A.V. / Chuang Y. (2005): Dancing with strangers: aspiration performance and the search for underwriting syndicate partners. Administrative Science Quarterly, Volume 50, pp. 536-575.

Burnes, B. (2004): Kurt Lewin and the planned approach to change: a re-Appraisal. Journal of Management Studies, Volume 41 (6), pp. 977-1022.

Burnes, B. (2005): Complexity theories and organizational change. International Journal of Management Reviews, Volume 7 (2), pp. 73-90.

Caves, R. E. / Porter, M. E. (1977): From entry barriers to mobility barriers: conjectural decisions and contrived deterrence to new competition. Quarterly Journal of Economics, Volume 91 (2), pp. 241-261.

Chattopadhyay, P. / Glick, W.H. / Huber, G.P. (2001): Organizational actions in response to threats and opportunities. Academy of Management Journal, Volume 44 (5), pp. 937-955.

Chuang, Y. / Baum, J.A.C. (2003): It's all in the name: failure-induced learning by multiunit chains. Administrative Science Quarterly, Volume 48, pp. 33-59.

Cohen M. D; / March, J. G. / Olsen, J. P. (1972): A garbage can model of or ganizational choice. Administrative Science Quarterly, Volume 17 (1), pp. 1-25.

Cook, S.D.N. / Yanow, D. (1993): Culture and organizational learning. Journal of Management Inquiry, Volume 2, pp. 373-390.

Cyert, R.M. / March, J.G. (1992): A Behavioral Theory Of The Firm, Massachusetts, USA.

Dial, J. / Murphy, K.J. (1995): Incentives, downsizing, and value creation at General Dynamics. Journal of Financial Economics, Volume 37, pp. 261-314.

Donaldson, L. (2001): The Contingency Theory Of Organizations. Thousand Oaks, California.

Eisenhardt, K. / Martin, J. (2000): Dynamic capabilities: what are they? Strategic Management Journal, Volume 21, pp. 1105-1121.

Eisenmann, T.R. / Bower, J.L. (2000): The entrepreneurial M-Form: strategic integration in global media firms. Organizational Science, Volume 11 (3), pp. 348-355.

George, E. / Chattopadhyay, V. / Sitkin, S.B. / Barden, J. (2006): Cognitive underpinnings of institutional persistence and change: a framing perspective. Academy of Management Review, Volume 31 (2), pp. 347-365.

Gersick, C.J. (1991): Revolutionary change theories: a multilevel exploration of the punctuated equilibrium paradigm. Academy of Management Review, Volume 16 (1), pp. 10-36.

Greve, H.R. (1998): Performance, aspirations, and risky organizational change. Administrative Science Quarterly, Volume 43, pp.58-86.

Greve, H.R. (2003a): A behavioural theory of R&D expenditures and innovations: evidence from shipbuilding. Academy of Management Journal, Volume 46 (6), pp. 685-702.

Greve, H.R. (2003b): Investment and the behavioural theory of the firm: evidence from shipbuilding. Industrial and Corporate Change, Volume 12 (5), pp. 1051-1076.

Greve, H.R. (2003c): Organizational Learning From Performance Feedback. A Behavioural Perspective On Innovation And Change. Cambridge, UK.

Haleblian, J., Kim, J. / Rajagopalan, N. (2006): The influence of acquisition experience and performance on acquisition behaviour: evidence from the U.S. commercial banking industry. Academy of Management Journal, Volume 49 (2), pp. 357-370.

Hamel, G. / Prahalad, C. K. (1989): Strategic intent. Harvard Business Review, Volume 67 (3), May/June 1989, pp. 63-76.

Hannan, M. / Freeman, J. (1984): Structural inertia and organizational change. American Sociological Review, Volume 49, pp. 149-164.

Houchin, K. / Maclean D. (2005): Complexity theory and strategic change: an empirically informed critique. British Journal of Management, Volume 16, pp. 149-166.

James, L.R. / Brett, J.M. (1984): Mediators, moderators and tests for mediation. Journal of Applied Psychology, Volume 69 (2), pp. 307-321.

Lant, T.K. / Hurley, A. (1999): Contingency model of response to performance feedback: escalation of commitment and incremental adaptation in resource investment decisions. Group and Organization Management, Volume 24 (4), pp. 421-437.

March, J.G. / Shapira, Z. (1992): Variable Risk Preferences And The Focus Of Attention. Psychological Review, Volume 99 (1), pp. 172-183.

McDonald, M.L. / Westphal, J.D. (2003): Getting By With The Advice Of Their Friends: CEO's Advice Networks And Firm's Strategic Responses To Poor Performance. Administrative Science Quarterly, Volume 48, pp. 1-32.

Ocasio, W. (1993): The structuring of organizational attention and the enactment of economic adversity: a reconciliation of theories of failure-induced change and threat-rigidity. Working Paper (Sloan School of Management) No.3577-93.

Pettigrew, A.M. (1987): Context and action in the transformation of the firm, Journal of Management Studies. Volume 24 (6), pp.649-670.

Poole, M.S. / Van De Ven, A.H. / Dooley, K. / Holmes, M.E. (2000): Organizational Change And Innovation Processes, Theory And Methods For Research. N.Y., USA.

Rajagopalan, N. / Spreitzer, G.M. (1997): Toward a theory of strategic change: a multi-lens perspective and integrative framework. Academy of Management Review, Volume 22 (1), pp. 48-79.

Ranft, A.L. / Lord, M.D. (2002): Acquiring new technologies and capabilities: a grounded model of acquisition implementation. Organization Science, Volume 13 (4), pp. 420-441.

Stacey, R. (2003). Strategic Management and Organizational Dynamics. The Challenge of Complexity, Harlow, U.K.

Staw, B.M. / Sandelands, L.E. / Dutton, J.E. (1981): Threat-rigidity effects in organizational behaviour: a multilevel analysis. Administrative Science Quarterly, Volume 26 (4), pp. 501-524.

Tushman, M.L. / Romanelli E. (1985): Organizational evolution: a metamorphosis model of convergence and reorientation. Research in Organizational Behaviour, Volume 7, 171-222.

Washington, M. / Ventresca, M.J. (2004): How organizations change: the role of institutional support mechanisms in the incorporation of higher education visibility strategies, 1874-1995. Organization Science, Volume 15 (1), pp. 82-97.

Wezel, F.C. / Saka-Helmhout, A. (2006): Antecedents and consequences of organizational change: 'institutionalizing' the behavioural theory of the firm. Organization Studies, Volume 27 (2), pp. 265-286.

Whittington, R. (2006): Completing the practice turn in strategy research. Organization Studies, Volume 27, 613-634.

Organizational Structure and the Trade Off Between Static and Dynamic Efficiency of the Firm
Federico Sallusti

1 Introduction

The literature on theory of the firm has developed significantly in the last decades, principally because of the debate between the institutional school and what will be defined as the traditional one.[1] The central matter of debate is the definition of the nature of a firm as a structure not entirely ruled by the mechanisms of the market, but rather as a replica, on a different scale, of the transactions of the market. Generally, the assumptive bases of the proposed theories are characterised by elements which would seem to authorise a prior distinction in terms of stability of the system of reference.[2]

Even though, as will be seen later, the debate about the theory of the firm can't be read merely in terms of the debate between institutional and traditional theorists, the basic distinction for the hypothesis of stability/instability allows for development of a path aimed at distinguishing the venues and issues of application of the different approaches.

A stable system is, by definition, incapable of having its own dynamic. This would seem to be confirmed by the a-temporal nature of traditional formulations and by the objective difficulty that those models meet in rendering endogenous such purely dynamic phenomena as dimensional, technological and structural mutations of the firms. From another perspective, authors who attempted to analyze such phenomena had to abandon both the logic of stability and that of the a-temporality of the formulations.

The principal aim of this work is to propose a schema consistent with the theories of instability, assuming that agents are characterised by bounded rationality and that the variations of the decisional context aren't entirely derivable. The abandonment of the logic of a-temporality will be reflected in the analysis of two different moments: one defined as static – with an unvaried environment – and one dynamic – with a varying environment, which will show how process phenomena can be developed in response to variations that have taken place.

---

[1] From here on, we will refer to traditional authors (traditional theory) to describe who, in the contest of firm theory, defines its nature in terms of contractual structure and derive a structure of efficiency (of incentives or rather of property rights) on the basis of market transactions.

[2] The absence of efficient coordination prevents the economic system from being stable, because the price system cannot correctly tell agents what behaviours to use in coherence with the needs of stability of the system. This is true also where agents will not be able to correctly interpret information signals coming from the market. From an assumptive perspective, this translates, in the first case, as the definition of linear models of price variations – which would allow the market to furnish very simple information for the agents to interpret – while, in the second, as the definition of full rationality of agents – which excludes the fact that they cannot interpret market signals correctly.

The logic followed will adhere to the theories which *Gibbons* (2005) defined as Adaptation Theories, that is the schemas which take into account the impossibility of solving ex-ante the incompleteness of contracts, so supposing that the firm must adopt an organizational structure whose principal role is to manage and coordinate the decisions and behaviours of the firm.

The definition of the nature of the firm will be that of cognitive capabilities. The organizational structure will be described in terms of its own capability to process and communicate the information acquired from the external environment. This choice essentially depends on the fact that the complexity of variations in the external environment and the limits of agents' rationality force the firm to create a scale economy of knowledge, aimed toward better acquisition, processing and communication of information, which no longer comes solely from the market.

The proposed model, departing from the theory of the dependent labour contract proposed by *Simon* (1951), will stress a trade-off relationship between static and dynamic efficiency conditions of the firm. This signifies that behaviours consistent with the principle of economic convenience (or rather survival) are inconsistent time-wise.

This trade-off relationship signals two elements of interest. The first is temporal asymmetry, unrecognised by traditional formulations, but perfectly consistent with the emergence of complexity. Second, the breakdown of this symmetry allows the emergence of the endogeneity of process phenomena.

2 Completion of Contracts and Processing of Information: The Role of the Internal Structure

The neoclassical firm is defined in terms of technological conditions and behavioural assumptions. The maximization of profits allows agents, rational in Savage's sense, to utilise the technology available in a fully efficient way. Such a firm receives the information needed to make its decision from the market, which provides decision-makers with all relevant signals for building and elaborating their decisional context.

This logical schema presumes some stringent starting assumptions: market mechanisms have to be able to play the role of coordination device efficiently; agents, who are decision-makers, have to be able to utilise efficiently those signals. On the other hand, if those conditions were not held, the system would not be able to generate an endogenous mechanism of coordination, with the consequence of becoming intrinsically instable, and the agents would be unable to interpret informative signals univocally.

This is the context in which the proposed analysis will be developed, as it will be supposed that variations in the external environment are complex – so it is not possible to build and maintain an univocal and fully determined context of decision and the price does not contain the fully relevant information – and that agents are limited by bounded rationality – so they are unable to devote the necessary cognitive effort to interiorize some form of certainty, intended as a full definition of their implicit utility function. Such a theoretical framework does not provide the system with the characteristic of stability, making necessary to analyse the absence of coordination and its implication on the theoretical level.[3]

The presence at once of bounded rationality and complexity of the dynamics of evolution of the external environment has as a consequence the need to introduce historical time into the analysis and to abandon the path of ex-ante completion of contracts, proposed by modern theorists of the general equilibrium theory.

It would in fact be impossible to establish ex-ante the structure of incentives,[4] or determine efficiently the structure of property rights,[5] consistent with determining an inter-temporal equilibrium which allows the achievement of full efficiency of the decisions and behaviours of firms.[6]

The incompleteness of contracts, hence, stresses the impossibility of describing the internal structure of a firm as a replica, on a different scale, of market mechanisms, because the limitations to agents' rationality prevent using those formulations. The nature of the structure seems rather to be determined within the institutional framework, where it holds a coexistence of market and non-market mechanisms, determined through the peculiarity of the assets subject to contract.[7]

The presence of complexity, on the other hand, imposes a step forward with respect to institutional analysis, because the resolution of the theoretical matter treated in this work – that is, the determination of a theoretical framework for treating the endogenous elements of the evolution of productive systems – goes beyond the mere comparison between market and non-market coordination.

This dialectic, though still an essential element for comprehending the nature and behaviours of the internal structure of a firm, does not allow, in fact, to stress completely the role it can play as both a means of coordination – which tends to represent a compensation-chamber of systemic instability[8] – and a means of processing information from the outside – thus revealing the evolu-

---

[3] Many authors have devoted themselves to the analysis of the causes and consequences of the absence of coordination and of instability. They refer to different schools of thought and historical periods. The authors of the Austrian school like *Hayek* (1945, 1948), *Mises* (1949), or *Kirzner* (1973), or rather institutionalists like *Coase* (1937, 1984), *Williamson* (1970, 1975, 1985, 1988, 1996). Other authors who dedicated their attention to instability have been *Knight* (1921), *Keynes* (1936) and the new theorists of instability like, for example, *Leijonhufvud* (2000).

[4] *Tirole* (1988), *Holmstrom/Tirole* (1991), *Holmstrom/Milgrom* (1994), *Anghion/Tirole* (1997), *Tirole/Maskin* (1999), *Holmstrom* (1999).

[5] *Arrow* (1964), *Alchian/Demsetz* (1972), *Hart* (1995), *Hart/Moore* (1990).

[6] *Alchian/Demsetz* (1972), *Masten* (1988), *Grossman/Hart* (1986), *Holmstrom/Tirole* (1989), *Gibbons* (2005).

[7] *Williamson* (1985, 1988), *Radner* (1992), *Menard* (1994).

[8] *Cohen/Levinthal* (1990).

tionary phenomena typical of productive systems, making them endogenous and visible in their working.[9]

Before introducing a theoretical analysis of the roles assigned to the organizational structure, it must be made clear that they cannot be completely disjoined, because the mechanisms of coordination and of the evolution of decisions and behaviours are strongly connected. Moreover, a preventive definition of the internal structure is needed.

As every complex structure, the organizational one of a firm is characterised by two basic elements: the agents who compose it – the nodes – and the relationships on the basis of which they interact – inter-connections. The existence of the nodes is obtainable through a contract which carries out the relationship between the agent and the structure – condition of existence of the structure – while the interactions will be ruled by both the contractual structure and the management of the capabilities contained within the structure itself.

Where the role of the structure is essentially coordinating and acquiring knowledge through the capability to process and communicate information, the capabilities abstractly referred to are summarizable on the level of the cognitive potentiality which the structure is able to profound.[10] The network of nodes and inter-connections can be, in fact, modelled in such a manner as to allow different degrees of flexibility, determining implicitly the capacity to process and communicate information.

The trade-off relationship between the amount of information processed and the capacity to communicate it in an efficient way within the structure will be dealt with in depth when the model is presented, but it seems opportune to introduce here the concept to be used in analysing such a central issue.

Cognitive distance can be defined, in an abstract way, as heterogeneity of feeling. More concretely, it represents a measure of the cognitive differences among the elements which compose the structure.[11] Since agents are generally heterogeneous, and the processing of information is a process of interpretation of signals, the more heterogeneous the agents are, the greater will be the intersection set of their capabilities to recognise different signals, augmenting the potential amount of information that can be processed. On the other hand, the more heterogeneous the set of cognitive capabilities of the agents, the harder it will be for the communication system to work efficiently, because the sharing of codes of communication becomes more complex as the amount of information and the heterogeneity of interpretations increase.

Hence, the concept of cognitive distance allows us to establish a trade-off relationship between the amount of information that can be processed and its communication within the structure. On the other hand, knowledge can be achieved only through a process that includes both processing and communication of information.

---

[9] *Simon* (1947).
[10]   March/*Simon* (1958), *Barney* (1991, 1996).
[11]   *Nooteboom* (2002).

A measure of cognitive distance can be determined in terms of, among other things, the degree of flexibility governing the relationships among the elements composing the structure. High degrees of rigidity will determine a greater incidence of homogeneous elements, reducing the amount of cognitive distance utilised, while, instead, high degrees of flexibility will determine the opposite result, that is, a rise in the cognitive distance utilised, amplifying the elements of heterogeneity present within the structure.

The expounded trade-off relationship is the consequence of the entropic determination of information.[12] The traditional theory of information, in fact, stresses the scarcity of information as the main element of its analysis. A greater amount of information determines, in such a theory, a better definition of the context of decision and, under the assumption of agents' full rationality, the determination of an efficient behaviour.[13]

In this work we will suppose indeed that information, or more properly informative signals, are by no means scarce, but we will assume that the context of decision is entirely defined by those signals present in the external environment, of which the market is simply a subset. Simon[14] has already proposed a similar scheme of reference, stressing that the concept of scarcity had to be referred to capabilities of processing information, rather than to the distribution of informative signals.

Further, the entropic theory of information introduces another complicating element in the analysis, that is, the fact that the increase in the number of signals produces the apparent paradox that the distribution of probabilities about states of the world, subsequent to the increase in the availability of information on the basis of which it is determined, becomes more blurry, because there are more informative elements that disturb the reception of relevant signals.[15]

Noise can be interpreted as the limitations of agents' cognitive capabilities, which prevent them from computing the right model for deriving a complete picture from the information available, or rather as the limit of the code of communication when there is too much information to be managed. Both interpretations can be viewed as a constraint on the organizational structure in efficiently managing the limited capabilities of the agents who compose it.

The limitation to the derivation of a certain solution, imposed by white noise, appears perfectly consistent with those traced through the definition of the concept of cognitive distance and its application to the organizational structure of the firm. The direct consequence of that frame of reference is that full knowledge cannot be attained and that the decisional context cannot be univocally determined. That is an obvious cause for systemic instability, because making erroneous decisions cannot be avoided, and hence full coordination fails, but it represents, at the same time, the main requirement for the vitality of the system

---

[12]   *Shannon/Weaver* (1949), *Bateson* (1972), *Zurek* (1989), *Santa Fe Institute* (1989).
[13]   *Guiso/Terlizzese* (1994).
[14]   *Simon* (1955).
[15]   *AA. VV.* (1996).

and the working of endogenous evolutionary mechanisms including variations of the productive structure and processes of innovation.

Thus, it is not surprising that similar schemas of reference have been utilised to analyse intrinsically dynamic and evolutionary elements of firms, including dimensional,[16] technological[17] and structural[18] ones.

On the other hand, authors such as Gibbons[19] and Williamson,[20] ever alert to developments in the literature on the theory of the firm, stressed the conceptual proximity of the approaches by many authors and schools of thought, which they have gathered respectively under the definition of adaptation theories and theories of ex-post resolution of incompleteness of contracts. Other authors have also noted that such theories can be gathered on the basis of a commonality of aims and starting hypotheses.[21]

This is a confirmation that the study of evolutionary phenomena of the firm passes for a re-definition of some starting hypotheses of models of general equilibrium theory, which have as a corollary the modification of some essential points of the traditional theory about firms: a description of the nature of the firm which includes the concept of cognitive capability, as well as contractual determination; a re-definition of the roles and mechanisms of the working of the internal structure, both in static and dynamic contexts.

The model will be presented moves from those considerations, with the goal to show how this characterization of the ambit of research can lead to conclusions which determine partially the confirmation of some results coming from the traditional theory, but, at once, the emersion of an inverse relationship between the static and dynamical needs in terms of the maintenance of efficiency, showing hence a space of analysis where the conclusions of the traditional theory do not seems to be valid.

In this context there is the vital space to analyse the evolutionary phenomena, which was the main result of the work presented, as well as that to be able to stress as the introduction of complexity and bounded rationality leads to the emersion of elements which remained hidden into the traditional analysis.

3 The Determination of the Condition of Static Efficiency

H. Simon[22] demonstrated that, under the hypothesis that action isn't entirely determinable ex-ante, or better there is uncertainty about the state of the world on the basis of which to define the most efficient response, the dependent labour contract is more efficient than the trade contract. Simon's idea is that,

[16] *Penrose* (1952, 1956).
[17] *Dosi* (1982), *Dosi et al.* (1988), *Teece* (1988, 1996), *Kogut/Zander* (1992, 1996).
[18] *March/Simon* (1958), *Cyert/March* (1963), *Nelson/Winter* (1973, 1982, 2002), *Conner/Prahland* (1996), *Garicano* (2000)
[19] *Gibbons* (2005).
[20] *Williamson* (2000).
[21] *Menard* (2005), *Garrouste/Saussier* (2005).
[22] *Simon* (1951).

even under the hypothesis of full rationality, if uncertainty prevents the possibility of completing the sale contract of the working performance, it is advantageous for both contractors to agree on the basis of a contract which involves acceptance of authority, determined through the comparison of the respective functions of satisfaction. Though the bounded rationality hypothesis is not explicitly present, it manifests itself in the idea that bargaining works within the area defined by satisfaction curves, rather than by curves of utility (indifference). Furthermore, the inclusion of limits to rationality – which will be presented in other terms as the work proceeds – would make Simon's conclusions stronger regarding the greater efficiency of this kind of bargaining with respect to the classical type, assumed by the general equilibrium theory.[23]

By using this model as a determinant of bargaining between employers and workers, we are able to obtain the dual result of defining the nature of the firm in transactional terms, which imposes a realistic base to our work, and letting organizational structure emerge as a management device of the contingencies which could not be inserted in the original contract.[24]

Following Simon's formulation, we are able to define the satisfaction function relative to firm S_I and workers S_L in the that way:

$$S_I = F(x) - a_I w$$
$$S_L = F(x) - a_L w$$

The functions of satisfaction are determined by the function of density of probabilities that workers are assigned to complete a particular task x, that is

---

[23]   The main idea, implicit in the Simon's formulation, seems to be that, to outline a sale contract, the object of trade must be univocally determinable by both contractors. In this case, being the employer uncertain about the effective tasks to require of employees, it should not be the univocal determination of goods contracted. The traditional theory skates around the problem, claiming that working time is the object of the transaction, a solution which is unsatisfactory seeing as we want to analyse the internal structure of the firm. In *Gibbons* (2005), as in *Holmstrom/Tirole* (1989) too, the logical justification of this assumption can be found. The internal structure of the firm, in fact, is not analysed because it is supposed to work according to market mechanisms. In this context, then, the derivation of a labour contract as a exchange between working time and wage is perfectly consistent with the hypothesis of incentive theory.

[24]   Before introducing the model, however, it is useful to clarify a simplification implicit within the formulation we are proposing, which will have the merit of facilitating comprehension and the formulation of subtended logic, at the same time avoiding the disadvantage of altering the proposed analysis. In the space of possibility defined by the functions of satisfaction, the relevant point selected by the entrepreneur is determined by x (task) and w (wage). In proceeding, we will suppose that the object of choice of the firm will be simply x, assuming that the definition of wage can be determined ex-post (or that it holds a range for each x selected). This should not alter the analysis and the conclusions which we want to highlight, because we can reasonably suppose that, within the area of acceptance, the determination of wage is formally indifferent to workers, seeing as they have a positive satisfaction from the definition of the point (x^*, w^*) and $A(x,w)$.

$F(x)$, and by the wage w, that, weighted by a constant, influences in an opposite way the respective functions of satisfaction (figure 3.1).

Figure 3.1: The Simon's Model

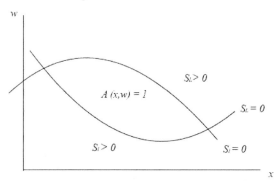

The area $A(x,w)$, determining the space where the functions of satisfaction of both contractors are positive, is posed as a whole unit and represents the area of acceptance of authority. This area represents the zone of discretion within the workers are willing to accept the discretional decision of the employers about the tasks to be completed. Such an area is posed as a unit because it reflects the greatest flexibility possible in bargaining, that is when the contract is entirely determined by ex-post contingencies. On the other hand, it represents the benchmark for subsequent analysis. The condition of vitality of the system presupposes that at least one of the relevant x falls into that area of acceptance,[25] otherwise it would be meaningless for parties to seek contractual agreement on the fixed elements of the contract.[26]

Seeing as generally this condition will hold, there is an incentive for both contractors to start the relationship. We are, then, able to suppose that the contractors would try to achieve an accord about the determination of those ele-

---

[25]   The obvious logic behind such a condition is that, if the contractors are reasonably convinced that none of the possible actions contained in the area of acceptance are significantly likely to be utilised, it would make no sense to bargain before functions of satisfaction are modified, in order to include the relevant actions within the space of possibilities. Obviously it is beyond the aim of this work to define and analyse what the implicit dynamics of such a process should be, so from now on we will suppose that the condition of vitality is generally satisfied.

[26]   This logical step can be interpreted in two ways. The first is considering the consistency of the function of satisfaction as a necessary condition to make the bargaining work. The second, probably more realistic, would be that the area of acceptance is an institutional framework determined by law, while the bargaining of fixed elements can be interpreted as a second stage of bargaining on a narrower basis. Whichever of these suggestions is accepted, the results of the proposed analysis do not change.

ments that can be defined ex-ante, thus narrowing the area of acceptance. So, the determination of fixed elements will define implicitly the remaining space of discretion once the bargaining is completed.

We can define a and b as the quote of the elements respectively fixed and discretional applied to the space of the x coherent with $A(x,w)$. Under the condition that $a + b = 1$, the determination of the fixed elements narrows the space of possibilities. Graphically it is possible to stress the narrowing of the space of discretion, once supposed that the space of the x coherent with $A(x,w)$ is constrained symmetrically, or admitting a symmetrical bargaining power (figure 3.2).

Figure 3.2: First Stage of Shrinkage

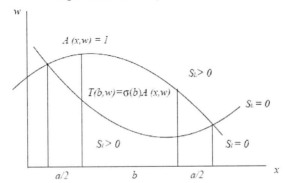

Formally we will have that:

$T(b,w) = \sigma A(x,w)$, where $0 \le \sigma = f(b) \le 1$, with obviously $0 \le b \le 1$.

We define $T(b,w)$ as the area of internal governance, while $\sigma(b)$ represents the quota of the discretional operative procedures managed by the governance, that is the space of the x determinable ex-post. The trend of the variation of b reflects the fact that when the discretional elements of bargaining are increased, so too the need increases for enlarging the zone of influence of the governance-managed operative processes. When $\sigma(b) = 0$ (or $b = 0$) we will have that all contingencies are included into the contract ex-ante, and so the space of the x will be restricted to a point, as in classical bargaining, with the consequence that the area of governance is reduced to zero, in coherence with the complete definition in terms of contract of the internal structure claimed by the contractual approach to the theory of the firm. If $\sigma(b) = 1$ (or $b = 1$) a symmetrical situation to the previous case will be determined. In this case the contract is entirely determined by ex-post contingencies, which implies that the structure of internal governance would coincide with the whole area of acceptance, that is, all operative procedures of the firm are managed by internal governance.

Defined as the area of operative possibility, $T(b,w)$ determines a constraint to the choice of the achievable x. We can then derive the existence of an x coherent with $T(b,w)$ as a condition of existence of the firm. If the x to be achieved were to fall outside the bounds of internal governance, in fact, the firm would not be able to achieve without modifying its contractual structure.

Within the area of governance, the firm will have to tend to the organization and management of the operative procedures. Being, in fact, an area of discretion for both contactors, employers will have to: organise operative procedures by trying to achieve maximum efficiency; limit as much as possible the elements of discretion of workers (control of effort and minimization of the possibility of dishonest behaviour). To achieve this goal we can suppose that the firm will try to gather operative processes within structures of routine that:

    a. limit the behavioural discretion of workers;

    b. allow greater control of operative procedures;

    c. provide a learning area for workers.

Generally, then, the structure of routine will define the area of coordination (E. Penrose), or of behavioural continuity (R. Nelson and S. Winter),[27] which is needed to allow operative processes to be conducted in a coordinated way, and the elements that compose the structure to interact within common schemas of action and communication. From an evolutionary perspective, such an operational environment determines faster learning for agents, and, further, as supposed, greater control for the employers over productive operations.

To arrive at such a definition of the structure of routine, the firm will have to define performance programs[28] (or substantive planning)[29] that involve a number of processes in response to the certain communications coming from the strategic direction. Linking the flow of information to schemas of response implies two consequences that characterise the structure of routines. On one hand, in fact, this produces a further reduction of discretion and thus a further narrowing of the possible x. On the other hand, because information can be channelled within the structure and can produce planned reactions, a code of communication must be defined and structured. This code can be viewed, implicitly, as a means of processing information.[30]

We can thus define c as the decisional variable that determines the restriction of the space of x with respect to the area $T(b,w)$ supposing, for sake of simplicity, that it is distributed symmetrically in the space previously determined by the variable b, as in figure 3.3. We can note that, while b is a variable which is not influenced only by strategic evaluations of the firm, being a bargaining rela-

---

27   *Nelson/Winter* (1973, 1982, 2002).

28   *March/Simon* (1958).

29   *Simon* (1947).

30   The consequences of this remark will be clarified as the work proceeds, when analysis will be made of the condition of dynamic efficiency of the firm.

tionship between workers and employers, the variable c can be considered a real strategic parameter.

Figure 3.3: Second Stage of Shrinkage

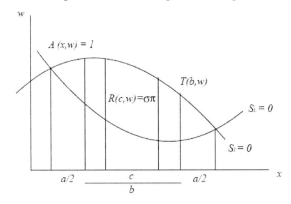

In a manner symmetrical to the first stage of narrowing of the operative possibilities, formally we will have that:

$R(c,w) = \pi T(b,w)$, where $0 \le \pi = f(c) \le 1$, with obviously $0 \le c \le 1$.

Through a process of simple substitution, we can determine:

$R(c,w) = \pi \sigma A(c,w)$ or $R(c,w) = \pi \sigma$.

The area $R(c,w)$ is the space of the possibilities of the x determined within the operative processes that, even if routinised, allow a complete flexibility, that is, they are equally achievable in coherence with the structure of the performance programs. The parameter $\pi(c)$ represents that which we define as the coefficient of flexibility of the routine. For $\pi(c) = 1$ we will have in fact that $R(c,w) = T(b,w)$. This implies that the structure allows maximum flexibility coherent with the condition of existence of the structure represented by the area $T(b,w)$. Symmetrically, for $\pi(c) = 0$ we will have that the area of routine is reduced to zero, or rather that the operative process is entirely standardised, involving that only one x is achievable. In this case the organizational structure have the greatest rigidity possible.

We have said that the variable c, which implicitly determines $\pi(c)$, can be considered a strategic choice entirely defined by the will of management. It remains, then, to define the determinants of this choice. Obviously, efficiency of operative processes is the main measuring stick for firms' decisions. It is worth noting that, by using the transactional schema proposed by general equilibrium theorists as a theoretical benchmark, full efficiency is achievable only when the efficient action x is entirely determined ex-ante, with the possibility of including only fixed elements within the original contract, thus leaving all contingent elements out of the contract. This conclusion is consistent with the idea that entirely standardised operative processes lead to more efficient carrying out of actions. The inefficiency deriving from the incompleteness of the contract is revealed through both the impossibility of initially determining the efficient x, and the narrowing of the space of the achievable x. Another source of inefficiency regarding contract theory is concealed by the problem of managing contingent elements that enter into the contract as discretional ones. To manage control of those elements, the firm must define a structure within which these discretional factors are limited, and the agents' behaviour is consistent with operative requirements. This implies a further restriction of possible x, but on the other hand it may tend to increase the relative efficiency of each achievable x.

If in fact the processes were entirely rigid, it would have just one achievable x, but this action should have the maximum possible efficiency. To demonstrate that a condition of efficiency, which we will call static, is definable with the minimization of the area of flexibility of the routine, we will use the concept of learning. With the adjective static, we will attempt to characterize a situation in which the firm does not need to acquire more new information than it already has, that is the agents are free to use the learning channel defined by the acquisition of greater skill at doing a given, fixed task (learning by exploitation). The idea is that by reducing as much as possible the number of discretional actions, that is, by making the routine as rigid as possible, agents' learning speed increases and with it their skills too. It is obvious that, if operative processes did not change, the action would be conducted with maximum possible efficiency, determined by the best possible learning and by management's greater capability of controlling the process. These determinants were both part of the definition of the condition of static efficiency. In this work, however, we decided to stress the learning variable, though obviously the demonstration could easily be conducted by taking into consideration the control variable, without any alteration of the results.

We define the speed of learning as a function of the area of routine in the following way:

$VA = f[R(c,w)]$, which maintains the trend illustrated in figure 3.4.

Figure 3.4: Learning Speed and Routine

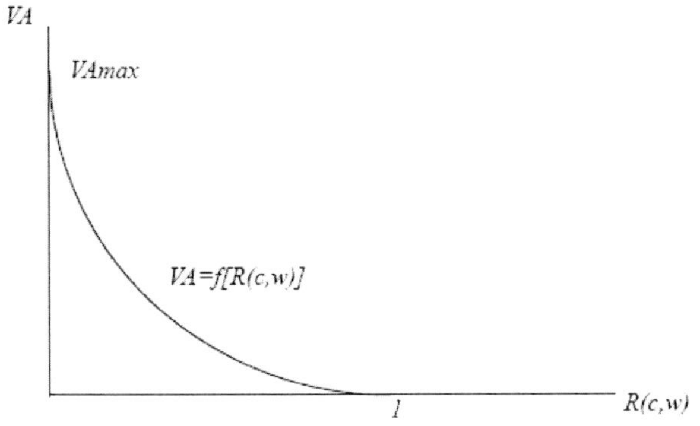

VA

VAmax

$VA=f[R(c,w)]$

1 $R(c,w)$

We then define static efficiency as a function of learning speed as:

$ES = g(VA)$, which maintains the trend illustrated in figure 3.5.

Figure 3.5: Static Efficiency and Learning Speed

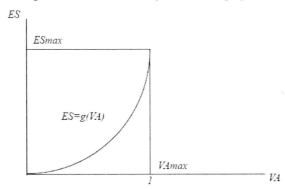

ES

ESmax

$ES=g(VA)$

VAmax

1   VA

Indicating the static efficiency in term of the area of routine we will have that:

$ES = g\{f[R(c,w)]\}.$

The trend of this function, illustrated in figure 3.6, shows evidence of the conclusion made above, or rather that the firm will increase its static efficiency to
the extent that it can make operative routine rigid, by recovering part of the efficiency lost due to the impossibility of completing the contract ex-ante. In this
case, in fact, the firm could maximize operative efficiency, even if it can't re-
cover what it lost by narrowing of space of possible x.

Figue 3.6: Static Efficiency and Routine

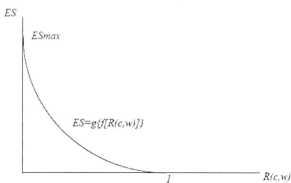

4 From Static to Dynamic

We have shown that, starting from the hypothesis of the impossibility to complete the contract ex-ante, it is possible to demonstrate the need for managing contingent elements determinable only ex-post. We have seen that the way to manage such elements is by defining a routinised operative structure that co-ordinates the firm's activities and allows it to achieve one of the x consistent with the limitation imposed by incompleteness of the contract. The routine processes, besides involving a further restriction of possible actions, also determines the possibility, by calibrating their degree of flexibility/rigidity, of recovering full efficiency with respect to the benchmark represented by classical bargaining and by the workings of the dynamics of the firm according to that schema. The incompleteness of contracts, however, reduces the possibility for action, imposing a constraint that apparently would operate only when events outside the firm made it necessary to achieve an x that was inconsistent with the space of possibilities. The limitation of actions is implicitly a limitation of possible operative plans, and thus a loss of efficiency in a dynamic sense, that is it manifests a constraint to the firm's possibility for adapting its operative behaviour to variations occurred in the external environment.

From this perspective, then, we can see the inconsistency in the legacy of traditional theory when it sought to analyse the dynamics of firms, in the sense of adaptation to the external environment. The ex-ante determination of contractual contingencies would thus have determined the greatest possible rigidity of operative processes, leading the firm to have maximum efficiency, while, on the other hand, changes in the external environment would have been anticipated, involving merely a variation in the sense of full efficiency of the perfectly determined operative program (maximum rigidity of routine). Such a schema, as we have already argued, remains true only under the hypothesis that agents are able both to foresee exactly variations in the environment and to sterilize the uncertainty caused by the flow of time. Once the analysis is made in the context of bounded rationality and complexity of variations in the external environment, that is when the market ceases to be an efficient venue for coordinating transactions, the model deriving from general equilibrium theory falters.

To give an image of the logic we are following, we can affirm that the traditional theory of the firm is lacking in the understanding of dynamic phenomena, because dynamics derive essentially from instability, and instability determines losses of efficiency which those models cannot include in their formulations. Innovation, like mutations in organizational structures, testifies to the vitality of the firm system and, by extension, of the whole economic system, much as organizational structures exist as a means of sterilizing the intrinsic instability of complex dynamic systems. The fact that the flexibility of the structure is a decisional variable shows this role quite clearly, though there still remains an apparent inconsistency regarding the conclusions we derived from the firm's condition of static efficiency.

The fact that the disappearance of the structure should determine maximum static efficiency does not lead us to rash conclusions about the absolute inefficiency of this element. The apparent contradiction comes from the fact that as yet we have taken into consideration only the static of the system, in other words, we have been analysing a system without variations in the external environment, that is, with a fixed level of information channelled within the structure.

From an evolutionary perspective, in fact, the dynamics of complex systems works toward adapting to the external environment. Such an adaptation is generated by the acquisition of new information, which makes it possible to interpret mutations in the environment and to derive (adaptive) behavioural responses. Models of full rationality suppose implicitly that such an adaptive process is instantaneous and that, in some way, agents are even able to anticipate and sterilize those variations with the aid of market mechanisms. It is evident that such models contain a logical contradiction. Such a system, in which dynamics are a-temporal and adaptation instantaneous, and which evolves along an equilibrium path determined ex-ante, is not vital from the perspective of the theory of complexity.

To include truly evolutionary dynamics within the system, we have to accept intrinsic instability and to assume that the elements that make up this system interact through structures that act as a compensation chamber for the instability produced by the system. Dissipation is obviously a loss of efficiency, but, on the other hand, its causes depend on an ontological element of reality, which renders blameless the agents operating in the system. They are, indeed, in keeping with the opinions of H. Simon about human rationality,[31] more rational, in the sense of their desire for survival, than the traditional, supposedly fully rational agent, who lives with the illusion of being able to dominate the complexity of reality, or reduce it to an approximation of general equilibrium models.

---

[31]   *Simon* (1956, 1978, 1984, 1986).

The presence of organizational structure, then, is justified by the need to manage the element of instability of the system during the flow of time, and to acquire and process the information necessary to provide a guide for evolutionary behaviour. The fact that its presence leads to a loss of efficiency is a consequence of the instability of the system and is, in fact, more than offset by the reality that it is the structure which allows the firm to develop and exist within a context of instability. The logic of static efficiency is not satisfactory to describe the necessity in terms of efficiency of a system which evolves in the time. We need, then, to determine the conditions of dynamic efficiency the system must obey to continue to adapt to a changing environment.

5 The Determination of the Condition of Dynamic Efficiency

We saw that the area $R(c,w)$ implicitly defines the flexibility of the firm's operative routines. We have shown that the narrower this area is, the faster the exploitation learning process, and thus the higher the static efficiency of operative processes will be. We will now derive a schema that allows us to define the determinants of dynamic efficiency. A firm's evolutionary process of adaptation can be defined in terms of acquisition and processing of new information. On one hand, this allows us to define a firm's dynamics in terms of variation of information, while, on the other, this logical step implies the possibility of conceptually superimposing innovation and evolution.[32] To derive such a schema we need to define the operative structure in terms of a size with features and behaviour allowing us to study its dynamics in terms of information contents.

When the firm has decided to hire a given number of workers, it has in fact defined the amount of maximum cognitive distance containable within the structure. The definition of cognitive distance is given by B. Nooteboom[33] as the capability of interacting elements to acquire information and communicate it to each other. When the number of elements that compose the net of interactions is increased, cognitive distance increases too. This signifies that it will be possible

---

[32]   Static efficiency was defined through the analysis of learning speed for a given set of information, or for a series of processes established on the basis of information possessed. Defining dynamics in terms of variations in a set of information derives from the consideration that the acquisition of relevant information should lead to a variation in some of the routinised processes, or should be influenced by the previous operative structure. By defining innovation in the Shumpeterian (*Schumpeter* 1935, 1947) terms of the creative process, we can prove that the condition necessary for innovation is that extra information be available compared to the past. To have innovation, then, it is necessary to acquire and process new information, which is the definition we used to characterize the dynamics of our model. Lastly, the mutation of the external environment implies an exogenous variation of the set of probability of the dynamic behaviour of the system. In this context, starting from the consideration that evolution signifies adaptation to the external environment, we will have that such a process can be defined in terms of the search for new information elements that were not available before. Generally, then, we will have an approximated overlap among dynamics, evolution and innovation, which can be seen to be consistent with the logical hypothesis used in the definition of the complex system.

[33] *Nooteboom* (1992, 2000, 2002).

to analyse more information, though, on the other hand, the process of communication will be more complex. This trade-off relationship between area of acquisition of information and the capability to communicate it reflects both the hypothesis of bounded rationality and the classical condition of the theory of information, implying that the code of communication must have a string of signals bigger than that of the information to be managed.

The capability to process information, that is the possibility of producing knowledge from available information, is influenced by the constraint imposed by bounded rationality, and by that imposed by distortions of communication (noise), which increase when the amount of information possessed increases.
Formally we can define the maximum cognitive distance that can be contained within the organizational structure as a function of the number of workers who make up the structure of operative interactions. On the other hand, the process of routine described limits the contents of cognitive distance of the structure by rigidly managing a quota of interactions. We will thus be able to define the contents of cognitive distance within the operative structure as a function of the degree of the structure's rigidity, as determined by $\pi\sigma$.
We define:

$Dc = f(\pi\sigma)$ – implicitly $R(c,w)$ – with the trend determined by $f'(\pi\sigma) = d$ and $f''(\pi\sigma) = 0$, or that shown in figure 5.1.

Figure 5.1: Contained Cognitive Distance and Routine

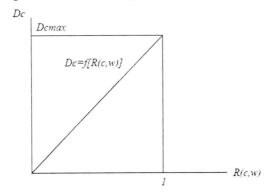

The choice of the degree of rigidity of the routine structure determines the use of potentially available cognitive distance. As an effect of the constraint imposed by the code of communication and by bounded rationality, we will have that the efficiency of the use of cognitive distance will have decreasing returns as the degree of use of available cognitive distance increases. We will thus be able to define:

$EDc = g(Dc)$ with the trend determined by $f'(Dc) \geq 0$ and $f''(Dc) \leq 0$ or that shown in figure 5.2.

Figure 5.2: Efficiency of Contained Cognitive Distance

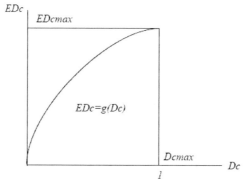

We are now able to explain the efficiency of contained cognitive distance in terms of the degree of flexibility imposed on the operative structure in the following way:

$EDc = g[f(\pi\sigma)]$, or as $g\{f[R(c,w)]\}$, whose trend is determined by $g'(.) \geq 0$ and $g''(.) \leq 0$, and it is shown in figure 5.3.

Figure 5.3: Efficiency of Container Cognitive Distance and Routine

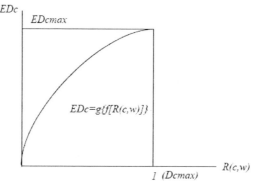

Once the degree of flexibility has been determined, the amount of cognitive distance utilised and the efficiency it allows are also implicitly defined.

Having defined cognitive distance in terms of capacity to process given information contents, the next stage will be to analyse the required cognitive distance for each level of information and the efficiency of cognitive distance required to process that given set of information. We thus define information in the classical terms of the formulation of C. Shannon and W. Weaver.[34] The entropic representation of information can be interpreted as the determination of resolved uncertainty by a certain distribution of the probabilities of events. An increase in information will tend to lead entropy to zero, or to produce certainty. The information, then, can be interpreted as a process of closeness to certainty, or step by step as an improved approximation of reality. We can thus define the information contents of a set of information in the following way:

$I = 1 - h(p)$, where $I = 1$ for $h(p) = 0$ represents the state of certainty.

If cognitive distance represents the means of processing information, when owned information increases, the necessity for cognitive distance required to manage the given informative set will also increase. We can define necessary cognitive distance in the following functional way:

$Dn = f(I)$ with the trend determined by $f'(I) = m$ and $f''(I) = 0$, or as depicted in figure 5.4.

Figure 5.4: Necessary Cognitive Distance

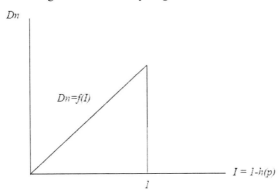

Processing the set of information is influenced by the fact that processing efficiency is limited by both bounded rationality and code of communication. The efficiency of the cognitive distance needed to process a volume of information that leads toward certainty has an asymptotic trend, which prevents the system from achieving the maximum degree of certainty, in a manner consistent with the hypothesis of this work.

We define the efficiency of required cognitive distance in terms of the amount of managed information in the following way:

---

[34]   *Shannon/Weaver* (1949).

$EDn = g(I)$ with the trend determined by $g'(I) \geq 0$ and $g''(I) \geq 0$ and asymptote as shown in figure 5.5.

Figure 5.5: Efficiency of Necessary Cognitive Distance

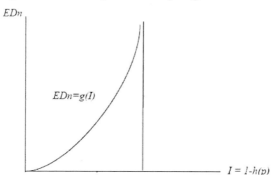

In this way we have determined the efficiency of available cognitive distance given the degree of flexibility/rigidity of the structure and that necessary to process a certain amount of information. In other words, we are now able to compare the capacity to process information that the firm can profound, and the need for this capacity which the analysis of a given amount of information implies. By analysing figure 5.6, we are able to draw some conclusions about the determination of the condition of a firm's dynamic efficiency.

Figure 5.6: Trade-Off Between Static and Dynamic Condition

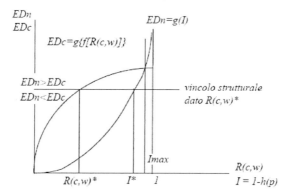

By expressing dynamics in terms of evolution, that is as acquisition of new information in response to variations in the external environment, we can agree that an essential condition for the firm to evolve is that it is able to process the information necessary to carry the dynamic process required. For the adopted definition of the capability to process information, or better, explained in terms of contained and required efficiency of cognitive distance, the condition that makes the evolutionary process possible is:

Given $R(c,w)*$ and the necessary information to be processed needed to achieve the evolutionary goals, $I*$ we must have that $EDc[R(c,w)*] \geq EDn(I*)$.

If this condition did not hold, the structure of the firm would not be able to process enough information to make the evolutionary process work, thus risking the firm's existence from a selection perspective, or, in any case, impairing operative performance and thus diminishing the efficiency of the firm. The structure of the firm can thus represent a constraint to the evolutionary process. In other terms, as is obvious from figure 1, the greater the rigidity of the structure, the less information the firm can process, and the less knowledge it can produce, which implies a lesser capacity to adapt and evolve. On the other hand, at least c, that is, implicitly $\pi(c)$, being a strategic variable, it is evident that to increase dynamic efficiency the management should tend toward greater flexibility of the structure, which poses the achievement of dynamic efficiency in a trade-off relationship with the symmetrical attempt to achieve static efficiency.

Another interesting element is the fact that there is a threshold value of the amount of information for which the condition of dynamic efficiency cannot be attained. This confirms the hypothesis that a certain level of uncertainty cannot be eliminated, which is a determinant factor for assuming the incompleteness of contracts. What is apparently only a validation of an hypothesis hides a deeper significance, that is, the process of adaptation is always an incomplete phenomenon that cannot be delineated in a complete way, leaving the system with the necessary instability for a vital dynamic.

6   Concluding Remarks

The work presented has some interesting aspects which it is useful to underline. First, from the perspective of firm theory, we have derived a model of analysis of the firm's internal structure as a device for coordinating decisions and processing information that is consistent with the Adaptation approach. This approach is broad and heterogeneous because of the different importance accorded to some features of analysis and hypothesis. Nevertheless, it seems possible to find a taxonomy that traces such schools of thought back to some common characterisations. Setting the processing of information as the main role of the organizational structure allows us to find a common denominator through which to render the theoretical framework consistent with the different nuances proposed by administrative, knowledge-based and evolutionary theories within the theory of the firm.

Each of these path of research presents many common ideas that presuppose a non-traditional analysis of the internal structure, the choice being implicit to assign it a more important role than the traditional theory does. Since the meeting point of such theories is the commonality of bounded rationality hypothesis and the need for internal coordination, choosing the process of acquisition of knowledge through processing of information as a feature element of the structure allows us to present a means of analysis that is perfectly consistent with the needs of research stressed by those theories.

As these are, in fact, theories of ex-post completion of contracts, as pointed out by Williamson, it is obvious that the models derived from this theoretical proposal must contain a dynamics that makes it possible to stress and analyse the process of managing contingencies and their coordination. The processing of information, being by definition a process that works in time, confers to the theoretical structure presented the feature of a dynamic analysis, responding both to the need to describe the process of internal learning (coordination) and that of adapting to mutations in the external environment (evolution by exploration learning).

Besides representing an element of strong differentiation from traditional models, this characteristic has evident consequences on the taxonomy of problems that can be analyzed through this approach. The simultaneous presence of learning and adaptation processes allows, on one hand, a definition of the sterilization of bounded rationality and management of complexity of interaction processes that determine the internal structure, and, on the other, a tool for describing and analysing the evolutionary path of firms, that is, their innovation capabilities and growth trends.

Furthermore, though this theoretical approach is evidently general in scope, it will be particularly suitable for analysing some categories of problems associated with peculiar forms of entrepreneurial organization. The strong link between knowledge and information in fact allows a better interpretation of the dynamics of the firm, which are strongly characterised by more flexible, rather than particularly mechanised, structures of interaction. From this perspective, there is an evident difference between firms in the industrial and service sectors.

On the other hand, such a model would also allow an interpretation of the capability of innovation of enterprises of different sizes, even in the same sector. This means we can analyse the structure in terms of flexibility/rigidity, both as independent and dependent variables, and in other terms both as a structural feature that differentiates firms, and as strategic variables that influence its path of development, in both innovation and growth.

From a strictly theoretical perspective, the work presented makes it possible to draws some important conclusions about the debate on the theory of the firm. Moving from a static to a dynamic analysis, formal emphasis can be made of the efficiency of the organizational structure, without which the dynamic evolution of the firm would not exist, or would not in any case be endogenous. On the other hand, in deriving conditions of efficiency we have stressed a trade-off relationship between static and dynamical conditions, which is completely consistent with the hypothesis and the conclusions of the theory of complexity, while from the point of view of the literal debate on firm theory, it explains in a quasi-exhaustive way the divergent opinions in the history of the literature on firm theory.

Since, in fact, traditional analysis has shown itself to be essentially static, in the sense of a-temporality explained above, it is evident that it lacks an entire portion of the picture of analysis, or better, that in which the structure shows its characteristics of efficiency. The negative conclusions about internal structure, derived from traditional models, are the result of this short-sightedness, though perfectly coherent in their approach, since we can also see from the model derived in this work that static analysis totally confirms the inefficiency of internal structure.

A last consideration should be dedicated to a direct consequence of the trade-off relationship shown. Since at least one of the parameters of flexibility is a strategic variable, there is an evident need to derive the choice processes adopted by entrepreneur/managers in deciding the degree of flexibility of the structures they manage.

The paths of research which would seem fulfil this need are essentially three: the analysis of decisional processes described in the literature of bounded rationality, trying to insert them within a model of acquisition and processing of information and creation of knowledge; the analysis of the relationship between the structure of property rights and the structural features of the firm, the former being an element which would have a dual impact on the structure, at the same time influencing strategic decisions and initial structural features, that, from a logic of evident path dependency of evolution, represents an important, interesting, field of analysis; the human-resource and social networks literature, which in recent years have been widely developed, can represent an important means of analysis of the interactive capabilities which the structure allows, characterising both agents and the structure of organizational connections.

Acknowledgement

The author wants to thank Guido Rey for the useful supervision on his work. I have Bart Nooteboom, Cristiano Antonelli and Brian J. Loasby to thank for the comments on the early versions of my work. I would like to thank also William Addessi. The author is the only responsible for mistakes and ideas contained.

References

AA. VV. (1996): Teoria dell'informazione. Cuen, Napoli.

Alchian, A.O. / Demsetz, H. (1972): Production, Information Cost, and Economic Organizations. American Economic Review, Volume 62, pp. 777-795.

Aghion, P. / Tirole, J. (1997): Formal and Real Authority in Organizations. Journal of Political Economy, Volume 105, pp. 1-27.

Arrow, K.J. (1964): Control in Large Organizations. Management Science, Volume 10, pp. 397-408.

Barney, J.B. (1991): Firm Resources and Sustained Competitive Advantage. Journal of Management, Volume 17, pp. 99-120.

Barney, J.B. (1996): The Resource-Based Theory of the Firm. Organization Science, Volume 7, pp. 469-469.

Bateson, G. (1972): Steps to an Ecology of Mind. Ballantines Books, New York

Coase, R.H. (1937): The Nature of the Firm. Economica, Volume 4, pp. 386-405.

Coase, R.H. (1984): The New Institutional Economics. Journal of Institutional and Theoretical Economics, Volume 140, pp. 229-231.

Cohen, M.D. / Levinthal, D.A. (1990): Absorptive Capacity: A New Perspective on Learning and Innovation. Administrative Science Quarterly, Volume 35, pp. 128-152.

Conner, K. / Prahalad, C.K. (1996): A Resource-Based Theory of the Firm: Knowledge versus Opportunism. Organization Science, Volume 7, pp. 477-501.

Cyert, R.M. / March, J.G. (1963): A Behavioural Theory of the Firm. Prentice Hall, Englewood Cliffs.

Dosi, G. et al. (1988): Technical Change and Economic Theory. Pinter, London.

Garicano, L. (2000): Hierarchies and the Organization of Knowledge in Production. The Journal of Political Economy, Volume 108, pp. 874-904.

Garrouste, P. / Saussier, S. (2005) Looking for a Theory of the Firm: Future Challenges. Journal of Economic Behaviour and Organization, Volume 58, pp. 178-199.

Gibbons, R. (2005): Four Formal(izable) Theories of the Firm? Journal of Economic Behavior and Organization, Volume 58, pp. 200-245.

Grossman, S. / Hart, O. (1986): The Costs and Benefits of Ownership: A Theory of Vertical and Lateral Integration. Journal of Political Economy, Volume 94, pp. 691-719.

Guiso, L. / Terlizzese, D. (1994): Economia dell'incertezza e dell'informazione. Hoepli, Milano.

Hart, O. (1995): Firms, Contracts, and Financial Structure. Clarendon Press, Oxford.

Hart, O. / Moore, J. (1990): Property Rights and the Nature of the Firm. Journal of Political Economy, Volume , pp. 1119-1158.

Hayek, F. (1945): The Use of Knowledge in Society. American Economic Review, Volume 35, pp. 519-530.

Hayek, F. (1948): Individualism and Economic Order. University of Chicago Press, Chicago.

Holmstrom, B. (1999): The Firm as a Subeconomy. Journal of Law, Economics and Organization, Volume 15, pp. 74-102.

Holmstrom, B. / Tirole, J. (1989): The Theory of the Firm. In: Handbook of Industrial Organization. North-Holland, Amsterdam, pp. 61-131.

Holmstrom, B. / Tirole, J. (1991): Transfer Pricing and Organizational Form. Journal of Law, Economics, and Organization, Volume 7, pp. 201-228.

Holmstrom, B. / Milgrom, P. (1994): The Firm as an Incentive System. American Economic Review, Volume 84, pp. 972-991.

Keynes, J.M. (1936): The General Theory of Employment, Interest and Money. Macmillan, London.

Kirzner, I. (1973): Competition and Entrepreneurship. University of Chicago Press, Chicago.

Knight, F.H. (1921): Risk, Uncertainty and Profit. Houghton Mifflin, New York.

Kogut, B. / Zander, U. (1992): Knowledge of the Firm, Combinative Capabilities and the Replication of Technology. Organization Science, Volume 3, pp. 383-397.

Kogut, B. / Zander, U. (1996): What Firms Do? Coordination, Identity and Learning. Organization Science, Volume 7, pp. 502-518.

Leijnohufvud, A. (2000): Macroeconomic Instability and Coordination, Edward Elgar, Chentelham.

March, J. / Simon, H.A. (1958): Organizations. Wiley, New York.

Masten, S. (1988): A Legal Basis for the Firm. Journal of Law, Economics, and Organization, Volume 4, pp. 181-198.

Menard, C. (1994): Organizations as Coordinating Devices. Metroeconomica, Volume 45, pp. 224-247.

Menard, C. (2005): A New Institutional Approach. In: Handbook of New Institutional Economics. Springer, Netherlands, pp. 281-318.

Mises, L. (1949): Human Action. William Hodge and Company, London.

Nelson, R.R. / Winter, S.G. (1973): Toward an Evolutionary Theory of Economic Capabilities. American Economic Review, Volume 63, pp. 440-449.

Nelson, R.R. / Winter, S.G. (1982): An Evolutionary Theory of Economic Change. Harvard University Press, Cambridge.

Nelson, R.R. / Winter, S.G. (2002): Evolutionary Theorizing in Economic. The Journal of Economic Perspective, Volume 16, pp. 23-46.

Nooteboom, B. (1992): Towards a Dynamic Theory of Transaction. Journal of Evolutionary Economics, Volume 2, pp. 281-299.

Nooteboom, B. (2000): Learning and Innovation in Organization and Economies. Oxford University Press, New York.

Nooteboom, B. (2002): A Cognitive Theory of the Firm. Paper for a workshop on theory of the firm, Paris, November 2002.

Penrose, E. (1952): Biological Analogies in the Theory of the Firm. American Economic Review, Volume 42, pp. 804-819.

Penrose, E. (1956): La teoria dell'espansione d'impresa. Franco Angeli, Milano

Radner, R. (1992): Hierarchy: The Economics of Managing. Journal of Economic Literature, Volume 30, pp. 1382-1415.

Schumpeter, J.A. (1935): The Analysis of Economic Change. The Review of Economic Statistics, Volume 17, pp. 2-10.

Schumpeter, J.A. (1947): The Creative Response in Economic History. Journal of Economic History, Volume 7, pp. 149-159.

Shannon, C. / Weaver, W. (1949): The Mathematical Theory of Communication. University of Illinois Press, Chicago.

Simon, H.A. (1947): Administrative Behaviour. Free Press, New York.

Simon, H.A. (1951): A Formal Theory of the Employment Relationship. Econometrica, Volume 19, pp. 293-305.

Simon, H.A. (1955): A Behavioural Model of Rational Choice. Quarterly Journal of Economics, Volume 59, pp. 99-118.

Simon, H.A. (1956): Rational Choice and the Structure of Environment. Psychological Review, Volume 63, pp. 129-138.

Simon, H.A. (1978a): Rationality as Process and Product of Thought. American Economic Review, Volume 68, pp. 1-16.

Simon, H.A. (1984): On the Behavioural and Rational Foundation of Economic Dynamics. Journal of Economic Behavior and Organization, Volume 5, pp. 35-55.

Simon, H.A. (1986): Rationality in Psychology and Economics. The Journal of Business, Volume 59, pp. 209-224.

Teece, D.J. (1988): The Nature of the Firm and Technological Change. In: Technical Change and Economic Theory. Pinter, London.

Teece, D.J. (1996): Firm Organization, Industrial Structure and Technological Innovation. Journal of Economic Behavior and Organization, Volume 31, pp. 193-224.

Tirole, J. (1988): The Multi-Contract Organization. The Canadian Journal of Economics, Volume 21, pp. 459-466.

Tirole, J. / Maskin, E. (1999): Unforeseen Contingencies and Incomplete Contracts. The Review of Economic Studies, Volume 66, pp. 83-114.

Williamson, O. (1970): Corporate Control and Business Behaviour. Prentice Hall, Englewood Cliffs.

Williamson, O. (1975): Markets and Hierarchies: Analysis and Antitrust Implications. The Free Press, New York.

Williamson, O. (1985): The Economic Institution of Capitalism. Free Press, New York.

Williamson, O. (1988): Corporate Finance and Corporate Governance. Journal of Finance, Volume 43, pp. 567-591.

Williamson, O. (1996): The Mechanisms of Governance. Oxford University Press, New York.

Williamson, O. (2000): The New Institutional Economics: Taking Stock, Looking Ahead. Journal of Economic Literature, Volume 38, pp. 595-613.

Zurek, W.H. (1990): Complexity, Entropy and the Physics of Information. Santa Fè Institute Studies Volume 8, Addison-Welsley, Reading .

Part III: Bounded Rationality in Price Theory, Environmental Economics and Public Management

A Horizonal Theory of Pricing in the New Information Economy

Frederic B. JENNINGS, Jr.

1 Introduction

The orthodox story of pricing assumes substitution of firms and products in organized markets separated by industry in a relentlessly static conception. There is no uncertainty clouding our vision of outcomes in this setting, and no irreversible changes so that the path of choices shall matter. Rising from this analysis is a case for *competition* as the organizational standard of efficient production and optimality in economic society. Yet there are a lot of legitimate questions to be asked about this scenario, with regard to assumptions and the images on which it rests.

For example, every real transaction is special, without any homogeneous units inviting aggregation. *Chamberlin* (1933, 1957) dealt with this problem by introducing an individualized firm in a population of imperfect substitutes. So would product diversity ever be joined to 'excess capacity' in an erroneous inefficiency argument tainting his seminal lead.[1] Problems of interfirm interdependence and network complexity – although opened – were never resolved through these models. The orthodox story – asserted by *Hicks* (1939) at the end of the 1930s debates – seized the minds of economists after World War II and prevails today. Yet new work on network communications systems suggests a novel look at this frame may be useful (e.g., *Elsner* 2004).

Another realm of questions about traditional models of thought derives from *Simon's* (1976, 1982-97) work on 'procedural' and 'bounded' rationality issues. Standard theories suppose away information and uncertainty problems in order to justify what has been called 'situational determinism,' meant to remove volition and cognition from models of choice.[2] Thus – according to this scheme

---

[1] The 'excess capacity' argument for inefficiency is a case of applying a standard of minimum cost – *ceteris paribus* for other changes – to a situation in which 'other changes,' such as an increase in product diversity with new entry, are *not welfare neutral*. Indeed, the defining characteristic of this market form – monopolistic competition – is *a preference for product diversity*, for which consumers are willing to pay some premium over minimum cost for a less standardized product! If so, then 'minimum average cost' is no longer an 'efficiency outcome' in social welfare terms. (The argument also unduly conflates short-run cost with long-run demand.)

[2] Cf. *Latsis* (1972); as *Nicholas Georgescu-Roegen* (1967, p. 104) put it:

From time indefinite, the natural sciences have cherished a positivist epistemology according to which scientific knowledge covers only those phenomena that go on irrespective of whether they are observed or not. Objectivity ... requires then that a proper scientific description should not include man in any capacity whatsoever. This is how some came to hold that even man's thinking is not a phenomenon. True, this ideal of a man-less science is gradually losing ground even in physics... However, for a science of man to exclude altogether man from the picture is a patent incongruity. Nevertheless, standard economics takes special pride in operating with a man-less picture. ...

– meaningful explanations emerge out of facts seen by rational agents seeking gain through optimization against some binding constraint. There is no need to incorporate theories of 'how we think' in this process (*Shackle* 1958; *Loasby* 1986): behavioral implications simply emerge out of visible options.

But the interdependence of everything in our world demands an ecological orientation to economics, where information networks and food webs share many features in common. Economists seem reluctant to embrace such interactivity, as it challenges some of our most cherished doctrines.[3] In information network contexts, scarcity undermines worth: 'the more, the merrier' is the rule. Substitution, homogeneity, additivity, independence, separability and convexity: all are opened to question once any one of them is relaxed. The restive fragility of orthodox suppositions is readily seen (*Stiglitz* 1985, p. 21).

2   A Static Concept of Pricing in Diverse Market Domains

One departure from mainstream models stems from an *inductive* version of firms' pricing decisions, setting aside the economists' standard deductive frame momentarily. What we observe from market transactions is that they entail a choice by each seller, asserting some P* as 'best.' Declaring P* in an open market determines Q* on that locus, so an observer can duly infer one single point on 'the market demand curve.' From what we know of maximum profit – assuming each seller is doing her best – we also find an M* point directly below (P*,Q*) on a graph, although we would *either* need the price-setter's marginal cost or demand elasticity to estimate where it is. In sum, we describe a stable P* = M* x E*, where unit cost M* ≡ MC = MR and the markup E* ≡ ε*/(ε* + 1) > 1 for demand elasticity ε* < -1. From a deductive vantage, this expression is just the familiar first-order condition of profit maximization within neoclassical theory, although derived differently here.[4]

This particular representation applies to all four market types – from 'perfect' through 'monopolistic' and 'oligopolistic' competitive firms to 'monopoly' – equally well. The problems secreted away behind this sort of explanation, however, rise from interdependencies seen in 'monopolistic competition' and 'oligopoly' markets, and throughout the new information economy. This is why a Chicago approach insists on just two endpoints: 'monopoly' and 'competition'

---

[3] Quoting *Lamberton* (2001, pp. 115, 117f), *Elsner* (2004, p. 1033) remarks that:
 "The limitations of information as a commodity... " call for a "thoroughgoing innovation in organizational design" to include "a very high level of collaboration." This renders economics a science of (...) adequate co-ordination mechanisms rather than a science of individual maximization, general equilibrium and 'optimality.'
[4] Demand elasticity ε ≡ dlnQ/dlnP ≡ (dQ/Q)/(dP/P) can be thought of as the percentage response of Q to a one-percent increase in P. In deductive terms, the whole expression emerges from the definition of MR as dR/dQ (where R ≡ PxQ) with respect to Q or P, which can be written simply as P = MR x [ε/(ε+1)], yielding P* = M* x E*, which price is adjusted until actual output Q* and growth g* ≡ dlnQ/dt are as expected (for a given horizon H*, as further discussed below).

(*Reder* 1982), dismissing all the rest of the rich field of industrial organization as "slightly differentiated microeconomics."[5] Problems of interdependence – in information networks and living ecologies – seem to open lacunae throughout the entire redoubt of established theory.[6] But there is another flaw that mainstream models slip by as well.

3   The Notion of Planning Horizons

Every economic conception involves a *flow-rate through time*. And every decision is made on imagined projections of unknown outcomes. The range of these projections – and the time-span they embrace – subsume the *planning horizon* in choice. The static curves on which we rely all include a 'given' horizon, though economists often ignore it: each relation is drawn from a larger horizonal family of like curves. The planning horizon (H*) in any decision is not observed directly: every contingency is projected by agents to a different extent, depending on knowledge, attention, importance, certainty, and other factors. The chief concern here is to see how H* affects the pricing decision, after a look at horizons themselves.

The choice of H* – the planning horizon – depends on social and personal inputs. If so, horizonal theory allows economists to entertain new relations in our ongoing causal analyses. For example, an agent's planning horizon is shifted by understanding, confidence, energy and attention, and by environmental factors such as stability, others' reliability, ethics and rates of change. Indeed, the way our horizons react to internal and external factors opens a whole new field for research by academics in many fields.

The impact of planning horizons on pricing is easier to define. The wider the range of planning perspective – the longer the time-frame of a decision – the lower will be both M* and E* and so P* as well. Each of these scalars falls with any extension of planning horizons (H*), but at a declining rate, within a specific context of choice.[7] In any particular situation, 'horizon effects' shall matter: as H*s shift, the ordinal impact on human choice can be seen. If so, horizon ef-

---

[5] *Koch* (1980, p. 2) remarks that "one of the modern giants in the field ... George Stigler, contends that ... industrial organization does not really exist, that it is nothing more than slightly differentiated microeconomics."

[6] As *Herbert A. Simon* (1976, pp. 140-41) put it, presaging the notion of planning horizons:

In the literature on oligopoly and imperfect competition one can trace a gradual movement toward more and more explicit concern with the processes used to reach decisions... There remains, however, a lingering reluctance to acknowledge the impossibility of discovering at last 'The Rule' of substantively rational behavior for the oligopolist. Only when the hope of that discovery has been finally extinguished will it be admitted that understanding imperfect competition means understanding procedural rationality.

[7] Formally, the relations of cost M*(Q,H), markups E*(Q,H) and price P*(Q,H) = M* x E* to planning horizons are represented thus: $dM*/dH < 0$ and $d^2M*/dH^2 > 0$; $dE*/dH < 0$ and $d^2E*/dH^2 > 0$; so $dP*/dH < 0$ and $d^2P*/dH^2 > 0$. On the assumption that the proportional growth rate of sales is $g* \equiv dlnQ/dt$, we can also infer that $dg*/dH > 0$ and $d^2g*/dH^2 < 0$.

fects shape pricing and growth, as well as efficiency, social welfare and ecological health.

Accepting interdependence suggests another way of viewing H* as a measure of 'bounded' rationality: if all we do ripples outward forever on everyone *ad infinitum*, then 'perfect knowledge' only applies to Gods enjoying complete Omniscience. We mortals see just so far and no further: we are contained by horizons. So H* in this sense should be viewed as an ordinal measure of 'rationality,' and of foresight, trust, time preference (impatience), sensitivity, ethics, socialization, maturity, conscience and general perspective. Recognition of interdependence sweeps us into another realm where reductionistic concepts fail to embrace our radiant impact: this is where Chamberlin's story applies to information network economies, ecological life and dynamic, complex systems of organization.

4   The Interdependence of Pricing Effects

Chicago's simplistic classification of markets into 'monopoly' and 'competition' denies any interdependence of firms in complex settings: we move from a single to many identical sellers and thus avoid dealing with 'oligopoly' or 'imperfect competitive firms' in network contexts. So when industrial organization is scorned as "slightly differentiated microeconomics," such a remark can be understood as a brazen evasion of interdependence. *Shubik* (1970, p. 415) observed that "there is no oligopoly theory" due to this problem; Simon (note 6 above) called for abandoning any search for regular rules in this setting. *Chamberlin* (1961) started in transportation, developing his approach. We live in an age of network clusters of firms in diverse settings interacting complexly and dynamically, yielding outcomes standing outside the purview of orthodox standards.

In networks, scarcity does not bring value, as in traditional economics: substitution is not the dominant feature in network contexts. Here the more users and interconnections you have, the greater the worth.[8] This situation is the reverse of what pertains under orthodox standards: substitution and diminishing returns cede to increasing returns and complementarity in this case. So where

---

[8] Information economies do not suffer from the same scarcity problems as do industrial economies; information is reproduced "at near-to-zero marginal costs. The 'new' economy, thus, has entered a stage of informational abundance which bears little resemblance to the conventional mainstream economic assumption of scarcity" (*Elsner* 2004, p. 1032). As *Angus Matthew* (2001, p. 2 of 7), writing on "The New Economy," put it:

> In the networked economy, the more plentiful things become, the more valuable they become. ... In a networked economy, value is derived from plenitude, the concept of abundance. ... Abundance is everything. Ubiquity drives increasing returns in a networked world. In fact, the only factor becoming scarce in a world of abundance is human attention.

Shapiro/Varian (1999, p. 6) suggest that : "Herbert Simon spoke for us all when he said that 'a wealth of information creates a poverty of attention.' Nowadays the problem is not information access but information overload."

externalities are an essential part of the interactive process, single agents act in response to interdependent effects. Separability is impossible: linkages are endemic.

The explanation of $P^* = M^* \times E^*$ applies to one firm, making decisions apart from externalities falling on neighbors. But if all we do ripples outward forever, then pricing is never in isolation. As *John Maurice Clark* (1955, p. 457) observed:

> "A theory of competition as dynamic process must be not a model but a framework within which many models may find their places, including equilibrium models as limiting hypothetical cases. ... The process includes initiatory action by a firm, responses by those with whom it deals, and responses to these responses by rival firms, to which one should add the subsequent rejoinders of the initiators, plus any actions that may be taken on a basis of anticipation. ... Fully dynamic theory needs to conceive these patterns as themselves subject to change, over longer periods of time."

Pricing decisions spill externalities out on neighboring agents. We must think of a group of firms shifting interdependently, in a 'monopolistic competitive' venue of interactive phenomena.

Transportation networks symbolize problems of interdependence (*Jennings* 2006), such as found between two extremes along a spectrum moving from substitution through independence to complementarity. These are cases of negative vs. positive feedback in our systems: parallel routes and serial linkages stand for these sorts of relation. Parallel lines *substitute* for each other in terms of use; serial linkages are consumed together, reflecting *complementarities*. Substitutes suffer a conflict of interests; they are like two brands of beer. Complements show a concert of value with their fortunes aligned: they thrive and decline together, like wine and cheese or pretzels and beer.[9]

Within network contexts, substitution and complementarity yield directly opposite implications. Substitution defines scarcity and exclusion as sources of *value*; rare items are dear, while ubiquity undermines worth. This scenario is reversed in the new information economy: here an abundance of interconnections serves to augment demand. This story is one of *complementarity*, positive feedback, common needs and public goods phenomena: the more users, the better. Here, interdependence cannot be ignored; it is the core of the matter! The way our decisions affect other agents shall be included thus.

---

[9] This invokes "The Richardson Problem" (*Richardson* 1959, pp. 233-34; also Earl 1983b, p. 29); *Shapiro/Varian* (1999, p. 10) give an informational version thereof:

> *Traditional rules of competitive strategy focus on competitors, suppliers, and customers. In the information economy, companies selling complementary components, or complementors, are equally important. ... The dependence of information technology on systems means that firms must focus not only on their competitors but also on their collaborators. ... The need for collaboration, and the multitude of cooperative arrangements, has never been greater than in the area of infotech.*

We will define P' as incorporating external profit effects. The impact of any single P_j on the earnings of neighboring firms i,j = 1,...,n is described through S_I, an aggregation of individual spillovers $s_{i\neq j} \equiv (Q_{i\neq j}/Q_j) \times (M_{i\neq j}^* - P_{i\neq j}^*) \times [\varepsilon_{ij}^*/(\varepsilon_j^*+1)]$, for any group I of firms i ≠ j.[10] Internalizing pecuniary externalities through a compensation process arising from joint profit maximization with respect to P_j yields the expression $P_j' = P_j^* + S_I$. S_I is a combinatorial of individual $s_{i\neq j}$'s within some group I of firms (which can be defined as needed). This is a composition rule allowing aggregation without any additivity, independence or substitution assumptions (Krupp 1963); it thus serves to circumvent economists' 'industry' concept.

In this construction, any firm j is surrounded by two other types of firms: substitutes and complements. For *substitute* products, si≠j > 0, so they prefer higher Pj' than Pj*: here collusion among them raises price (the orthodox story). For *complementarities*, on the other hand, si≠j < 0 implies a concert of interest: here cooperation reduces Pj' below Pj* allowing greater sales for both. This is the case with beer and pretzels, which are consumed together. In transportation networks such equate to serial linkages, so contrast to rival brands of beer akin to parallel routes. Economists' substitution assumptions only include the latter.

Rival lines are important, but they are only one side of interdependence. Network complexities shall extend beyond the range of orthodox standards; interdependence comes in two flavors: substitution or complementarity, conflicts or concerts of value, and negative vs. positive feedback. Equilibrium models call for the former in order to work. Complex skeins of interdependence – such as information networks, systems of education or research, and vital living ecologies – are not described by substitution. Social welfare is not confined exclusively to opposing concerns. The question is whether common needs surpass those that diverge: which is stronger in human relations, substitution or complementarity? Where does each best apply?

5   Substitution or Complementarity: Increasing Returns and Horizon Effects

Kaldor (1975, p. 348) argued increasing returns in production were general and not special, making complementarity "far more important" than substitution;[11] he drew this finding from macroeconomic models of growth. *Myrdal* (1978, pp. 772-74) called this 'cumulative causation,' but neither economist tied it to information network connectivity or knowledge economies. The introduc-

[10] $S_I \equiv \Sigma s_i$ only with all s_i's independent, which cannot be assumed in the presence of fully interdependent phenomena. S_I is derived from maximizing *joint* profits for firms in group I with respect to P_j, while ε_{ij} is the cross-elasticity of $Q_{i\neq j}$ with respect to P_j, and ε_j is the own-elasticity of demand for Q_j.

[11] *Kenneth J. Arrow* (1969, p. 495) acknowledged long ago that a theory of monopolistic competition "is forcibly needed in the presence of increasing returns, and is superfluous in its absence."

tion of planning horizons into our theory of pricing gives another route to Kaldor's sweeping conclusion from microeconomics.

How planning horizons shape pricing and growth was shown above. The bearing of substitution and complementarity on the pricing decision has also been detailed. The question now turns to what is the impact of longer horizons on the balance of substitution and complementarity in any group I, i.e., on the 'feedback term' S_I. The answer is surprisingly general: $dS_I/dH_j^* < 0$ in (nearly) all cases. As planning horizons extend, the balance of interdependencies shifts away from substitution to complementarity at the margins of choice. In other words, horizontal lengthening amplifies shared desires while reducing conflicts of value: longer horizons make everyone better off by augmenting common needs. There is, however, a vital assumption on which this finding relies.

Planning horizons interact directly across individuals, both through role model effects and diverse socio-cultural links. If I extend my horizons through learning, I become more predictable or reliable in my decisions: those around me can plan better too. If I become more mature, ecologically conscious or ethical in my behavior, others in my sphere of influence are affected thereby. Everyone constantly interacts, affecting each others' states of mind, trust, devotion and diversions, in an ongoing flow. One can directly observe this interhorizonal complementarity in any close (romantic or other) relationship, when our vantages shrink or expand together as stresses or insecurities seize or relax their grip on us. Planning horizons move in unison: all our horizon effects are contagious. If so, then generally $dH_{i\neq j}^*/dH_j^* > 0$.[12]

Such interhorizonal complementarity yields the implication that $dSI/dH_j^* < 0$.[13] As horizons extend together (through contagious horizon effects), the balance of interdependencies shifts to favor complementarities and away from rivalrous substitution. If so, then institutions must segue from competition to cooperation to support this horizonal lengthening or it will not be sustainable: competition is inefficient in complementary settings. Since learning goes best through cooperation (due to its concerts of interest), the impact of competition on knowledge and research is counterproductive. Competition – indeed – is actively *keeping horizons short.*

---

[12] A case of interhorizonal substitution ($dH_{i\neq j}^*/dH_j^* < 0$) might be a jealous reaction to rivals' successful learning.

[13] Interhorizonal complementarity means $dH_{i\neq j}^*/dH_j^* > 0$. If so, then $dS_I/dH_j^* < 0$: a rise in H_j^* yields – through contagious horizon effects on $H_{i\neq j}^*$ – a shift of S_I away from substitution in favor of complementarity. For any $i\neq j$ element of S_I, namely $s_{i\neq j} \equiv (Q_{i\neq j}/Q_j) \times (M_{i\neq j}^* - P_{i\neq j}^*) \times [\varepsilon_{ij}^*/(\varepsilon_j^*+1)]$, an extension of H_j^* will likely reduce the magnitude of both $Q_{i\neq j}/Q_j > 0$ (as a weighting scalar) and $|(M_{i\neq j}^* - P_{i\neq j}^*)| < 0|$, while increasing own-elasticity $|\varepsilon_j^* < -1|$ and thus the negative magnitude of $|(\varepsilon_j^*+1)| < 0|$, while the cross-elasticity (ε_{ij}^*) is shifted away from substitution ($\varepsilon_{ij}^* > 0$) toward complementarity ($\varepsilon_{ij}^* < 0$), such that $d\varepsilon_{ij}^*/dH_j^* < 0$ as well. So regardless of the sign of S_I (as a combinatorial of $s_{i\neq j}$ across any group I around member j), $\underline{dS_I/dH_j^* < 0}$: a mutual lengthening of horizons shifts our social relations away from substitution ($S_I > 0$) in favor of greater complementarity ($S_I < 0$) in virtually all economic contexts.

The evidence abounds. As some wise soul once said: "Fish discover water last" (*McGregor* 1960, p. 317). The symptoms of a persistent, dangerous short-sightedness seem ubiquitous throughout modern society. We drown in narcissistic concerns, while life-support systems cede to entropy and erode the carrying capacity of a rapidly shrinking earth with population expanding unchecked. Ignoring concerns of this kind – in denial – leaders seldom acknowledge, much less address themselves to these problems: solving them *before* they are crises has no political value, as such foresighted solutions stay invisible to a myopic electorate. *All human-caused ecological losses are horizonal,* almost by definition. The short horizons stemming from competition threaten all life. In the presence of network complexity, the case for cooperation is strong (*Elsner* 2004): it rises out of the complementary interdependence of information and ecological life.

6   So Information Network Economies Have a Lesson for Us

The features of interdependence – substitution vs. complementarity, inter-horizonal linkages – show why orthodox standards have failed us so badly: rivalrous systems do not only founder under increasing returns; they also reduce our planning horizons. There are more than just substitution and conflict of value in an economy; information networks stretch beyond parallel lines. Serial linkages (complementarities) may even dominate over opposing concerns in human affairs. Such is the argument here: increasing returns make complementarity "far more important" than substitution for "understanding ... economy" (*Kaldor* 1975, p. 348).

Prevailing complementarities make competition *inefficient*: here we seek cooperation to realize common aims. If planning horizons – horizon effects – play any role in social welfare, longer horizons are 'better,' and so we must learn to extend them. One direction is through education, encouraging ethics and trust: these goals are complementary and thus served through cooperation, not by rivalrous strife. These insights suggest that Kaldor and Myrdal were right in their basic claim. More recent work on information networks supports such views.

If complementarity is the dominant feature of human relations, then economists' substitution assumptions have led us severely astray. If value increases with interconnections, scarcity and exclusion don't work; gifts and cooperation – generosity and expansion of vision – are how we achieve economy. In this situation, orthodox suppositions shall not apply. An inescapable economic conclusion is that competition – economists' standard for 'optimality' – in reinforcing myopic concerns, is *fostering inefficiency*. In the presence of complementarity, rivalries shorten horizons. Increasing returns mean complementarity; horizon effects are complementary; information networks and ecological systems show complementarities. If our relations are ruled by increasing returns and horizon effects, such as in networks and living ecologies, substitution assumptions are wrong. And this is what transportation networks – and ecological living systems

– have to teach the economist about the new information economy: such settings are ruled not by substitution but complementarity. A remaining unanswered question is whether economists will pay heed, due to their own economic culture.

One important information network is found in a university, in academic communities. The process of learning, in transacting knowledge, is surely complementary (*Boulding* 1968, pp. 133-34): here collusion advances output and growth, while fragmentation impedes them. Competition in complementary settings is sure to fail, producing counterproductive (if not demonstrably pathological) outcomes. Examine the impact of competition in academic contexts, where new ideas are routinely opposed and dogmas stay in control. This is not a real 'learning environment': true inquiry always seeks out difference as a chance to explore and overcome personal limits. What we see in academics is symptomatic of failure: rivalry in the presence of complementarity is the cause; short horizons are the result.

Thus information network economies show why orthodox standards have foundered due to substitution assumptions. How we emerge from mounting crises stemming from this error is through an institutional change in favor of cooperation, not competition. This, in turn, will lengthen horizons and encourage learning activities, so will lead to more intelligent choices based on greater ethical and ecological conscience. A dramatic cultural change is required, away from myopia and acquisitive values toward a maturity and generosity almost inconceivable in today's society. The way to start is with a reform of our educational institutions and information networks, since its social effects should thereby extend more rapidly into our cultural lifestyles.

Substitution is not the essence of human interdependence in the new information economy; *complementarity is*. Value rises from multiple use and not from mere exclusion: 'what goes around, comes around' here. If so, efficiency, equity, ecological conscience, social awareness and longer planning horizons stem from cooperation, not competition (*Jennings* 2005). The theme in neoclassical economics showing competition as optimal is incorrect: the new information economy yields an efficiency case for cooperation. The question turns on economists and their reluctance to adapt, due to the harmful impact of competition on academic incentives. Sadly, one cannot be too sanguine about any awakening (*Earl* 1983a; *Morishima* 1984, pp. 69-70).

One note of optimism – among the otherwise urgent dangers – lies in horizon effects. Since yours and mine interact so readily, we can change ourselves and others simply with longer horizons. Perhaps that is all we can do, namely, to share what we know and take care of each other. These contagions should diffuse, as learning and information grow, extending their social fruits. *Walt Kelly* (1987) identified "the enemy" as "us." We *can* heal ourselves, and learn new ways that might diffuse.

References

Arrow, K.J. (1969): The Organization of Economic Activity: Issues Pertinent to the Choice of Market Versus Nonmarket Allocation. as reprinted in Edwin Mansfield, ed., Microeconomics: Selected Readings, 4th ed. (New York: Norton 1982).

Boulding, K.E. (1968): Beyond Economics: Essays on Society, Religion and Ethics. University of Michigan Press, Ann Arbor.

Chamberlin, Edward H. (1933): The Theory of Monopolistic Competition: A Reorientation of the Theory of Value. Harvard University Press, Cambridge.

_____ (1957): Towards a More General Theory of Value. Oxford University Press, New York.

_____ (1961): The Origin and Early Development of Monopolistic Competition Theory. Quarterly Journal of Economics, Volume 75, (4), pp. 515-43.

Clark, J.M. (1955): Competition: Static Models and Dynamic Aspects. American Economic Review, Papers and Proceedings, Volume 45, (2), May.

Earl, P. (1983a): A Behavioral Theory of Economists' Behavior. *Eichner, A.S.* ed., Why Economics is Not Yet a Science, M.E. Sharpe, Armonk, NY.

_____ (1983b): The Economic Imagination: Towards a Behavioral Analysis of Choice. M.E. Sharpe, Armonk, NY.

Elsner, W. (2004): The "New" Economy: Complexity, Coordination and a Hybrid Governance Approach. International Journal of Social Economics, Volume 31 (11/12), pp. 1029-49.

Georgescu-Roegen, N. (1967): Analytical Economics: Issues and Problems. Harvard University Press, Cambridge, MA.

Hicks, J.R. (1939): Value and Capital. 2nd ed., Oxford University Press (1942), Oxford.

Jennings, F.B., Jr. (2005): How Efficiency/Equity Tradeoffs Resolve Through Horizon Effects. Journal of Economic Issues, Volume 39 (2), June, pp. 365-73.

_____ (2006): A Horizonal Challenge to Orthodox Theory: Competition and Cooperation in Transportation Networks. *Pickhardt, M. / Sarda Pons, J.* eds., INFER Research Perspectives, Volume 1: Perspectives on Competition in Transportation, LIT Verlag, Berlin, pp. 207-19.

Kaldor, N. (1972): The Irrelevance of Equilibrium Economics. Economic Journal, Volume 82, pp. 1237-55.

_____ (1975): What Is Wrong With Economic Theory. Quarterly Journal of Economics, Volume 89 (3), pp. 347-57.

Kelly, W. (1987): We Have Met the Enemy and He Is Us. Simon and Schuster, New York.

Koch, J.V. (1980): Industrial Organization and Prices. 2nd ed., Prentice-Hall, Englewood, NJ

Krupp, S.R. (1963): Analytic Economics and the Logic of External Effects. American Economic Review, Papers and Proceedings, Volume 53 (2), pp. 220-26.

Lamberton, D.M. (2001): The Knowledge Based Economy: Better Living or Bigger Profits? Innovation, Economic Progress and the Quality of Life, ed. G. Sweeney, Edward Elgar, Cheltenham, pp. 111-19.

Latsis, S J. (1972): Situational Determinism in Economics. British Journal for the Philosophy of Science, Volume 23, pp. 207-45.

Loasby, B.J. (1986): Organisation, Competition and Growth of Knowledge. Economics as a Process: Essays in the New Institutional Economics, ed. *R. N. Langlois*, Cambridge University Press, Cambridge.

Matthew, A. (2001): The New Economy – Truth or Fallacy? Pool: Business and Marketing Strategy, Issue 13, Winter, http://www.poolonline.com/archive/issue13/iss13fea4.html.

McGregor, D. (1971): Theory X and Theory Y. in Organization Theory, ed. D. S. Pugh, Penguin, New York, pp. 305-23.

Morishima, M. (1984): The Good and Bad Uses of Mathematics. ch. 3 of *Wiles, P. / Routh, G.* eds., Economics in Disarray, Basil Blackwell, Oxford, England.

Myrdal, G. (1978): Institutional Economics. Journal of Economic Issues, Volume 12 (4), pp. 771-83.

Reder, M.W. (1982): Chicago Economics: Permanence and Change. Journal of Economic Literature, Volume 20 (1), pp. 1-38.

Richardson, G.B. (1959): Equilibrium, Expectations and Information. Economic Journal, Volume 69, 1959.

Shackle, G. L. S. (1958): The Economist's Model of Man. Occupational Psychology, Volume 32; reprinted in his The Nature of Economic Thought: Selected Papers, 1955-1964, Cambridge University Press, 1966, Cambridge, pp. 123-30.

Shapiro, C. / Varian, H.R. (1999): Information Rules: A Strategic Guide to the Network Economy. Harvard Business School Press, Boston.

Shubik, M. (1970): A Curmudgeon's Guide to Microeconomics. Journal of Economic Literature, Volume 8 (2), June, pp. 405-34.

Simon, H.A. (1976): From Substantive to Procedural Rationality. *Latsis, S.J.* ed., Method and Appraisal in Economics, Cambridge University Press, Cambridge, England.

_____ (1982-97): Models of Bounded Rationality, Volumes 1-3, MIT Press, Cambridge.

Stiglitz, J.E. (1985): Information and Economic Analysis: A Perspective. Economic Journal, Volume 95.

Horizon Effects, Sustainability, Education and Ethics: Toward an Economics of Foresight

Frederic B. JENNINGS, Jr.

1 Introduction

Interdependence stands at the center of ecological economics: substitution is only half of its story; the other is complementarity. Orthodox economics stands critically on substitution assumptions; complementarity swamps standard theory in nonconvexities and other intractabilities. The notion of planning horizons suggests a sweeping case for complementarity, and not just a minor exception to substitution in economics. Even increasing returns supports a complementary interdependence (*Kaldor* 1972, 1973, 1975), where prior anticipation of outcomes sets our rational limit. The introduction of planning horizons strengthens the claim for complementarity, yielding new insight on how economics affects sustainability, education and ethics in human society. Horizon effects show how competition is keeping us immature, relentlessly fixed on narcissistic concerns.

In an interdependent world, where every act has a radiant impact, the relevant bound is that of our rational anticipation thereof (*Simon* 1982-97). Once in motion, results spread outward beyond the range of expectation, neither reversible nor remedied by offsetting correction. Our planning horizons thus reflect the bounds of rationality in decisions we make continually: the more we understand the world – the better the fit of frames to fact[1] – the more efficient we are in the use of resources for human needs. Perhaps the greatest failure of neoclassical economics is its objectification of human decision: a reintroduction of cognitive factors (cf., e.g., *Georgescu-Roegen* 1967, p. 104) suggests some major revisions in how we think about economics in its relation to ecology, education and ethical issues.

Choice is a normative process of multidimensional causal projection. We cannot choose among outcomes; we sift through imagined depictions thereof, from beliefs of how things work. If our ideas are wrongly applied – or incorrectly conceived – we squander resources on unrealistic goals. The fit of theory to realms of application is vital to all success. Suppositions specify applications for economic conceptions: the 'ifs' surrounding our 'then' conclusions. If so, unrealism brings a cost to the practical worth of knowledge.

---

[1] Cf. *Boulding* (1956). As *Simon* (1981, p. 132) put it: "The artificial world is centered precisely on this interface between the inner and outer environments; it is concerned with attaining goals by adapting the former to the latter." *Pylyshyn* (1984, p. 251) adds this:

It is my view that there is only one empirical hypothesis responsible for the productive success of the entire range of imagery models...: when people imagine a scene or an event, what occurs in their minds is, in many ways, similar to what happens when they observe the corresponding event actually happening.

2   Horizon Effects in Economics

Planning horizons signify the range of projection in choice. We cannot observe or measure them in any cardinal way. Instead, they are treated in ordinal terms: as longer or shorter, broader or narrower, bigger or smaller, but not by 'how much.' Within this frame, planning horizons exist (in our minds at each moment of choice), and any adjustment to their range shall be called a 'horizon effect.'

Demand curves in economics state an inverse relation of P to Q, with $\underline{dQ/dP < 0}$ (assuming *ceteris paribus*). When MR crosses MC from above, a stable market price can be framed as $\underline{P^* = M^* \times E^{*2}}$ with $\underline{Q = Q^*}$.[3] Horizons state a similar inverse relation of P to H. Every economist knows that long-run demand, supply and cost curves are flatter than short-run equivalents (e.g., cf. *Stigler* 1939; *Clark* 1940, 1955; *Turvey* 1969), so all static conceptions of price include an implicit planning horizon (within the pound of *ceteris paribus*). Here we open economists' theory of price to a shift in planning horizons, making H^* explicit and asking how it affects P^*. In any and all economic contexts, P^* is a *falling* function of H, while Q^* and g^* (the proportional growth rate of output Q) are *rising* functions of H.[4] If so, the orthodox static conception of pricing is incomplete without any explanation of H and why a particular H^* is chosen.

The planning horizon (H^*) in any decision occurs at the balance of factors such as knowledge, attention, importance, impatience, stability, energy, interest, stress, distraction, exhaustion, etc. Indeed, these and many other determinants cause horizon effects. This is so for an individual price such as described; the same pattern applies across any interdependent domain, due to contagiously spreading horizon effects. If you and I interact, then our horizons shift together. You, in this respect, are a 'disturbance' in my sphere. So if you learn something making you more predictable (or if you just calm down), I am more able to plan, and thus to project my outcomes better and further (*ceteris paribus*, for whatever I bring to that choice myself). In other words, for any group including both i and j, $\underline{dH_{i \neq j}{}^*/dH_j{}^* > 0}$ in the general case. I call this spread of horizon effects 'interhorizonal complementarity.'

---

[2] Formally, $M^* \equiv MR = MC$ at Q^* (the maximum profit condition), with $E^* \equiv [\varepsilon^*/(\varepsilon^*+1)]$ where $E^*>1$ because $-\infty < \varepsilon^* < -1$ [and here $\varepsilon \equiv d\ln Q/d\ln P \equiv (dQ/Q)/(dP/P)$, the elasticity of demand, which can be thought of as the percentage response of Q to a one-percent increase in P]. The whole expression can be derived very simply by substitution from the definition of MR as dR/dQ (where $R \equiv P{\times}Q$) with respect to Q or P, which can be written simply as $P = MR \times [\varepsilon /(\varepsilon+1)]$, yielding $\underline{P^* = M^* \times E^*}$.

[3] The asterisk (*) denotes the level actually chosen as best by an agent.

[4] This conclusion can be derived – if done properly – from Alchian's (1959) nine propositions on cost, despite the erroneous effort by *Hirshleifer* (1962) and its acceptance by Oi (1967) and *Alchian* (1968): cf. *Jennings* (1985, ch. 5). The outcome may be summarized thus: $dM^*/dH < 0$ with $d^2M^*/dH^2 > 0$; $dE^*/dH < 0$ with $d^2E^*/dH^2 > 0$; so $dP^*/dH < 0$ and $d^2P^*/dH^2 > 0$. If so, then for $g \equiv d\ln Q/dt$, the growth rate of sales, $dg^*/dH > 0$ with $d^2g^*/dH^2 < 0$. Also cf. Margolis (1960).

All this implies that longer horizons shift the balance of interdependence in any setting away from substitution in favor of complementarity. Defining 'groups' as aggregations of substitutes – as economists do – is simply begging the question about the nature of interdependence (by assuming substitution and ignoring complementarity). We need a rule of composition (Krupp 1963) that includes them both. This is done by comparing independent pricing (P_j^*) with the impact on P_j^* of internalizing its profit effects (S_I) on any group I (with i≠j = 1,... n) of substitutes and complements (which yields some P_j').

For i≠j substitutes a higher P_j^* raises sales, so internalizing profit effects would *increase* P_j^* to P_j'. For complements, the reverse applies: they prefer reductions in P_j^* to boost demand; internalizing these effects will *reduce* P_j^* to P_j'. The net compensatory impact on P_j will serve as a measure (S_I) of *net interdependence* within any group *I* of firms (i≠j) with respect to one member (j). It offers a method of aggregation free of substitution assumptions (unlike grouping by 'markets').[5] Within this compensatory frame, interhorizonal complementarity yields another relevant truth about horizon effects: interdependence within a group with respect to any member thereof adjusts to favor complementarity over substitution as group members' horizons extend: $\underline{dS_I/dH_j^* < 0}$.[6] The institutional implications of this shift are very important.

3   The Institutional Implications of Horizon Effects

In a world of pure substitution, such as supposed by orthodoxy, competition increases output and therewith social well-being. If people drink either beer

---

[5] So we escape the aggregation dilemma of most 'market' theory through a Kaldor-Hicks compensation process, as introduced by *Kaldor* (1939) and *Hicks* (1939). Formally, the aggregate 'feedback term' discussed in the text as the difference between the compensated P_j' and the independent P_j^* is simply $S_I = \Sigma s_{i \neq j}$ (or the combinatorial $\Omega s_{i \neq j}$ in cases of nonadditivity), where compensation $s_{i \neq j}$ to or by each i≠j member is: $s_{i \neq j} \equiv (Q_{i \neq j}/Q_j) \times (M_{i \neq j}^* - P_{i \neq j}^*) \times [\varepsilon_{ij}^*/(\varepsilon_j^*+1)]$, whose sign is that of the cross-elasticity of demand for i with respect to j, $\varepsilon_{ij} \equiv dlnQ_{i \neq j}/dlnP_j$, where the own-elasticity of demand for j is $\varepsilon_j^* \equiv dlnQ_j/dlnP_j < -1$. Then $\underline{P_j'}$ (compensated) $= P_j^*$ (independent) + the 'feedback term' S_I.

[6] $P_j' = P_j^* + S_I$ for any group I of firms, where S_I is the difference between the compensated (joint-profit maximizing) P_j' and the P_j^* set independently of its pecuniary impact on the other (i≠j) firms' profits. Interhorizonal complementarity means $dH_{i \neq j}^*/dH_j^* > 0$. If so, then $dS_I/dH_j^* < 0$: an increase in H_j^* yields – through its contagious effects on $H_{i \neq j}^*$ – a shift of S_I away from substitution in favor of complementarity. For any i≠j element of S_I, namely $s_{i \neq j} \equiv (Q_{i \neq j}/Q_j) \times (M_{i \neq j}^* - P_{i \neq j}^*) \times [\varepsilon_{ij}^*/(\varepsilon_j^*+1)]$, an extension of H_j^* will likely reduce the magnitude of both $Q_{i \neq j}/Q_j > 0$ (as a weighting scalar) and $|(M_{i \neq j}^* - P_{i \neq j}^*) < 0|$, while increasing own-elasticity (ε_j^*) and thus the negative magnitude of $|(\varepsilon_j^*+1) < 0|$, while the cross-elasticity (ε_{ij}^*) is shifted away from substitution $(\varepsilon_{ij}^* > 0)$ toward complementarity $(\varepsilon_{ij}^* < 0)$, so $d\varepsilon_{ij}^*/dH_j^* < 0$ as well. So regardless of the sign of S_I (as an aggregation of $s_{i \neq j}$ across any group I around member j), $\underline{dS_I/dH_j^* < 0}$: a mutual lengthening of planning horizons shifts our social relations away from substitution in favor of greater complementarity (in virtually all economic contexts).

or wine,[7] these sales are inversely related in a basic conflict of interests. Standard theory finds that collusion between them brings a restriction of output with higher prices and profit on both. This is the compensation effect described above for substitutes, where $S_1 > 0$.

But what of wine and cheese, consumed together as complementary goods, where $S_1 < 0$? When they collude, prices fall from mutual profits achieved thereby. Here we find not conflict, but a *concert* of financial interest. Among complements, social well-being is served by cooperation. The proper realm of application for competition is substitution; in the presence of complementarity, competition fails: here the route to efficiency is through cooperation.

Figure 3.1

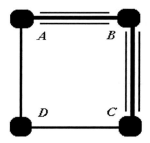

A general theory of interdependence, on which any boundedly rational ecological economics must stand, includes an intractable mix of substitution together with complementarity. Outcomes spread, for better or worse, to others from every act. 'Do no harm' is the best advice, and that is a matter of conscience, so of ethics and planning horizons. Selfishness – so richly rewarded in a competitive frame – is self-defeating from a cognitive vantage: horizon effects show why.

A useful way to think about interdependence is in a systems setting. Imagine a transportation network, in its simplest form, as four routes between four towns in a square, without diagonal shortcuts (see *Figure One*). Now consider the interdependence of routes *AB* and *BC*: how will a merger between them affect the prices charged by each? We've already shown that if they are rivals, a merger raises their rates, and for complements such will reduce them. But how do we know whether these two routes are 'wine vs. beer' or 'wine and cheese'? Substitution cannot be asserted, as with theories of markets. Here we must face the question.

---

[7] Even this simple example, however, reveals that interdependency is contingent and purpose-specific: if the relevant choice is to throw a party or do something else instead, then beer and wine – in this situation – are complementary goods.

The issue is one of parallel vs. end-to-end lines in transportation; the first are rivalrous substitutes, where the second are complementary. What then is the linkage of routes *AB* and *BC* in this setting? The answer is not absolute: it turns on *direction of traffic*. Travel between *B* and *D* uses these routes as substitute means, whereas anything moving between *A* and *C* encounters them both as complements. And this square is part of a system, making it almost impossible to unbundle these effects. Substitution and complementarity often are not decomposable; it is a rare exception when mostly one or the other prevails.

The institutional challenge is to structure this situation. Do we encourage competition or cooperation here? Which incentives are more efficient? We cannot just blindly impose substitution and competition: that is precisely the wrong answer wherever complementarity rules. So what do we do, once we admit to complex interdependence? Substitution assumptions steer us well through oppositions of interest, but will serve as an unreliable guide whenever aims are aligned. This is where horizon effects shine new light on the problem.

As noted already, longer horizons shift the mix of interdependence in any economic case toward complementarity and away from substitution. Thus economic development calls for a parallel shift in our institutions, favoring cooperation over incentives for competition, to facilitate this advance. Threatened people get selfish, if foiled in their basic concerns (*Maslow* 1954, 1968); similarly, we become more generous as we age and mature. Indeed, the acquisitive values so rewarded by competition are a symptom of immaturity in society and ourselves.[8] The various failures of competition in complementary settings show up in organizational stress, short horizons and systems collapse. Such is always the case with theory unfit to its sphere of use. Examples can be found in ecology, education and ethics.

4   The Ecological Economics of Sustainability

Ecologies serve as a good example of complementary interdependence. Sure, rivalry can be found in narrow realms of focus, but to enter a larger frame makes complementarity more important. The same is seen in economics: only by looking at tightly-defined domains with short-term models does substitution dominate all. Long-term, broader representations show the importance of com-

---

[8] Cf. *Wachtel* (1989) and *McGregor* (1960). *Argyris* (1960, pp. 262-63) observes that conventional organization treats its members too much like children; mature people in these settings show symptoms of ill health, including "frustration, failure, short time perspective and conflict." He expresses concern about the problem of organizational fragmentation on pp. 268-69: "The nature of the formal principles of organization causes the subordinates, at any given level, to experience competition, rivalry, intersubordinate hostility and to develop a focus toward the parts rather than the whole." *McGregor* (1960, p. 310) warned:

The deprivation of needs has behavioral consequences. ... The man whose needs for safety, association, independence or status are thwarted is sick, just as surely as he who has rickets. We will be mistaken if we attribute ... passivity, or ... hostility, or ... refusal to accept responsibility to ... inherent 'human nature.' These forms of behavior are symptoms of illness – of deprivation of ... social and egoistic needs.

plementarity: this is a key distinction of micro- from macroeconomics. So let us consider sustainability in horizonal terms.

First, every human-caused ecological loss is *horizonal*. If all we do ripples outward forever in its spreading effects, then the bounds of rationality are an issue we ought to address. This is the notion of planning horizons, which are not only an ordinal measure of knowledge, time-perspective and effort, but also reflect our levels of socio-ecological conscience. Sustainability asks us to *internalize externalities* spilling outward and onward from our decisions. Such is only attainable with longer planning horizons, so we ought to examine our institutions for their horizon effects. Again, a shift to cooperation is needed in this sphere.

If ecological life reflects a complementary interdependence, then competition – efficient with substitution – does not work. The optimal organizational form in this situation is cooperation, to preserve and protect the cohesion of fully integral systems. The abortive fragmentation of firms inherent to a competitive venue will not meet the needs of any integrative frame. Observe what competition is doing to ecological systems, if you need examples of this. An economics of competition fails in the presence of complementarity.

This is not to dismiss worthy endeavors supported by The Natural Step, *Paul Hawken* (1994) and others. It is rather to warn that competitive forms – by marginalizing and decentralizing economic decisions – subvert these undertakings. Shortsighted behavior, reinforced through rivalrous systems, is incompatible with sustainability. Horizons extend with more integration through a cohesive view. The case for competition rests on substitution assumptions; rivalry is doomed to fail in complementary settings. Myopic concerns are symptoms of failure, revealing economic guidance sundering ecological health. Another realm of similar relevance is in knowledge and information: namely, our educational system.

5   A Horizonal Look at Education and Information Exchange

Information transactions certainly illustrate complementarity. When we engage in discussion, no one loses what they give away, and new ideas often emerge (*Boulding* 1968, pp. 133-34). "What goes around, comes around," as we say. In this situation, again, competition totally fails. Indeed, the new information economy yields a reversal of the most basic canon of orthodoxy, on the relation of value and scarcity. Instead of value rising with scarcity, information network economies show worth enhanced by ubiquity and more interconnections.

> "In the networked economy, the more plentiful things become, the more valuable they become. ... Value is derived from plenitude, the concept of abundance." (*Matthew* 2001, p. 2 of 7)

Due to the reproduction of information "at near-to-zero marginal costs," as *Elsner* (2004, p. 1032-33) put it: "The 'new' economy, thus, has entered a stage of informational abundance which bears little resemblance to the conventional mainstream economic assumption of scarcity." Quoting *Lamberton* (2001, pp. 115, 117f), Elsner continues:

> "'The limitations of information as a commodity...' call for a 'thorough-going innovation in organizational design' to include 'a very high level of collaboration.' This renders economics a science of (...) adequate co-ordination mechanisms rather than a science of individual maximization, general equilibrium and 'optimality.'"

This is what complementarity means, suggesting a fundamental shift in the way economists ought to think about trade-offs and human relations. The flip from orthodox standards of materialistic constraint to realms of information abundance and intangible sources of value is profound and deeply unsettling. *Among complements, scarcity is created through rivalrous systems.* Think about grading by the curve as an example of this: If I do worse when you succeed, I will not help you learn (and may even misinform your efforts). Sabotage and predation are rewarding in this scheme; myopia is the effect.

In the presence of complementarity, your fate is tied to mine, where "rising tides shall lift all boats." If so, withholding information pours sand in the gears of advance. Imposing a rivalrous system of incentives on information exchanges suffocates our learning, keeping us stupid and immature. Even a glance at commercial TV and the sort of fare relentlessly offered is striking proof of the point. The effect of competition in education – on cultural learning in general – is nothing short of fatal.[9]

---

[9] *Kohn* (1986), pp. 55, 61-65, 108, 110, 113, 123, 129-31 and 143 (original emphasis):
The simplest way to understand why competition generally does not promote excellence is to realize that <u>trying to do well and trying to beat others are two different things</u>. ... <u>Competition ... precludes the more efficient use of resources that cooperation allows.</u> ... Beyond the greater efficiency of cooperation, it is also true that <u>competition's unpleasantness diminishes performance.</u> ... At best, the stressfulness of a competitive situation causes us to try to avoid failure. And trying to avoid failure is not at all the same thing as trying to succeed. ... Competition does not promote excellence. ...
Whereas cooperation apparently contributes to high self-esteem, competition often seems to have the opposite effect. ... Psychological health requires unconditionality... In competition, by contrast, self-esteem is conditional. ... Something very like an addiction is at work here... : the more we compete, the more we <u>need</u> to compete. ... In sum, the security that is so vital to healthy human development is precisely what competition inhibits. ... Competition does not promote ... substantial and authentic ... individualism. On the contrary, it encourages rank conformity [and] ... dampens creativity. ... Creativity is anticonformist at its core; it is ... a process of idiosyncratic thinking and risk-taking. Competition inhibits this process ... [and] affects the personality. Turning life into a series of contests turns us into cautious, obedient people. ... The chief result of competition ... is strife.

Part of the problem is fear of failure, equivalent to a fear of learning: errors are opportunities for review which should be encouraged and not punished through poor grades. The educational system must be purged of competitive features and transformed by cooperation: knowledge – like any complementarity – promulgates best when shared. Understanding ought to be fun; we have made it a chore. No wonder that our competitive culture reflects an avoidance of learning. Short planning horizons – steering us straight into ecological crises – stem from rivalrous systems of education and knowledge transmission. All originate in economists' substitution assumptions, due to selective exclusion of complementarity and positive feedback.

Indeed, the grip of dogmatic conformity in academics is part of this story; in education, of all places, science should be inclusive, first and foremost devoted to learning. Instead what we find is strictly orthodox standards set in place and defended against departures therefrom (*Reder* 1982). Look at what chaos theory encountered (*Gleick* 1987), or at the fate of increasing returns (*Kaldor* 1972; *Waldrop* 1992), if verification is sought. Neoclassical economics stubbornly ignores its own flaws, rather than addressing them in an open or forthright manner.[10] *Leontief* (1982, p. 105) likened the "tight control" by seniors over their junior colleagues in economics departments to Parris Island for the Marines!

Teaching ideological dogma over intellectual inquiry – answers instead of questions – is indoctrination, not education. A flexibly open mind is axiomatic to honest science, and there is no place in a learning environment for narrow-minded defense. The strictures reported by many economists (*Earl* 1983; *Georgescu-Roegen* 1967, p. 104; *Leontief* 1982; *Waldrop* 1992, p. 18) show why competition has failed: its substitution assumptions do not apply to information economies. Pathological organizational forms are the result (*Burns* 1963); these

---

[10] *Mueller* (1984, p. 160) noted that: "Neoclassical economics reigns supreme, not because it refutes challenges to it, but because it ignores them," to which *Hart* (1984, p. 189) replied thus: "I think that most economists retain the neo-classical methodology [because] ... there is at this point no satisfactory alternative to neo-classical theory," a claim also made by *Hahn* (1981, p. 129). But *Simon* (1979, p. 510) disputed this view in his 1978 Nobel Lecture: "...There is an alternative. If anything, there is an embarrassing richness of alternatives." *Earl* (1983, p. 121) offered the following explanation for the enduring persistence of orthodoxy in economics:

Our analysis leads to two connected ways of explaining the dominance of neoclassical economics. One is that it is safer and more rewarding to be an equilibrium theorist of the conventional kind. The other is that upbringings affect the constructions young economists form of what it is that economists do and they then act in conformity with this image unless given an exceedingly strong cause to behave otherwise. Kuhn's suggestion that a scientific revolution will not succeed until older scientists have died off seems entirely reasonable from a behavioral standpoint. If a mature scientist is to undergo a personal scientific revolution she will have largely to dispense with a well-formed world view. Since the choice will not usually be clear-cut, such a transition, if made, would entail a period during which she suffered nothing short of a scientific nervous breakdown.

symptoms show across society. As some wise soul once said: "Fish discover water last" (*McGregor* 1960, p. 317). The cultural implications shall matter.

6   Ethics and Planning Horizons

Standard theory in economics simply ignores ethics; *Smith's* (1776, p. 423) 'invisible hand' depicts self-interest as sufficient, due again to substitution assumptions. *Lux* (1990, pp. 87-89) says Smith's mistake consisted of leaving out "one little word ... the absence of [which] could ... unmake a world" by culling morality from economics. Suppositions of substitution and independence swim together,[11] inviting neglect of externalities and interdependence. So we economists justify ignoring cultural and ecological impacts of our claims. Most economists see no reason to worry about these things.

A recognition of complementarity and the role of planning horizons in all economic conceptions shows a way to escape this syndrome. Materialism is part of the problem: *Maslow* (1954, 1968) explained that human needs are ranked from basic (clothing and food) to higher-order ambitions (such as love, art and community) as we grow beyond mere physical wants – once met – to intangible aims. Such advances suggest development – through its social and personal links – shifts ambitions away from material things to more evanescent demands, out of scarcity into sharing, against substitution to favor complementarity, so – as already explained: $dS_y/dH_i* < 0$.

Framed this way, it is easy to see why competition is keeping us stupid and socially immature: organizational management theorists showed this some time ago (*Argyris* 1960; *Burns* 1963; *McGregor* 1960; *Whyte* 1967). Others suggest the myopic consumptive frenzy all around us stems from higher-order need deprivation due to a loss of community (*Argyris* 1960; *Kohn* 1986; *McGregor* 1960; *Scitovsky* 1976; *Wachtel* 1989). All such issues are rightly addressed through a theory of planning horizons and of their role in an economics of complementary interdependence. An economics of love frames another instance of complementarity, in which how we foster abundance is to give love freely![12]

The social effect of substitution assumptions has been deeply harmful, keeping us stupid and immature (*McCloskey* 1994, pp. 21-24 and 396). The ecological and economic consequences are equally dire, in vital losses stemming

---

[11] *Krupp* (1982, p. 388) remarked that:
> Axioms of independence ... lead directly to the laws of substitution... Independence means that the behavior of the elementary unit can be described without reference to the behavior of other units.

[12] *McCloskey* (1990, pp. 142-43) described the problem thus:
> ... There is an ethical problem in the theory and practice of economics. The problem is deeper than mere distaste for calculation of selfishness or greed. ... Economics was once described as the science of conserving love. The notion is that love is scarce, and that consequently we had better try to get along without it, organizing our affairs to take advantage of the abundant selfishness instead. The argument is economic to the core. ... The problem is that conserving on love, treating it as ... scarce ... may be a bad way to encourage its growth.

from short horizons spawned through competition. A cultural shift toward cooperation is needed to reverse such trends, to lengthen planning horizons through learning, conscience and personal growth. This is an optimistic conclusion, where hope promulgates effort. The welcome promise of cooperation to engage us in our community offers solutions otherwise set out of reach by competition. The healing process starts with each individual, and develops from there.

7   Conclusion

The point of this paper is: substitution is not our most general interrelation; complementarity is. If so, an economics standing crucially on substitution assumptions steers us wrongly in all applications where complementarity rules. Substitution assumptions may apply in the allocation of fixed stocks of physical goods, where competition directs them to best use, or even in a production economy under rising cost technology. Increasing returns show complementarity (*Kaldor* 1972, 1975); introducing planning horizons simply strengthens the claim for cooperation and concerts of value.

Ecology, education and ethics show cases of competitive failure in complementary settings. Economists' substitution assumptions may yet "unmake a world," to use *Lux's* (1990, pp. 87-89) phrase for the matter. *Kaldor* (1972, p. 1240) put it more robustly, calling for "demolition," namely "destroying the basic conceptual framework" of orthodox economics. Such is the promise offered by a horizonal economics.

Interdependence is the defining characteristic of ecology and of planning horizons. Any useful economics should incorporate both its forms: substitution and complementarity. Organizational crises occur – stress, selfishness, short-sightedness – when our theories do not fit the facts, squandering goods and nurturing conflict. This is what competition does, socially and intellectually: it keeps us stupid and immature, retarding economic growth while despoiling our world. The remedy is shifting socioeconomic cultures from competition to cooperation; the process starts with us. Interhorizonal complementarity means that we influence social horizons by extending our own. That is a nicely optimistic conclusion in a hazardous world destroying itself through wrong economics. So one might proceed...

References

Alchian, A.A. (1959): Costs and Outputs. The Allocation of Economic Resources, ed. *Abramovitz, M.*, Stanford University Press, Stanford, pp. 23-40.

_____ (1968): Cost. the International Encyclopedia of the Social Sciences, Volume 3, Macmillan and Free Press, New York, pp. 404-15; reprinted as ch. 12 of his Economic Forces at Work, Liberty Press (1977), Indianapolis, pp. 301-23.

Argyris, C. (1960): The Impact of the Organization on the Individual. Organization Theory, ed. *Pugh, D.S.*, Penguin (1971), New York.

Boulding, K.E. (1956): The Image: Knowledge in Life and Society. University of Michigan Press, Ann Arbor.

_____ (1968): Some Questions on the Measurement and Evaluation of Organization. Beyond Ethics: Essays on Society, Religion and Ethics, University of Michigan Press, Ann Arbor.

Burns, T. (1963): Mechanistic and Organismic Structures. Organization Theory, ed. *Pugh, D.S.*, Penguin (1971), Baltimore.

Clark, J.M. (1940): Toward a Concept of Workable Competition. American Economic Review, Volume 30 (3), pp. 241-56.

_____ (1955): Competition: Static Models and Dynamic Aspects. American Economic Review, Papers and Proceedings, Volume 45 (2), pp. 450-62.

Earl, P. (1983): A Behavioral Theory of Economists' Behavior. Why Economics Is Not Yet a Science, ed. *Eichner, A.S. / Sharpe, M.E.* Armonk.

Elsner, W. (2004): The 'New' Economy: Complexity, Coordination and a Hybrid Governance Approach. International Journal of Social Economics, Volume 31 (11/12), pp. 1029-49.

Georgescu-Roegen, N. (1967): Analytical Economics: Issues and Problems. Harvard University Press, Cambridge.

Gleick, J. (1987): Chaos: Making a New Science. Viking Penguin, New York.

Hahn, F. (1981): General Equilibrium Theory. The Crisis in Economic Theory, ed. *Bell, D / Kristol,I.* Basic Books, New York.

Hart, O. (1984): Comment. on Mueller in Economics in Disarray, ed. *Wiles, P. / Routh, G.* Basil Blackwell, Oxford.

Hawken, P. (1994): The Ecology of Commerce: A Declaration of Sustainability. Harper Business, New York.

Hicks, J.R. (1939): .The Foundations of Welfare Economics. (Economic Journal, Volume 49), in The Economics of John Hicks, ed. *Helm, D.*, Blackwell (1984), Oxford and New York.

Hirshleifer, J. (1962): The Firm's Cost Function: A Successful Reconstruction? Journal of Business, Volume 35, no. 3.

Jennings, F.B., Jr. (1985): Public Policy, Planning Horizons and Organizational Breakdown: A Post-Mortem on British Canals and Their Failure. Ph.D. dissertation, Stanford University.

Kaldor, N. (1939): Welfare Propositions in Economics and Interpersonal Comparisons of Utility. Economic Journal, Volume 49, pp. 549-52.

_____ (1972): The Irrelevance of Equilibrium Economics. Economic Journal, Volume 82, pp. 1237-55.

_____ (1973): Equilibrium Theory and Growth Theory. Economics and Human Welfare: Essays in Honor of Tibor Scitovsky, ed. *Boskin, M.J.*, Academic Press (1979), New York, pp. 243-91.

_____ (1975): What Is Wrong With Economic Theory. Quarterly Journal of Economics, Volume 89 (3), pp. 347-57.

Kohn, A. (1986): No Contest: The Case Against Competition. Houghton Mifflin, Boston.

Krupp, S.R. (1963): Analytic Economics and the Logic of External Effects. American Economic Review, Papers and Proceedings, Volume 53 (2), pp. 220-26.

_____ (1982): Axioms of Economics and the Claim to Efficiency. The Methodology of Economic Thought: Critical Papers from the Journal of Economic Issues, ed. *Samuels, W.J.*, Transaction Books, New Brunswick.

Lamberton, D.M. (2001): The Knowledge Based Economy: Better Living or Bigger Profits? Innovation, Economic Progress and the Quality of Life, ed. *Sweeney, G.*, Edward Elgar, Cheltenham, pp. 111-19.

Leontief, W. (1982): Academic Economics. Science, Volume 217, (9) also 'Foreword' to Why Economics is Not Yet a Science, ed. *Eichner, A.S.* / *Sharpe, M.E.*, Armonk, NY.

Lux, K. (1990): Adam Smith's Mistake: How a Moral Philosopher Invented Economics and Ended Morality. Shambhala Publications, Boston.

Margolis, J. (1960): Sequential Decision Making in the Firm. American Economic Review, Papers and Proceedings, Volume 50 (2), pp. 526-33.

Maslow, A. (1954): Motivation and Personality. Harper and Row, New York.

_____ (1968): Toward a Psychology of Being. Van Nostrand, New York.

Matthew, A. (2001): The New Economy – Truth or Fallacy? Pool: Business and Marketing Strategy, Issue 13, http://www.poolonline.com/archive/issue13/iss13fea4.html.

McCloskey, D.N. (1990): If You're So Smart: The Narrative of Economic Expertise. University of Chicago Press, Chicago.

_____ (1994): Knowledge and Persuasion in Economics. Cambridge University Press, Cambridge.

McGregor, D. (1960): .Theory X and Theory Y. Organization Theory, ed. *Pugh, D.S.*, Penguin (1971), New York, pp. 358-74.

Mueller, D. (1984): Further Reflections on the Invisible-Hand Theorem. Economics in Disarray, ed. P. Wiles and G. Routh, Basil Blackwell, Oxford.

Oi, W.Y. (1967): The Neoclassical Foundations of Progress Functions. Economic Journal, Volume 77, pp. 579-94.

Pylyshyn, Z.W. (1984): Computation and Cognition: Toward a Foundation for Cognitive Science. MIT Press, Cambridge.

Reder, M.W. (1982): Chicago Economics: Permanence and Change. Journal of Economic Literature, Volume 20 (1), pp. 1-38.

Scitovsky, T. (1976): The Joyless Economy. Oxford University Press, Oxford.

Simon, H.A. (1979): Rational Decision Making in Business Organizations. American Economic Review, Volume 69 (4), pp. 493-513.

_____ (1981): The Sciences of the Artificial. 2nd edn, MIT Press, Cambridge.

_____ (1982-97): Models of Bounded Rationality. Volumes 1-3, MIT Press, Cambridge.

Smith, A. (1776): An Inquiry into the Nature and Causes of the Wealth of Nations. Modern Library (1937), New York.

Stigler, G.J. (1939): Production and Distribution in the Short Run. Journal of Political Economy, Volume 47, pp. 305-27.

Turvey, R. (1969): Marginal Cost. Economic Journal, Volume 79, pp. 282-99.

Wachtel, P. (1989): The Poverty of Affluence: A Psychological Portrait of the American Way of Life. New Society Publishers, Philadelphia.

Waldrop, M.M. (1992): Complexity: The Emerging Science at the Edge of Order and Chaos. Simon and Schuster (Touchstone), New York.

Whyte, W.F. (1967): Models for Building and Changing Organizations. Human Organization, Volume 26, (1)-(2), pp. 22-31; reprinted as ch. 8 in Management of Change and Conflict, ed. *Thomas, J.M. / Bennis, W.G.*, Penguin (1972), Baltimore.

Reconciling Bounded Rationality with the Search for Performance in Public Administration: Herbert Simon's Perennial Ideas vs. the New Public Management?

Laurent Percebois

1 Introduction

Current public administration reforms often aim to introduce management techniques initially developed in private enterprises. To describe this trend, the academic community has coined an acronym, known as "NPM", for "New Public Management". Hence, the NPM is understood as a patchwork of devices designed to improve efficiency in public administration by transferring, when necessary, private Human Resource Management (HRM) strategies into public bureaucracies, as well as budgeting techniques likely to be an incentive for better management. Eventually, better management is conceived to improve legitimacy and acceptation for political choices, and to enhance democratic norms. Moreover, NPM reforms are often – but not always – considered as economically liberal reforms, since they try to bypass traditional flaws of public management through good practices from both business and the market.

However, NPM reforms generally attach little importance to the question of rationality, which is nevertheless crucial for the implementation of reforms and policies. The NPM approach is often developed by public management academics and practitioners, whereas the rationality problem is a privileged field for economists. Thus, this lack of emphasis on the discussed congruence of efficiency and rationality probably constitutes the interest of this research.

Indeed, several topics should be addressed around the articulation of the efficiency goal and the inner bounded rationality environment of public bureaucracies. The core of this paper is to try to define common paths for both increased efficiency and better understanding of bounded rationality. The assumption of pure rationality in economic models applied to public management sometimes results in excessive confidence in the ability of decision-makers to manage administrations, which is perhaps detrimental to the possibility of reforms to curb bureaucratic biases. Despite this point, one should not infer it is impossible to reform public management. There are certainly opportunities for reform, provided that decision-makers remain modest in their aspiration for change. This should probably limit some ambitious views about NPM reforms, notably considering performance-related devices in administrative fields. As private management, public administrations are submitted to imperfect information, structural uncertainty and bounded rationality of decisions. But, in addition to these characteristics, public management is regulated by specific institutional norms. Even if the NPM tends to adopt performance-related pay or delegated management, one should not forget that administration is yet driven by intangible goals, such as what is referred to as "general interest", access to essential services, democratic representation of people through recruitment, and so on; it does not rule out these reforms, but it limits any trend to generalization.

So, this paper will particularly stress the probable insufficient use of the rationality topic in the NPM field. As such, it hopes to reconcile classical analysis of public administration, notably Herbert Simon's insights and his followers', and current empirical reforms and theoretical views[1]. The method displayed here will be mainly a discussion of the rationality hypothesis in public administration in the light of the modern impetus towards efficiency-prone reforms taken from private management. Consequently it will be necessary to confront theoretical analyses about the administrative institutional background, by evoking some real life reforms in OECD countries and their results. The demand for efficiency will require moderating some reform hopes; no change is likely to enhance public management performance in such a dramatic way that it becomes perfect. The rationale for this assertion is that no reform is designed in a pure rationality and perfect information environment, which is – probably – not enough stressed in current reforms. This should remind academic researchers in the field of public management that Simon's breakthroughs, now refined by means of modern analyses of bounded rationality, should be a reference for reformers and decision-makers; this is necessary to moderate hopes in a pure administrative science for the optimal design of public administration.

To deal with this relationship between efficiency and rationality, five sections will follow.

First, a presentation of the incidence of the assumption of bounded rationality will be necessary to draw the actual institutional design of administrative bureaus. This section should temper some implicit ambitions of pure rationality analyses towards increased efficiency, especially in public management.

Second, a description of efficiency-prone NPM reforms will aim at focusing on current reforms in most OECD countries, so as to capture the search for efficiency and better adequacy to citizens' needs through managerial norms transposed from private management.

Third, reflections on the indispensable association of hypotheses of efficiency and bounded rationality should bring new insights on the current paths of reforms.

Fourth, a short analytical model will try to depict the consequences of bounded rationality in public administrative design; this should enlighten the necessity of a trade-off between increased delegation of management, usually claimed by NPM reforms to improve knowledge of costs and production func-

---

[1] Note that this work does not intend to oppose Simon's view of bureaucracies (and notably public ones) to modern NPM reforms, or to suggest that Simon opposes public and private administrations. Rather, it aims to show that Simon's approach of imperfect rationality in public or private administrations should have greater importance when administrative reforms are designed following some of the NPM rules. The key point is to say that bounded rationality in decision-makers is perhaps not enough emphasized in the modern literature on public administration. Of course, due to the paper's topic, Simon's view of administrative behaviour will be that in public administrations here.

tions in administration by means of better information and rationality, and some decisional centralization in order to cope with spillovers and externalities among bureaus.

Finally, last section presents a conclusion and summary of the results.

2 Persistent Doubts about the Rationality of Administrative Behaviour; Herbert Simon's Breakthroughs and his Followers

This section will be divided into two subsections. The first one will recall the advances of Herbert Simon's thought in terms of bounded rationality applied to public and private administration, collected in his classical Administrative Behaviour (1983/1976). This will be a logical beginning for this work, since Simon is among the first economists to insist on institutional peculiarities of bureaucracies.

Second, later works drawing on Simon's insights will be discussed so as to measure the consequences of bounded rationality for the modern quest for efficiency as the ultimate goal to achieve budgetary and service provision performance.

2.1 Administrative management: the need for Simon's approach to bounded rationality

According to Simon, and as it is accurately shown by Xavier Greffe in his presentation of the French translation of his classical opus, it is a critical error to suppose that the traditional *Homo oeconomicus* approach to individual agents may be applied to bureaucracies.

Simon restricts the likelihood of optimization to attain efficiency, mainly because of information biases and knowledge limitations in agents. There, the usual distinction between "pure" rationality and "bounded" rationality is of value to understand his reasoning.

If "pure rationality" depicts the theoretical or fictional ideal reasoning that should be displayed to reach optimality, "bounded rationality" captures the limited capacities of agents to process effective decisions, due to uncertainty, risk or simply imperfect understanding. As he puts it (*Simon* 1997, p. 291),

> "The term 'bounded rationality' is used to designate rational choice that takes into account the cognitive limitations of the decision maker – limitations of both knowledge and computational capacity. Bounded rationality is a central theme in the behavioral approach to economics, which is deeply concerned with the ways in which the actual decision-making process influences the decisions that are reached."

This dichotomy of "rationality" bears upon the assessment one may make of microeconomic maximization. Under the bounded rationality assumption, the validity of optimization calculus in its traditional form is undermined, since individuals cannot practically draw complex analytical solutions from the information set they are endowed with. Complexity is thus necessarily too high in general problems in everyday life to succeed in pure optimization. This is as true for the state bureaucracy as for private enterprises.

Consequently, the epistemological effect of the bounded rationality hypothesis is to raise scepticism about the complicated computations described in many works in the literature. Nevertheless, one should not conclude that the search for efficiency in

management, be it public or private, would be irrelevant[2]; but Simon asserts that some theoretical views of optimality would require to be amended so as to meet the facts. For practical purposes, the state cannot really avoid using some kind of – even imperfect – optimization.

In his seminal and perhaps most famous paper, *Simon* (1955) insisted on the impossibility of reasoning through perfect rationality, which explains and legitimizes the use of "satisficing"[3] yields in organisations. Indeed, it is of value for public management. Later, in the 1970s, he criticized the development of the rational expectations theory developed by Lucas and Sargent, since, according to him, it was grounded on so unrealistic hypotheses on information processing that it made it impossible to translate its conclusions into "everyday" real organizations (*Simon* 1978, 1979). Individuals and organizations hardly perceive general aspects of the present, so it would be excessive to suppose they can predict efficiently the future to always adopt the right thing to do now. Summing up Simon's views, it appears that the 1978 Nobel Prize winner calls for a less formal but more realistic view of economics, even if it induces less sophistication in economic and management models (*Simon* 1979).

Simon's view is that administrative behaviour does not always translate into a search for efficiency. He considers that efficiency would be the ultimate criterion of administrative action, if the agents experienced pure rationality. Yet real life organizations substantially differ from their theoretical counterpart, an assertion which is probably consistent with Simon's approach.

Overall, administrative management should focus on an efficiency criterion rather than an efficacy one, which is true for private and public management. Let it be recalled that "efficiency" stands for maximum ratio of outputs to inputs, whereas "efficacy" only concentrates on the attainment of given outputs, without paying specific attention to inputs. This procedural recommendation

---

[2] To some authors, especially within the "Public Choice" approach developed *infra* (*e.g.* Buchanan and Tullock (1962), Niskanen (1971)), even more than private management, public administration would be submitted to efficiency problems, because of the lack of a need for profit, and due to annual and guaranteed budgets. But considering these "bureaucratic biases" in public management, even added to bounded rationality, should not make the reader think that public administration is *per se* condemned to insufficient results. One should conceive public management and its reforms as opposed to the unrealistic ideas of a structural lack of efficiency or that of perfect efficacy and rationality; this is at least the thesis developed here.
[3] Of course, the so-called "satisficing" approach of economic behaviour is part of Simon's theoretical legacy.

made by Simon to decision-makers is notably justified in public administration by scarce budgetary resources, funds mainly produced by taxation, that is, social consent for state intervention. It would be detrimental to rule out the budgetary issue and the so-called inputs it allows, on behalf of the mere respect of output objectives.

The above presentation of Herbert Simon's approach to – notably public – administrative behaviour, particularly about the rationality frame, is the key to understanding some limitations reformers will face through implementing schedules to enhance efficiency in public bureaucracies. Even more than private firms, public administration seems to obey political and institutional constraints and environments that model its operation. In the following lines, it will be interesting to consider what bounded rationality implies for reforms in an era of constrained budgets worldwide. From now on, it will be relevant to develop Simon's idea of decision-making "rationality", with references to other authors about administrative behaviour; current research on administrative behaviour and rationality will be emphasized in Section Four in order to show the possible compatibility of bounded rationality and the search for increased performance in public management. The following discussion of the adequacy of bounded rationality for public management will be crucial for the exposure of NPM theories for current administrative reforms worldwide on behalf of increased efficiency and performance (Section Three).

2.2 Bounded rationality in public administration: A longstanding academic dialogue with Simon

The main idea to admit from Simon in the field of administrative management is certainly that there is no optimal decision in terms of efficiency; there are just sufficient alternatives, constrained by information limits and uncertainty. Truly optimal decision only could be reached through perfect rationality, which is only a pure theoretical benchmark, irrelevant for the administrative practitioners and reformers. This might be true as well for public management reforms leading to Performance-Related Pay (PRP) or increased personnel management delegation. This point will be developed later. Now it is necessary to stress the extent of the intellectual debt of administration academics and practitioners to Simon.

Klaes/Sent (2005) present recent research on bounded rationality as a general topic; the authors emphasize Simon's breakthrough in the field of the decision-making economic theory, by insisting on the general consensus created around the notion of "bounded rationality" he coined in the 1950s. Before this decade, there was no such agreement on any similar economic concept. One may add that this is certainly as correct for public administration as for private management.

However, in the sociological field of bureaucracy, Simon was preceded by Max Weber concerning the opposition between, on the one hand, administrative rationality and, on the other hand, "efficiency" as it is recurrent in modern New

Public Management (NPM) analyses of public reforms nowadays. Moreover, sociologists develop an idea of ambivalent "expertise" in bureaucrats, which translates into public institutional economics with the notions of "private knowledge" and "opportunistic risk" for the hierarchy. This suggestion of Simon's intellectual debt to Weber is due to emphasize that administrative science is a social science benefiting from multiple and heterogeneous contributions, especially from sociology or economics. *Albrow's* (1994, pp. 63-64) classical sociological work allows drawing a link between Weber and Simon, by interweaving "rationality" and "expertise":

> "This procedure of expert application of rules was central to what Weber called the *formal rationality* of bureaucracy. It would be quite misleading to equate Weber's concept of formal rationality with the idea of efficiency. It certainly comprised techniques, such as accounting or filing. But it also meant legal expertise, the interpretation of law by lawyers. Administrative action was not guided by technique alone, but also by norms."

So, even if Simon was the father of the modern economic analysis of rationality, he was necessarily aware of the rising influence of microeconomic works on decision-making, especially in the field of public decisions and public bureaucracies. As early as the 1960s, the positive theory of the "Public Choice" analysis was set up by such prominent authors as James Buchanan and Gordon Tullock. In The Calculus of Consent (1962, p. 32), their classic opus and perhaps the foundation of the modern microeconomic view of politics, they indicate the way they consider "rational collective action"; this is that "which is consistent with the achievement of [commonly shared goals for all members of the group]".

What is important to note is that Buchanan and Tullock have paved the way for the development of the computational economics of political behaviour, for topics ranging from the public bureaucracy to electoral issues. The use of very complex models sometimes yields nontrivial or unexpected results. Yet, Simon probably criticized this overuse of complex analytics in modern economic science, because it was based on excessive confidence in the ability of organizations or individuals to reproduce optimum calculus in real life. Famous French political scientist Raymond Aron (1993/1983, pp. 454-455) was very sceptical about the development of a microeconomic theory of politics based on utility, maximization and pure rationality when he said "il n'y a pas pour celui qui gouverne un État d'équivalent de la maximisation de l'utilité visée par l'acteur économique et supposée par les schèmes de la théorie économique[4]".

The advantage of pure rationality lies in its propensity to allow complex computational economics through mathematical formulas. Simon considers that

[4] This may be translated as "For who governs a state there is no equivalent to the utility maximization aimed at by the economic agent and supposed by the models of economic theory".

decision-makers and administrative agents do not act in such a way, and he denies the right of social scientists to develop inferences from sophisticated models. Yet, the study of bounded rationality has kept refining Simon's analyses, incorporating the assumption of limited knowledge or calculus into mathematical or computational frameworks. In a way, Simon's idea of limited propensity to use calculus to apprehend organizations and individuals has been bypassed by current research. It is notably true for Kiel and Seldon, *in Earl's* (2001, p. 546) contribution to honour Simon's legacy; they consider that public organizations are particularly fitted for the use of the bounded rationality concept and they assert that

> "The environment of public organizations may produce both deterministic and nonlinear dynamics. When such dynamics are present in the environment of public organizations public managers will find themselves contending with levels of complexity that generate surprises and inhibit understanding."

Of course, current research on bounded rationality is not limited to public administration analysis[5]. But it is especially relevant for this field of analysis.
One major point to address would be the issue of the persistence of standard optimization in spite of well-known reservations about its conclusions. *Kirchgaessner* (2005) presents a fruitful discussion of bounded rationality in economics. Indeed, Simon's perennial view of bounded rationality in decision-making, and particularly in public administration, is well-admitted and it advocates a thoughtful and moderate search for efficiency in organizations, because of institutional imperfections.

The modern public management approach understood as "New Public Management" (NPM) is a management approach of public administration, and it also benefits from economic, sociological and legal approaches so as to enhance efficiency and performance in public bureaucracies. In order to attain this objective, the NPM often transposes entrepreneurial norms to public management, which is one of the main subjects of debates among authors. Besides, the possibility of bounded rationality seems to be rather scarcely envisaged in current reforms, whereas Simon stressed its importance for administration. The performance goal is almost a motto in the NPM, and it supposes that administrations may be reformed into significantly more efficient organizations by following, if necessary, the example of private corporations.

---

[5] For instance see *Crawford* (2003) for an application of bounded rationality to conflicts; *Huck* (2004) also provides some reflections on bounded rationality, and the book mainly focuses on computational models of game theory. Klein's article *in Gigerenzer/Selten* (2001) provides an interesting view of the theoretical problems arising from standard optimization, that is implicitly in a pure rationality world. For an epistemological approach to bounded rationality, the reader may refer to recent papers, such as *Vanberg* (2004), *Lagueux* (2004) or *Redmond* (2004).

Section Three aims to present the NPM arguments in search of performance in public management, and it will appear that information theory and
bounded rationality is not really a central topic of the NPM. Later on, Section
Four will try to reconcile the informational imperfections underscored by Simon
in administrations and the need for high efficiency.

3 The NPM Efficiency-Prone Reforms in Administrations

Where does this demand for performance in administrations come from?
For simplification purposes, it may be asserted that the adoption of NPM reforms results from the combination of several political and economic reasons.
Among them, two reasons seem to be particularly important. First, since the late
1960s and the beginning of a slowdown in growth rates, economic liberalism
gained new attention, and public administration had to show its efficiency in
minimizing the opportunity cost of taxation; *Fourcade-Gourinchas/Babb* (2002)
speak about "the rebirth of the liberal creed" to capture this ideological trend
(*Buchanan/Tullock* (1962) certainly constitute a trigger for the rise in interest for
reducing interventionism and for the need for ever-increasing "value for money"
of public services). Second, the debt burden was generally high in several countries after the oil crisis in the 1970s and its consequences for public policies,
leading to improve public management efficiency.

Nevertheless it would be a gross approximation to consider that NPM only
represents a critical viewpoint of public administrations. Indeed, it includes a
very vast range of methods, as well as a wide range of authors, but all sensibili-
ties seem to be present in the NPM. Some approaches believe in the need for a
change in public administration, so as to meet the citizens' wishes, and to provide better quality without necessarily using efficient private management practices. Others consider that traditional public management is quite obsolete and
think it is accurate to transfer business rules of promotion, pay and personnel
management to public administrations; these views often stem from Public
Choice critical articles or books such as Niskanen's (1971), which emphasizes
the flaws of public bureaucracies. Of course, most approaches adopt a pragmatic
view of reforms since they hope to improve public regulations without losing the
raison d'être of public bureaucracies. In fact, the NPM acronym is overused in
public management literature which eventually depletes its content. But overall
it is a common and useful way to speak about current managerial reforms of
administrations, which explains why it is referred to here.

One striking point about NPM reforms is the belief in the ability to make
administrative routines more efficient, through a better ratio of outputs to inputs.
Actually, the NPM constitutes a practical way of dealing with a very heterogeneous set of methods aiming at improving public administration, notably
through private corporation procedures.

The search for efficiency appears to be a shared ambition among most
academics and practitioners in public administration. There is a true desire for
increased performance in administration, which is of course a legitimate cause to

defend. The problem is that ideological values, whether interventionist or market-oriented, are often present in this debate, which sometimes lessens the impact of arguments. Historically, the beginning of the NPM wave of reforms – still ongoing for some, already over for others – dates back from *Osborne/Gaebler's* (1992) book entitled Reinventing Government; it even initially inspired Bill Clinton's reforms in the USA, before being referred to as a standard management opus to reform administrations abroad. Yet it is necessary to admit that bounded rationality is probably too little emphasized in this debate.

To briefly describe the main areas of NPM reforms, several paths for efficiency-prone reforms may be quoted. Unfortunately, this paper does not allow describing them extensively, since it mainly intends to focus on the insufficient use of the bounded rationality concept.

The first path is probably the transformation of Human Resource Management (HRM). Authors often refer to the need for improving and opening recruitment beyond standard examinations, so as to make access to public employment easier for private agents, in order to allow competence transfers. Moreover performance-related pay is often referred to as a means to increase the public servants' motivation and involvement in public service. Nevertheless, this efficiency-prone device is far from being neutral in terms of detrimental side-effects, since it may excessively amplify the so-called "crowding-out effect" (*Percebois*, 2006a)[6]. Furthermore, the issue of adequate performance indicators is an important debate among academics, since individual performance data is not always simple to collect in public management and because of disputes over the relative importance to give to quantitative and qualitative indicators in public services[7].

Another path consists in increasing decentralization and public management delegation. The interest of delegation is to empower public servants with everyday management. This is likely to increase participation and personnel involvement into human resource management, some local decisions and so on. "Delegation" refers to a downward transfer of competence inside a hierarchy, while "decentralization" implies some spatial reallocation of the decisional power[8].

---

[6] The modern approach to the crowding-out effect was established by the groundbreaking work of *Deci/Ryan* (1985): the central idea is that too many external incentives paradoxically lessen motivation, as people excessively focus on external rewards instead of personal motivation for the work itself, which might result in decreasing quality or work involvement. Experimental studies seem to confirm this effect.
[7] *Emery/Giauque* (2005) are convincing when they argue that modern reforms excessively emphasize quantitative performance indicators detrimentally to qualitative ones. Indeed, evaluating public services is probably often more a question of substantive perception than one of objective measure, when compared with other economic activities.
[8] Scholars and reformists often advocate delegation and increased autonomy for "street-levels" agents or administrations. For example, *Saint-Etienne* (2007, p. 77) explains that efficiency as much as quality would be promoted through delegation in hospitals, schools, universities or social services; according to him, three elements have to be delegated: a goal, an empowered manager and a budget. Moreover, performance-related pay is necessary to instill

Besides, improving public management often means modernizing its procedures through the use of Information Technologies (IT). That is why one may observe a trend towards the so-called Internet-based "electronic administration", or simply "e-administration" (or "e-government") to refer to this growing use of new technologies in the transmission and diffusion of administrative information to citizens and businesses. For example, every developed country currently expands its government Internet portal so as to make access easier for individuals, which is supposed to be a precondition for enhanced democratic ambitions.

This is but a mere sketch of the main areas of public management reforms, now designed to both improve service quality and increase budgetary efficiency[9]. In Section Five, a simple model of the underlying stakes of NPM reforms for delegation will be presented so as to understand how current reforms could use the bounded rationality concept in defining optimal or "satisficing" management reforms. But in the meantime, it is probably necessary to focus on the difficult task of joining up the "bounded rationality" reality and the "efficiency" norm within public bureaucracies.

4 Combining Administration Efficiency and Rational Design

Bounded rationality constitutes the real institutional environment of organizations. In public administration as elsewhere, economists and other social scientists often admit Simon's views. And no reform aiming at efficiency, as important as it may be, might successfully wipe out the fringe of inherent uncertainty to achieve optimality. That's an important point underlined by *Chevallier* (2002, p. 500):

"L'information n'accède en effet jamais directement au décideur: elle transite par des canaux administratifs, ce qui allonge les délais de transmission et crée des risques de rétention ou de désinformation; chaque acteur filtre l'information en fonction de ses intérêts propres et l'absorption d'incertitude interdit au décideur de disposer d'une information parfaitement fiable. Et l'informatisation n'a, à cet égard, pas changé fondamentalement les choses[10]."

This quote sheds some light on information management and its use within any bureaucracy. Actually, any top-level decision-maker is submitted to information

---

performance. Many scholars agree with this opinion, a mainstream view nowadays within what is referred to as "NPM" (despite the aforementioned restrictions about this acronym).
[9] To develop public administration reforms, the reader may refer to *Bartoli* (2005) or *Horton et al.* (2002).
[10] This may be translated as:
"Indeed information never directly reaches the decision-maker: it is transmitted through administrative channels, which lengthens transmission delays and creates retention or disinformation risks; all agents screen information according to their personal interests and uncertainty absorption prevents the decision-maker from benefiting from perfectly reliable information. And in this regard, computerization has not brought about significant change."

biases due to multiple interferences in the diffusion of information. Besides, bounded rationality makes it difficult for the decision-maker to clearly understand reality. Knowledge of "street-level activity" is necessarily distorted by the gap between decision-making and implementation. This is another conception of public administration through the bounded rationality conceptual apparatus. In order to counter this detrimental effect on public sector efficiency, one may advocate increased management delegation and empowerment of street-level public servants for day-to-day management, as advocated by NPM reforms. One may indeed suppose that the inferior hierarchical levels will be better informed of real production conditions and that they will better understand citizens' needs. Bounded rationality probably does not affect in a similar way street-level agents and top-managers in public management, due to specific ways of information transmission inside bureaucracies. Yet there is another problem: public administration, as an extended organization, deeply relies on the coordination of activities to achieve efficiency. For instance, in a centralized approach to cooperation, the ministry of education should often interact with the ministry in charge of employment policy issues. But it is even true in a local view: municipal police forces should be coordinated with social workers in underprivileged districts. Moreover, coordination not only involves public administrations, but also the third sector and private corporations.

Consequently, managing efficiency in a bounded rationality environment implies taking into account the advantages of delegation-prone reforms to cope with citizen's needs, and the advantages of some centralization of activities to enhance coordination of public services. Then a trade-off is relevant, which is of course common practice in economics and in its specific public administration subfield.

The question of bounded rationality is not only linked to the delegation policy in public management though. *Alford/Friedland* (1992, p. 437) pinpoint frictions around efficiency – via ambitions towards "rationalization" – and bounded rationality within public administration, which is of full value for the present discussion, and as such deserves to be quoted:

> "The rationalization of each state agency renders the state bureaucracy as a whole increasingly irrational. Efforts are made to establish coordinating bodies, including corporatist structures, but because these bodies frequently lack sufficient authority to rationalize the total structure they become one more source of unpredictability."

Excessive stress on efficiency yields unwanted effects according to the above quote. Efficiency should be conceived as a global approach before being envisaged at local levels; to put it differently, following Alford and Friedland, the sum of "rationalized" public agencies does not result in a "rationalized" set of public agencies. There lies the risk of the emergence of an anarchically-managed bureaucracy, following its own goals and uncontrolled by the citizens.

Thus modern public management reforms should combine elements of delegation so as to minimize risks of biased decisions due to bounded rationality and information processing, and centralization for coordination of different horizontal or vertical levels in order to maintain a common direction for reforms. For instance, *Chibber* (2002) considers that the specific bureaucratic rationality benefits from the existence of what is referred to as a "nodal bureau" to coordinate different administrative departments so as to impulse a common approach for the economic role of the state, especially in developing countries. Consequently, satisficing – if not optimal – efficiency should be reached through an association of satisficing – if not optimal – delegation and satisficing – if not optimal – centralization. This is a lesson to be drawn from Simon and the social scientists interested in bounded rationality that specialized in public administration design.

The arising question is then: should one blame traditional public administration for being insufficiently likely to adopt efficiency norms as private management does? Is the rationality problem so excessive in public management to justify drastic changes as advocated by some promoters of NPM reforms?

The necessity to replace public bureaus with private firms to provide public-interest services is only a last resort option, at least in "administrative" or "red-tape"-processing activities. Besides, Public-Private Partnerships (PPP) become more and more common, but they are restricted to activities where society accepts that the state has no greater legitimacy to intervene than firms.

In his now classic opus, *Goodsell* (1994, p. 84) advocates public management and considers that its specificity in terms of rationality and efficiency insulates it from managerial-oriented NPM reforms. To him,

> "...bureaucracy is in a no-win situation because it responds not to a single rational calculus or even to net market demand. As part of government, it responds (...) to the political process. Since that process involves the pursuit of competing values and claims, some values inevitably go unfulfilled and some claimants inevitably go unsatisfied. The resulting frustrations are multiple and disparate, but they are nonetheless aggregated under the rubric of bad bureaucracy, bound in red tape."

Actually, Goodsell denies the ability of public management to display levels of rationality as high as perhaps private management does. Yet this should not be sufficient motivation to reform it in a market-like way as some NPM reforms intend to. Even if bounded rationality is still more acute in public administration, one should not consider that, in the name of efficiency, public management should transpose all efficiency-prone devices from the firm; and, due to bounded rationality, it should not be supposed that reforms have to be automatically implemented following "technocratic" and general rules, so popular consensus should be reached as much as possible. These subjects remain controversial among public management experts and one possible way to overcome them is certainly to proceed through experimentation and step-by-step reforms[11]. For instance, Sweden has recently tested a system of congestion tax in Stockholm, from January 2006 to July 2006, before holding a referendum on whether or not to implement it permanently: since decision-makers could hardly anticipate if Swedish citizens were going to consent to it, this procedure may be seen as a democratic approach to urban policies as much as an efficient administrative view of congestion and environmental issues; in the September 2006 referendum, the "Yes" prevailed in central Stockholm but the "No" prevailed in the suburban areas; this referendum made it possible for local decision-makers to compensate for some lack of information and to avoid an illegitimate and maybe irrational decision due to disregard for the citizens' voice[12].

Poor rationality is sometimes invoked as a structural flaw of public management. It would be an inescapable problem as well as a justification for private management when it is possible. On the contrary, *Grandguillaume* (1996), in an original way, considers that absence of strong rationality grants public bureaucracy its independence as much as its valuable "checks and balances", *i.e.* its necessary equanimity. In other words, this means that some authors see public management as an efficient organization, but in a different manner from that of private management. This pleads for different reforms than those generally promoted by reform policies nowadays. Thus there is no consensus yet on the correct articulation of efficiency and specific bounded rationality within public management.

The next section will now illustrate the interaction of notions like "optimization", "bounded rationality", institutional "design" and management "delegation" in a context of public administration reforms.

5   A Simple Model of Administrative Design in a Bounded Rationality Frame

The following model is a simple presentation of a public institutional design assuming bounded rationality of the decision-maker, following part of the analytic framework of Public Choice theorists.

Two public bureaus referred to as "1" and "2" produce each a different composite public good, respectively Y_1 and Y_2. They are financed through a common budgetary basis B, which a central decision-maker shares out[13] between B_1 and B_2.

---

[11] For strong and quite unusual – but stimulating – criticism of excesses in NPM reforms, see *Farazmand* (2002).

[12] To get more information about the Stockholm congestion tax experiment, see also: http://www.stockholmsforsoket.se/templates/page.aspx?id=183; furthermore, the reader might refer to *Percebois* (2006b) for a study of specific public management reforms in Scandinavian countries.

[13] An alternative way to develop this model would be to suppose that the common budgetary basis is split into three parts, instead of two: bureau 1's budget, bureau 2's budget and the central decision-maker's budget. In the present model, this latter budget does not appear, because it is supposed to be determined *ex ante*. Yet, adding the personal interests of the central

Production functions yielding Y_1 and Y_2 display some complementarities between both bureaus. Production in each bureau is then a composite supply, whose value depends on the specific combination of both outputs X_1 and X_2, each one being produced by a different bureau. Production Y_1 depends on specific output of service 1, called X_1, of course, but also on a specific output of service 2, called X_2. Similarly, production Y_2 relies on both X_2 and X_1. Production costs for X_1 and X_2 are identical and equal to x. The interdependence relationship between these outputs is given by the following equations:

(5.1) $$Y_1 = X_1 \left(1 + X_2\right)$$

(5.2) $$Y_2 = X_2 \left(1 + \alpha X_1\right)$$

Parameter α represents the importance given to the complementarity of outputs X_1 and X_2 in producing the aggregate output of bureau 2 (i.e. Y_2), and it is a positive or null number (yet, negative values could be conceivable, but this does not seem to bring significant added value to this presentation). To simplify the model, the number representing the complementarity of outputs for bureau 1 has been valued one. Parameter α is likely to have values ranging from zero to more than unity. Consequently, the model exclusively distinguishes bureaus in terms of parameters for output interdependences[14].

Bounded rationality occurs because the central decision-maker cannot observe or infer parameter α, due to complexity in public administration and because of biases in information diffusion, as notably mentioned in Section Four. This generates problems for designing optimal decisions within public management. To solve this problem of insufficient information-processing ability, the central decision-maker may choose to delegate management to each bureau, and thus each will optimize its production with respect to its own budget, still determined by the initial decision-maker. NPM reforms often advocate increasing decentralization and delegation, thus this model may be coherent with this reforming frame[15]. Before this possible delegation, the central decision-maker can

---

decision-maker into budget sharing would introduce a new dimension; this is certainly a possible extension of the model.

[14] The multiplicative shape of these production functions and of the decision-maker's utility function (see *infra*) denotes that the central decision-maker cannot share the global budget very unequally without side-effects for production levels, and that he prefers that both composite outputs be produced in sufficient quantities. Contrarily, an additive function could result in corner solutions. So, this hypothesis on the multiplicative shape of functions is made to avoid any unrealistic null production of an administrative good.

[15] With some restrictions, this theoretical frame could be applied to private management, where – obviously – bounded rationality and management dilemmas also exist. Nevertheless, the economic literature insists on the strong difference between private and traditional public management, that is the importance given to profits. If one follows *Buchanan/Tullock* (1962) and others, organisational and informational biases are far stronger in public management. So, the possible differential intensity of bounded rationality and other problems perhaps justifies different assumptions in public and private management contexts.

try to "optimize" its utility function inasmuch as it is possible, despite the aforementioned informational bias on output complementarity[16].
The decision-maker's utility function is simply given as:

(5.3) $$U = Y_1 Y_2$$

Thus, the optimization programme of the central decision-maker is:

(5.4) $$\max_{B_1} U$$
$$\text{s.t. } B = B_1 + B_2$$

This optimization programme is solved such that the decision-maker ignores the true value of α, because of bounded rationality. The calculus is then straightforward:

(5.5) $$\max_{B_1} U = Y_1 Y_2$$
$$\Rightarrow \max X_1 (1 + X_2) X_2 (1 + \alpha X_1)$$

Replacing X_1 and X_2 by, respectively, $\dfrac{B_1}{x}$ and $\dfrac{(B - B_1)}{x}$, gives another presentation of the decision-maker's utility function, which leads to optimize (under hypothesis $x = 1$, for simplicity):

(5.6) $$\max_{B_1} B_1 (1 + B - B_1)(B - B_1)(1 + \alpha B_1)$$

Solving the programme yields optimal sharing of budgets[17], where $B_1{}^*$ is the optimal budgetary endowment for service 1, and it is implicitly given as the root of the following expression, for $B_1{}^* \in [0, B]$:

---

[16] Simon's reserves to infer strong results from maximization are not conceived here as an interdiction to use optimization calculus, insofar as such a calculus provides here the result of a purely and very improbable theoretical computation. The bounded rationality assumption will be a way to depart from the presumptive general validity of such an optimization, in the second step of this model. So, this optimization is necessarily biased, and this optimization calculus would only be successful for a perfectly rational decision-maker.

[17] Verifying second-order conditions is quite straightforward: from the objective function, one obtains 4 trivial roots in terms of B_1. These roots are $B_1 = 0$, $B_1 = B + 1$, $B_1 = B$, and $B_1 = -\dfrac{1}{\alpha}$; of course $-\dfrac{1}{\alpha} < 0 < B < B + 1$; then, due to the fourth-order polynomial to maximize, one obtains that the polynomial is negative for $-\dfrac{1}{\alpha} < B_1 < 0$ and for $B < B_1 < B + 1$ and positive for $B_1 < -\dfrac{1}{\alpha}$, $0 < B_1 < B$ and $B_1 > B + 1$. Obviously the only economically relevant interval is $0 < B_1 < B$, which allows concluding the extremum is ef-

$$4\alpha B_1^3 * +3\left[1 - \alpha\left(1 + 2B\right)\right]B_1^2 * +2B_1 *\left[\alpha B^2 - B\left(2 - \alpha\right) - 1\right]$$
$$(5.7) \quad +B\left(1 + B\right) = 0$$

Optimal values B_1 * constitute the locus of optimal budgetary endowment by the decision-maker, but he does not know the true α. Consequently, a bounded rationality choice might as well lead to suppose the interdependences between production functions are equal, that is $\alpha = 1$. But this bounded rationality choice will probably lessen the decision-maker's utility relatively to the choice he would have made under both pure rationality and information[18].

Graphically, for different true values of α, it is possible to determine the optimal sharing of budgets in order to maximize the decision-maker's utility function (for the example, one posits $B = 10$), for a perfectly rational decision-maker. But the reader must remember that the decision-maker cannot infer correctly information on α, due to bounded rationality, as aforementioned in Section Four. Thus, the graph below shows the utility surface of the decision-maker and his choice of B_1 * on the optimal locus, had he both perfect rationality and information, which is just a theoretical hypothesis.

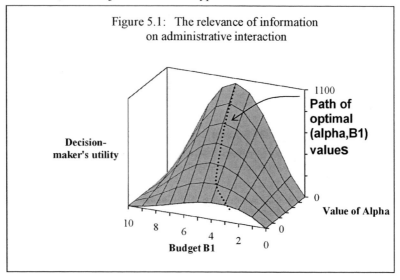

Figure 5.1: The relevance of information on administrative interaction

fectively a maximum (because of the function's continuity, a necessary hypothesis for Rolle's Theorem); but in this bounded rationality framework, the decision-maker cannot reach this optimum, for organizational and informational reasons. More algebraic proofs may be provided by author upon request.

[18] Note that assuming another parameterization leads to similar results in terms of utility loss.

The path of optimal values is simply the optimal locus, defining the optimal choice of budgetary allocation, for any true value of α. It is a three-order function, whose determination or approximation does not seem to be straightforward for a decision-maker in an imperfect rationality environment.

Because of bounded rationality, the decision-maker may suppose for simplicity that both bureaus are identical in terms of production costs, which means $\tilde{\alpha}$ equals one, where $\tilde{\alpha}$ is the estimation of $\alpha*$ (true value of α) under bounded rationality. Consequently, one obtains from the optimal locus that $B_1 = 5$, under bounded rationality (it is a trivial case, since, to the decision-maker, bureaus do not seem different). If haphazardly $\tilde{\alpha} = \alpha*$, there is no estimation error, and no bias due to bounded rationality; but it is highly improbable. If $\tilde{\alpha} \neq \alpha*$, bounded rationality results in an error in budget allocation because the true value of α is not incorporated into the algebraic optimal locus. Thus, in most cases, the decision-maker undergoes a utility loss whose value is:

(5.8) $$U\left(\tilde{\alpha} = 1; B_1 = 5\right) - U\left(\alpha*; B_1*\right)$$

Consequently, it is possible to define graphically the total utility loss, conceived as the negative effects of bounded rationality. It is given by the graph below:

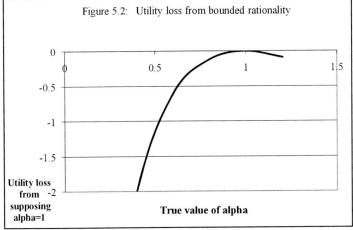

Figure 5.2: Utility loss from bounded rationality

In order to avoid this utility loss, the decision-maker may choose to delegate management to both bureaus, as often promoted by modern reforms of public management[19]. However, this transfer of management has not only advantages. Admittedly, NPM reforms often advocate delegation, as section two showed, but this is not a panacea in all cases.

---

[19] It would be interesting to develop the model further so as to show the trade-off between delegation and centralization in a bounded rationality framework. It constitutes a possible future extension to this paper.

The main advantage of delegation is certainly that it empowers bureaus with the ability of determining their economic policy. Local management allows increasing the amount of available information and it gives an opportunity for lessening bounded rationality because information is more directly accessible.

Yet, there are also limits to delegation, which are at least twofold. First, public management delegation might justify delegating public budgets as well, and one may wonder whether bureaus would agree on the sharing of budgets. Second and perhaps main restriction to delegation, the issue of coordination of public outputs; since bureaus are strongly interdependent in terms of both budgets and outputs, there is probably a need for cooperation among them. Precisely, management centralization could enhance coordination better than delegation.

To sum up arguments, there is actually a trade-off between increasing delegation, which is notably legitimized by the need to overcome bounded rationality problems, and increasing centralization, which is perhaps less often advocated by NPM theories but might be justified by specific requirements of coordination due to interdependences. What may be reproached to current reforms is perhaps that they do not sufficiently insist on advantages and drawbacks of their propositions: delegation is not always a fruitful solution, for coordination reasons. It is also true for other propositions emphasized by NPM: performance-related pay also introduces elements of competition in terms of salaries for public servants, and it may be negative for what is referred as *esprit de corps*. And e-government also results in "street-level" job destructions besides job creations related to Information Technologies (I.T.), inside public administrations; it is also sometimes argued that e-government may increase what is referred to as the "digital divide" between citizens familiar with IT and others. For all those reasons, and in order to cope with the bounded rationality hypothesis, public management should receive NPM propositions in the light of their possible drawbacks, and step-by-step reforms should be adopted as much as possible, instead of "once and for all" and "universal" solutions for every country and every administration.

Incorporating bounded rationality in the study of NPM reforms is probably of value to improve the knowledge of "satisficing" public administration design. So, Herbert Simon's pioneering works are still relevant today, in the era of NPM, as a recall of the intrinsic imperfections of public management. In other words, no public management reform is likely to provide an efficient solution, conceived as a definitive improvement. This is certainly additional backing for modesty in public reformers, as well as a justification for step-by-step reforms.

6 Conclusion

Overall, bounded rationality remains relevant for theoretical public management, now that the NPM constitutes the mainstream efficiency-prone approach to reforms. Hypotheses on the rationality of decision-makers do not seem very frequent in this field of analysis, so insisting on these subjects would certainly be interesting ground for new developments.

There is probably no general opposition between the search for efficiency as promoted by NPM reforms and the real informational environment of public management, which is a bounded-rationality approach. Limited ability to make optimal decisions should be food for thought before implementing reforms. Bounded rationality may plead in favour of delegation or decentralization, as in this presentation, and perhaps against it in other contexts; and "step-by-step" reforms should probably be used as much as possible, in spite of possible unanticipated side-effects. Finally, taking into account bounded rationality probably contributes to the refinement of theoretical research on reforms.

References

Albrow, M. (1994): Bureaucracy. London, Macmillan.

Aron, R. (1993/1983): Mémoires. Paris, Julliard.

Alford, R.R. / Friedland, R. (1992): Powers of Theory: Capitalism, the State, and Democracy. Cambridge, Cambridge University Press.

Bartoli, A. (2005): Le management dans les organisations publiques. 2nd edition, Coll. Management public, Paris, Dunod.

Buchanan, J.M. / Tullock, G. (1962): The Calculus of Consent: Logical Foundations for Constitutional Democracy. Ann Arbor, University of Michigan Press.

Chevallier, J. (2002): Science administrative. 3rd edition, Coll. Thémis, Paris, Presses Universitaires de France.

Chibber, V. (2002): Bureaucratic Rationality and the Developmental State. American Journal of Sociology, Volume 107 (4), pp. 951–989.

Crawford, V.P. (2003): Lying for Strategic Advantage: Rational and Boundedly Rational Misrepresentation of Intentions. American Economic Review, Volume 93 (1), pp. 133–149.

Deci, E. / Ryan, R. (1985): Intrinsic Motivation and Self-Determination in Human Behavior. New York, Plenum Press.

Earl, P.E. (ed.) (2001): The Legacy of Herbert Simon in Economic Analysis. Volumes I and II, Coll. Intellectual Legacies in Modern Economics, 8, Cheltenham, UK and Northampton, MA, Edward Elgar.

Emery, Y. / Giauque, D. (2005): Paradoxes de la gestion publique. Paris, L'Harmattan.

Farazmand, A. (2002): Administrative Ethics and Professional Competence: Accountability and Performance under Globalisation. International Review of Administrative Sciences, Volume 68 (1), pp. 127–143.

Fourcade-Gourinchas, M. / Babb, S.L. (2002): The Rebirth of the Liberal Creed: Paths to Neoliberalism in Four Countries. American Journal of Sociology, Volume 108 (3), pp. 533–579.

Gigerenzer, G. / Selten, R. (eds.) (2001): Bounded Rationality: The Adaptive Toolbox. Cambridge, Mass.; London, England, The MIT Press.

Goodsell, C.T. (1994): The Case for Bureaucracy: A Public Administration Polemic, Chatham, NJ, Chatham House.

186 L. Percebois

Grandguillaume, N. (1996): Théorie générale de la bureaucratie. Paris, Economica.

Horton, S. / Hondeghem, A. / Farnham D. (eds.) (2002): Competency Management in the Public Sector: European Variations on a Theme. Amsterdam, Berlin, Oxford, IOS Press, IIAS-EGPA.

Huck, S. (ed.) (2004): Advances in Understanding Strategic Behaviour: Game Theory, Experiments, and Bounded Rationality. Houndmills, Basingstoke, Hampshire and New York, Palgrave Macmillan.

Kiel, L.D. / Seldon, B.J. (1998): Measuring Temporal Complexity in the External Environment: Nonlinearity and the Bounds of Rational Action. American Review of Public Administration, Volume 28 (3), pp. 246–265. In *Earl, P.E.* (2001), *supra*, Volume II, pp. 537–556.

Kirchgaessner, G. (2005): The Weak Rationality Principle in Economics. CE-SIFO, 1410, Research Working Paper.

Klaes, M. / Sent, E.-M. (2005): A Conceptual History of the Emergence of Bounded Rationality. History of Political Economy, Volume 37 (1), pp. 27–59.

Klein, G. (2001): The Fiction of Optimization. In *Gigerenzer, G. / Selten, R.* (2001), *supra*, pp. 103–121.

Lagueux, M. (2004): The Forgotten Role of the Rationality Principle in Economics. Journal of Economic Methodology, Volume 11 (1), pp. 31–51.

Niskanen, W.A. (1971): Bureaucracy and Representative Government. Chicago, Aldine Publishing Company.

Osborne, D. / Gaebler, T. (1992): Reinventing Government: How the Entrepreneurial Spirit is Transforming the Public sector. Reading, MA, Addison-Wesley.

Percebois, L. (2006a): Incentives for Performance in Public Management: Theoretical Mechanisms and Empirical Evidence in OECD Countries. Conference presentation, Caledonian University, The 10th International Research Symposium on Public Management, Glasgow, Scotland, April.

Percebois, L. (2006b): La promotion de la performance de l'administration publique dans un contexte d'Etat interventionniste: le paradoxe scandinave [Promoting Public Administration Performance in an Interventionist State Context: the Scandinavian Paradox], CES – Matisse, Université Paris 1, Conference on the State and Social Regulation, Paris, France, September.

Redmond, W.H. (2004): On Institutional Rationality. Journal of Economic Issues, Volume 38 (1), pp. 173–188.

Saint-Etienne, C. (2007): L'Etat efficace. Paris, Perrin.

Simon, H.A. (1955): A Behavioral Model of Rational Choice. Quarterly Journal of Economics, Volume 69 (1), pp. 99–118.

Simon, H.A. (1978): Rationality as Process and as Product of Thought. American Economic Review, Volume 68 (2), pp. 1–16.

Simon, H.A. (1979): Rational Decision Making in Business Organizations. American Economic Review, Volume 69 (4), pp. 493–513.

Simon, H.A. (1983/1976): Administration et processus de decision. Coll. Gestion, Paris, Economica (translated from Administrative Behaviour, 1976).

Simon, H.A. (1997): Models of Bounded Rationality. Volume 3: Empirically Grounded Economic Reason, Cambridge, Mass.; London, England, The MIT Press.

Vanberg, V.J. (2004): The Rationality Postulate in Economics: its Ambiguity, its Deficiency and its Evolutionary Alternative. Journal of Economic Methodology, Volume 11 (1), pp. 1–29.